"*Green Enough* is a fun, direct, user-friendly guide to a healthier lifestyle. You will want to give this book to those you love, because Leah is that best friend telling you exactly what you need to hear."
—Robyn O'Brien, founder of AllergyKids Foundation
and author of *The Unhealthy Truth*

"This is the perfect starting point for people who want to detox their lives from harmful chemicals. Often, the fear of not doing it right, not doing enough, or not knowing enough about toxic chemicals paralyzes people who are interested in taking better care of themselves. Fear no more. Leah Segedie has you covered: You *can* be green enough!"
—Amy Ziff, founder and executive director of MADE SAFE

"Leah Segedie is a force to be reckoned with. I've know Leah for years and even though she began her journey fighting for cleaner food and household products well before I began to understand the importance of it all, I always marveled at her energy, dedication, drive, and fierce never-say-die attitude. Leah is so sincerely passionate about uncovering mistruths and problems that most of us have *no* idea about. I credit her with being one of *the* forces of massive change in the non-GMO movement that has made a significant impact on the CPG industry at large. I have mad respect and gratitude for this woman who fights for our protection every day. We all owe her a debt of gratitude that cannot be measured. Keep fighting, Leah. You've so got this."
—Kelly Olexa, founder and CEO of FitFluential.com

"I'm smitten with *Green Enough,* and Leah Segedie's brilliant, witty approach in dissecting the science behind why going green can help you to eat better, live better, and raise healthier kids."
—Jennifer McGruther, creator of Nourished Kitchen
and author of *The Nourished Kitchen*

"I've been waiting a long time for somebody to write this book!
Leah Segedie's *Green Enough* is an irreverent bible for powerful living—
packed of straight talk about science and practical tips for taking charge
of our own health and the health of our personal environments. Best of
all, the book feels like a cathartic confab with a good girlfriend, someone
who knows what it's like to be a busy mom grappling with an increasingly
complex and crazy world, who has our backs and knows just what to say
to keep us fired up to keep taking the next step forward into our own
power. Bravo Leah, and thank you."
—Stacy Malkan, co-founder of The Campaign for Safe Cosmetics
and author of *Not Just A Pretty Face*

"Riveting, fact-based, and utterly hilarious. *Green Enough* is the perfect
book for anyone curious about how to make their home safer, without
drastically uprooting life as you know it."
—Lindsay Dahl, activist and former deputy director
of Safer Chemicals, Healthy Families

"When you realize everything in your life
that affects your family's health it can feel overwhelming!
Get *Green Enough* to relax and start making better (but not perfect)
choices daily that will help keep you all healthy."
—Ashley Koff RD, CEO of The Better Nutrition Program

"Eco-wellness pioneer Leah Segedie speaks candidly and boldly
reveals so much valuable, thoughtful, and mind-boggling information
that should make you stop and say *WTF*. After reading this book, you'll
want to take a closer look at your home, your pantry, and probably,
yourself in the mirror. Leah shares her knowledge based on personal
experience and from the heart. Plus, the best part is that her mantra is
that it's not about not being perfect but being aware, present, and
proactive when it comes to your home environment. And if you
appreciate a few f-bombs every now and then, this may be up your alley."
—Barbara Jones, founder and CEO of Blissful Media Group

WITH
50 MOM & KID
FRIENDLY RECIPES

GREEN ENOUGH

EAT BETTER

LIVE CLEANER

BE HAPPIER

(ALL WITHOUT DRIVING YOUR FAMILY CRAZY!)

LEAH SEGEDIE

Green living expert & founder of mamavation.com

RODALE.

RODALE **wellness**

Live happy. Be healthy. Get inspired.

Sign up today to get exclusive access to our authors, exclusive bonuses,
and the most authoritative, useful, and cutting-edge information
on health, wellness, fitness, and living your life to the fullest.

Visit us online at RodaleWellness.com
Join us at RodaleWellness.com/Join

© 2018 by Leah Segedie

Rodale books may be purchased for business or promotional use or for special sales. For
information, please e-mail: BookMarketing@Rodale.com.

Printed in the United States of America

Rodale Inc. makes every effort to use acid-free ∞, recycled paper

Illustrations by Andrew Broznya

Book design by Jordan Wannemacher

Library of Congress Cataloging-in-Publication Data is on file with the publisher.

ISBN 978-1-62336-760-2

Distributed to the trade by Macmillan

2   4   6   8   10   9   7   5   3   1   hardcover

We inspire health, healing, happiness, and love in the world.
Starting with you.

This book is dedicated to my father, who died of cancer.
I promise to always make you proud!

CONTENTS

INTRODUCTION

TOXIC FOOD? TOXIC HOME?

WHEN I WAS GROWING up, there was a plaque on my grandma's wall that said it all:

> *This home is clean enough to be healthy, and dirty enough to be happy.*

Maybe you've seen this saying on a decorative plate or framed needlepoint. It's still everywhere, and it would be a total cliché if it weren't so true. Creating a home environment that is healthy and happy is not about perfection and driving your family batshit crazy. It's about finding a balance between the choices that keep y'all healthy and the sanity-preserving allowances that keep everybody happy too.

In other words, do what you can and then just chill out.

But here is some reality you need to understand. If you thought that the food and products you purchase are independently safety-tested before they hit the shelves, you are wrong. Your family is not protected the way you thought, and it has to do with what crazy chemicals y'all are exposed to, day in and day out. Chemicals that, in many cases, are banned or restricted overseas, but here in the good old U.S. of A. end up on our dinner plates and in products inside our homes.[1] Yes, there are rules and regulations governing this shit, but some of that bureaucratic mumbo jumbo is more about shielding manufacturers from legal liability than it is about looking out for you and your family—so who's to say you're actually being protected? It also doesn't mean the powers that be have to tell you what they are *not* regulating for your safety.

In some cases, you've been flat-out lied to; in others, no one bothered to tell you about the fine print. And let's face it: Had someone pointed out that fine print, would you have really read it? You've been a bit busy making awesomeness happen, and those sneaky chemical companies are banking on you being too busy to check that shit out.

So what chemicals are we talking about, and where are they? The answer to that is complicated as fuck, but I'm going to break it down for you. That is what this book is all about.

I'm here for you, girl.

In today's world of seemingly endless options and totally relentless marketing, it has become more and more difficult to make good, careful choices. The supermarket has become a place of confusion for most people, and when you have a family to protect and care for, you need *real* answers, really quick.

Well, my dear, you have come to the right place! I am here to end the confusion and get you started on the right track.

Let's get a few things out of the way first.

Full disclosure: I didn't used to be a "green mom." You know, those total killjoys you encounter at playgrounds, parties, and everywhere you want to just relax. ("Everything is toxic! Everything is giving us cancer! You can't do this because of that, and you can't do that because of this!") I *hate* to be told what to do, so I avoided green moms like the plague. Back in the day, I even worked for politicians who voted against regulations that would have helped protect our children and environment. My life was full of chemicals. I went green slowly, as I learned about chemical contamination in products and food and witnessed the avalanche of chronic disease and cancers, including in my own family.

I'm sure you've noticed something similar happen with your family and friends. People are dying and getting sick, and it's everywhere.

Today, I'm green enough, which means far from perfect, but light-years better than before. I'm the founder of Mamavation, a mom-focused social-media community dedicated to cutting through the marketing bullshit and discovering what's truly healthy for ourselves, our families, and our environment. I'm a rabble-rouser, and a speaker of truth to power, and I'm here to help you find your way to a greener path. No judgment, just love and compassion—plus need-to-know information leavened with a lot of humor and more than a few cuss words.

I am challenging you to read this book and take action to make things better for yourself and your family; learn as much as you can and share your knowledge with your loved ones and friends; and also help make a difference with your dollar bills by buying more products from companies that are creating a better, healthier world. We *will* change the system through sharing knowledge and supporting the good guys who are doing things in a better way right now.

And I'll tell you what this book is *not* about. This book has not been written to make you feel bad about how you are raising your family. How can I possibly look down on you when I used to eat fast food every single day? On the other hand, you ain't no badass in my book if you use any of this information to make other moms feel like shit. This book is about us all rising up together, each on her own timeline and in her own way. So take what you want and leave what you don't. I don't care. I just want you to have the information so you have *true* choices.

We are going to update that corny but wise philosophy:

> *This home is GREEN ENOUGH to be healthy, and*
> *CHILL enough to be happy.*

So buckle up, my friend. It is time to get real and get busy.

TOXIC FOOD? TOXIC HOME?

What would you say if I told you . . .

That cinnamon oat square cereal you bought because it's chock-full of fiber and protein is not only loaded with sugar—more than 2 teaspoons per half-cup serving—but also butylated hydroxytoluene (BHT, a scary, petroleum-derived preservative that's banned in Australia, Canada, New Zealand, Japan, and throughout Europe),[2] genetically modified organisms (GMO) galore in the sweeteners, maybe some monosodium glutamate in that mystery "flavor" listed on the label, and potentially a huge dose of pesticides in the oats and wheat.

If you'd say that's un-freakin'-believable, I'd totally understand (personally, this makes me want to rip my hair out.)

OR THIS:

When you microwave that handy bag of popcorn, you are unleashing tons of toxic substances inherent in the packaging materials and chemicals that are strongly suspected of being potent hormone disrupters and carcinogens.[3]

If your response to the oh-so-convenient bag o' hormone hackers and cancer is a big eye roll and a heavy sigh, I'm right there with you.

ALSO THIS:

Ninety-nine percent of conventionally grown strawberries tested by the USDA in 2014 and 2015 came up positive for contamination with pesticides—and that's *after* the berries were washed. On 20 percent of samples, the pesticides included a fungicide that has been banned in the European Union because of its intense toxicity.[4]

It's a total horror show.

PLUS THIS:

Eighty-two percent of ground-turkey samples collected for a study in 2012 were contaminated with *E. coli*—and more than half of the bacteria found on the ground turkey were resistant to at least three classes of antibiotics, according to FDA scientists.[5]

Shrieking is totally understandable at this point, as are gagging noises.

AND HOW ABOUT THIS:

Ninety percent of household dust samples from multiple studies of American homes contain 10 harmful chemicals that may be linked to infertility, birth defects, autism, early puberty, obesity, diabetes, and hormone-related cancers, as well as a flame-retardant (TDCIPP) that is known to cause cancer. But wait, there's still more! One-hundred percent of the dust samples contained large amounts of substances called phthalates, which are believed to interfere with hormones in the body and are linked to declines in IQ and respiratory problems in children, poor sperm quality (among other reproductive problems), and many other health hazards.[6]

I'd hazard a guess that you're mighty tempted to slap this book shut and go vacuum the bejesus out of your entire domicile.

AND (LAST ONE. FOR NOW.):

Most shampoo, soap, lotion, and other personal care products we slather all over ourselves and our children on a daily basis contain hormone-disrupting chemicals that have been linked to asthma, attention deficit hyperactivity disorder (ADHD), obesity, type 2 diabetes, low IQ, neurodevelopmental issues, behavioral issues, autism spectrum disorders, breast cancer, altered reproductive development, and male genital defects and fertility problems. These chemicals are called phthalates. And they only rarely are listed on product labels.[7]

Are you thinking, Leah, could just shut up?! I feel ya. But no.

If it sounds like I'm telling you that your food and the packages it comes in are polluted, and so are your home and your family's personal care products, that's because I am. These everyday toxic exposures we are contending with add up, eventually burdening our bodies with a toxic load that can lead to serious health problems.

The good news is that there are a lot of reasonably easy ways that you can dial your family's toxic load way down.

First, we'll cover everything you need to know to get smart about your food choices, including issues about processed food and food packaging (Chapters 1 and 2, respectively), followed by produce, meat, and dairy (Chapters 3 and 4). Chapter 5 is all about setting you up with great foods and easy ways to prepare them. Then comes Chapter 6, a room-by-room guide to reducing toxic exposures at home. Finally, there's Chapter 7, where I'll help you navigate the treacherous terrain of personal care products.

If you want to get right to the part where we open up a can of whoop-ass on those toxic exposures, just turn to page 208.

However, if you want more background on what kind of chemicals we're concerned about here; how they're getting into our food, our household items, and our grooming products; how little we are protected by the powers that be; and what the potential health consequences are, then dig in to the rest of this chapter.

This is where I'm going to get you acquainted with the main chemical offenders and important details on exactly how they threaten your health. I'll also dish up some dirt on chemical companies and the government agencies that are falling down on the job of protecting you and your family, or straight-up ignoring it. Basically, I'm going to give you a whole slew of reasons to get serious about lightening your family's toxic load—complete with some seriously scary science. You can refer back to this information as you make your way through the practical steps you'll get into in the chapters that follow.

So, are you ready to kick the toxic shit to the curb? Brace yourself. (And I wouldn't discourage you from pausing to pour yourself a glass of organic wine, either.)

HELLO, HAZMATS

From preservatives, flavorings, and fragrances to pesticides, plasticizers, and flame retardants, there are thousands upon thousands of synthetic chemicals in the products we consume and use on a daily basis—more than 85,000, according to the Environmental Protection Agency. The vast majority of these chemicals have not been proven safe for human and environmental health.[8] In fact, every day we are learning about more chemicals that are more dangerous than they are useful. Mind you, a chemical doesn't have to be synthetic to be dangerous—lead, arsenic, and mercury are just a few examples of naturally occurring elements that cause grievous harm.

Basically, we live in a toxic soup, and still we wonder why so many people are having trouble conceiving children, so many others are dropping dead of cancer, and chronic disease is becoming so prevalent among young children that our offspring have been dubbed "Generation Rx." Check out these seriously scary stats (as of 2017):

1 in 3 children are overweight[9]
1 in 6 children have a learning disability[10]
1 in 9 children have asthma[11]
1 in 10 children have ADHD[12]
1 in 13 children have food allergies[13]
1 in 27 male children have autism[14]

What the actual hell is going on here?

PUBLIC ENEMY NO. 1: ENDOCRINE DISRUPTORS

The chemical culprits I am going to give top billing to here and throughout this book are endocrine-disrupting chemicals (EDCs), substances that, depending on the chemical, interfere with hormones and sometimes entire hormone systems.

We tend to think of hormones mostly as important factors in sexual development and reproduction. Well, they're certainly vital in those ways, but it goes way beyond that.

If you thought the brain was unilaterally responsible for ruling the rest of the body, guess again. The endocrine system is an exquisitely complex and finely tuned system that works at a grassroots level to control the body's other systems, which in turn deal with the business of vital functions such as development, growth, metabolism, immune response, reproduction, intelligence, and behavior. To manage this feat, the endocrine system uses a variety of chemical messengers, including hormones.

If these chemical messengers could be hijacked, just imagine the severity and extent of the mayhem that could ensue. Unfortunately it's not a matter of if, but when—because that's what's going down in our bodies.

These hijackers are devious; they mimic, thwart, disorient, and otherwise interfere with hormones, and they can change the way our cells develop and grow. Some of these chemicals mess with sexual development. Certain ones can diminish intelligence and derail behavior. Others have the potential to throw our metabolic function and/or immune systems out of whack.[15, 16]

In terms of fertility, the consequences can be horrendous. Men may have declines in sperm count, increases in malformed sperm, and sperm that lack the requisite swimming skills to get the job done.[17] Worldwide, sperm counts have tanked by as much as 50 percent in recent decades, while rates of testicular cancer have surged.[18] In women, endocrine disruption can cause egg production or ovulation to malfunction, pregnancy to terminate, or fetal development to go awry. Hormone-related cancers, endometriosis, and other reproductive disorders are on the upswing among women.[19]

For those fortunate enough to conceive, there are grave concerns about chemicals that can pass through the placenta and/or can be passed from mother to infant through breast milk. In the womb, exposure to EDCs during pregnancy can be dire because hormones play a programming role during fetal development, and the damage is irreversible if this is tampered with at such an early stage.[20] For example, the entire male sexual-differentiation process depends upon certain hormones (androgens) arriving on the scene during a very specific window of time. Any interference—which can happen when the mother is exposed to phthalates via plastic food containers and fragrances, among many other things—has been linked to increased incidence of undescended testicles and malformations of the penis (such as the urethra coming out the side rather than the end), both of which are on the rise in baby boys.[21] Similarly, the disruption of thyroid hormones (from pesticides, for one) before birth has been associated with all manner of neurodevelopmental problems, from learning disabilities and impaired IQ to ADHD and autism.[22]

Once a kid is born, several distinct factors come into play. As we all know, most children spend their first few years

THE MIND-BLOWING COSTS OF EDCS

A recent scientific analysis calculated the annual costs of various EDCs in terms of both dollar and IQ points and added cases of intellectual disability. The findings? The researchers estimated that, in the United States, the medical costs and loss of wages in the United States was over $340 billion and Europe was about $270 billion.[23] Some of the findings looked at exposure to a class of flame retardants called polybrominated diphenyl ether or PBDEs accounts for 11 million lost IQ points in children, 43,000 more cases of disability, and total health costs of $266 billion. The tab for pesticide exposure: 1.8 million lost IQ points, an additional 7,500 intellectual disability cases, and health costs of $44.7 billion.

exploring life low to the ground, so they have a lot of opportunities to come in contact with potentially contaminated soil and dust; they also love to put just about everything in their mouths; and they eat, drink, and breathe more per body weight compared to adults, while undergoing many rapid body changes. All this leaves kids susceptible to even minute doses of environmental toxins.

Standard testing logic assumes that higher doses of anything cause greater harm, but many EDCs—heavy metals, solvents, polychlorinated biphenyls (PCBs), organophosphate pesticides, phthalates, and bisphenol A (BPA)—have been found in animal and human studies to result in ill effects at lower doses.[24] At low doses, EDCs cause adverse effects by interfering with specific receptor systems.[25] At high doses, those receptor systems shut down, so then the EDCs find different targets with different effects. Basically, **if you are testing for EDC effects at high doses, you won't see the low-dose consequences.** And what might result from many different doses combining and accumulating—especially in children's smaller and much more vulnerable bodies—is an unanswered and truly terrifying question.

Did you catch that? In this case, **dose does *not* equal the poison.** Teeny-tiny parts per trillion can affect the future of your family.

Even in adults, minuscule amounts of an endocrine-disrupting chemical can have a disproportionate effect, and small amounts of different ones may have a cumulative effect. In some cases, the by-products of EDCs (when the body's enzymes break it down) may have greater harmful effect than the parent chemical.[26]

Speaking of ill effects being passed along from a parent—and being amplified in the process—some of the most god-awful news about endocrine-disrupting chemicals is coming from an emerging science called epigenetics. This new science indicates that children inherit more than just DNA from their parents—studies suggest that EDC exposure may leave chemical marks on a parent's genes that manifest later in the child's life, triggering an array of health problems that run the gamut from asthma, autism, diabetes, and obesity to infertility and reproductive diseases, cardiovascular dysfunctions, and schizophrenia.[27] And let's not forget one of the most terrifying: cancer. There is also evidence that the alterations these EDCs make on our own genes may be passed down to subsequent generations, so the reality is your children—and quite possibly your grandchildren, great-grandchildren, and great-great-grandchildren—could inherit a lot more than your eye color and dimples![28]

ENVIRONMENTAL POLLUTION

News flash: There are some—ahem!—*problems* with the way we've been treating the planet. You know that already. But what you may not realize is exactly how much this is coming back to bite us in the ass. Environmental pollution is a huge source of EDC exposure. Chemicals that were banned decades ago are still in the air, the ground, the water, and the food chain. They've been in our bodies since day one, when our mothers started pumping blood into us in the womb.[29]

It's bad enough to introduce highly toxic chemicals into the environment without proper safety testing, but what's up with not even bothering to pay attention to what goes down after? Well, one really clear sign that you have seriously messed with Mother Nature is when little boy tadpoles grow into female frogs and male fish start producing eggs. You did not misread that: Male animals become fertile females.[30]

And let me tell you, that little bit of science about EDCs is probably all you need to get the men in your household on board with whatever toxin-avoiding strategies you want to implement. When I talked with my husband and kids about going plastic-free, I described it to them as my "Save the Swimmers" campaign. I essentially explained that I want grandchildren one day, and if they

> ## BIG FAT MESS
>
> So many EDCs have been implicated in the obesity epidemic that scientists have made up a new word for them: obesogens. These are compounds we're exposed to in daily life—via pesticides, industrial and household products, plastics, detergents, flame retardants, and grooming products—that can cause weight gain. As with other effects of EDCs, exposure to obesogens in utero and in early infancy can be especially harmful because they might preprogram the body to make more fat cells, which then can store more fat, leading to a lifelong struggle with weight and making poor diet and insufficient exercise even more obesity-inducing than they already are. Bottom line: Exposure to even very small amounts of EDCs might trigger obesity later in life, as well as insulin imbalances that increase risk of type 2 diabetes. At high doses, EDCs can cause weight loss because at those doses, they are overtly toxic.

want to breed without the use of two-headed monster sperm, they need to avoid phthalates. Now my boys literally roll their eyes at me and say, "Yes, Mom, avoiding endocrine disruption saves my swimmers. I know." #truestory

I know this is all scary news that probably makes you just want to run away and hide, but here's what you need to do instead of getting overwhelmed and freaking out: Try to get out there and stick up for the environment in whatever ways you can, whether you engage in activism, get your recycling act fully together, climb aboard public transportation more often, boycott products from companies with bad practices, or all of the above and even more. And instead of letting your awareness of unavoidable exposure shut you down, use it to empower and motivate you to tackle the exposures you *can* do a lot to dial down. Because while you can't go live in a bubble somewhere, you can most definitely make some changes in day-to-day life to reduce EDC exposures within your home.

GENERALLY RECOGNIZED AS ~~SAFE~~ BULLSHIT

Wondering how the hell it is possible we aren't being protected from these contaminants? Well, to put it mildly, our government's review practices are inadequate in general, and downright ludicrous for chemicals with hormone-like actions. Here's the lowdown on how poorly the system works to keep the citizenry safe from exposure to toxic chemicals. The FDA is the branch of our federal government that regulates the safety of drugs, medical equipment, and stuff that emits radiation, as well as our food supply. Basically, they're in charge of testing and approving all kinds of things, which essentially boils down to protecting our health.

The thing is, the FDA has this program they call GRAS. The letters stand for "generally recognized as safe," but what it actually adds up to is a monumental loophole for the chemical industry.

Seriously, here's how it works. Let's pretend for a second that you are a chemical *aching* to become a useful and productive member of our nation's food supply. You need to get into one of three lines to receive approval under the GRAS program.

LINE NO. 1: Before you start, ask yourself if you were born before the year 1958. If you answer yes, congratulations! You are grandfathered into the system and zip right into the express line, which puts you straight into the food supply, pronto. How very nice for you.

LINE NO. 2: If you love to do *tons* of paperwork, conduct legitimate scientific studies that are published in peer-reviewed science journals, hold a public comment period, and follow the spirit of the law, then this line is for you. What—no takers? Okay. Well, here's the third option.

LINE NO. 3: Get in this line if you don't want to bother with rigorous science. Just do up your own safety studies and notify the FDA that you want a review. You can involve legit scientists if you want, but you don't have to. The FDA has 120 days to do a complete review of whatever you give them, but it takes them about that long just to get ink in one of their printers, so chances are they won't pull off a review in that time—and in that case, you're good to go, because it means automatic approval is yours.

On the off chance the FDA gets their act together and denies your petition, don't worry your pretty little chemical head because a) they are reviewing *your* safety studies that you did with people you paid to get the results you wanted, and b) even if they are about to reject your petition, they will tell you beforehand so you can withdraw it *before* any news goes public. Then it's like nothing ever happened—no one will ever know there were any questionable safety issues, not even when you try again and, one way or another, eventually get approved.[31]

Hey! Look at you all jumping into the third line. You know that's not nice. That's not how the law was intended to be carried out.

Absurd, right? Unfortunately, this is a pretty accurate summary of how things truly work. Was this process intended to make it possible for more than 1,000 chemicals to be approved without FDA review from 2000 to 2014?[32] No. But because it provides the chemical industry with a super huge loophole, that's exactly what happened. Why get into line No. 2 when No. 3 is clearly easier and cheaper?

LAME DOES NOT EVEN BEGIN TO DESCRIBE . . .

With hundreds (if not thousands) of new chemicals being developed every year, and industry interests exploiting every loophole and blind spot in the regulations that are supposed to ensure our safety, the Environmental Protection Agency (EPA) can't possibly provide us with remotely adequate protection. They can't even ban asbestos, for crying out loud! This is a substance that is known all too bloody well to cause cancer—its very own special kind of horribly lethal cancer, mesothelioma, which still kills 3,000 people per year in the United States.[33] In 2006, my very own father was one of them.

THIS IS WHAT CONFLICT
OF INTEREST LOOKS LIKE

Another outrageous example to lay before you: BPA, which has been a real headline-grabber for going on a decade now. As the piles of science linking this estrogen-mimicking chemical to a long list of serious health problems grew higher, public outcry got louder. BPA was banned in baby bottles because the industry was getting so much bad press about it, and manufacturers eventually felt the pressure about other especially notorious products, so nowadays store shelves are stacked with canned foods and plastic products prominently labeled BPA-free. At first glance, that seems like a win—but watchdog groups are clueing us in about the replacement chemicals manufacturers use instead: essentially, other bisphenols, like BPS. From there it's all been downhill, as emerging research indicates this next generation of chemicals are estrogenic (just like BPA) and may have even more harmful effects.[34]

Say *what*? Yeah, this is how evaluations work when they are based, as is the case in the United States, on "risk assessment." Such assessment involves profoundly unreliable assumptions about how people are going to use products. This approach protects products from legal liabilities; it does *not* protect people from chemical harm.[35]

> *Judging a chemical's safety without knowing its EDC characteristics is like looking at credit scores and teaching credentials for a person you are thinking of hiring to teach at a high school without having access to a database of sexual predators.*

Knowing if a teaching candidate were a sexual predator would be *very* important, right? Yeah. That's exactly my point.

Meanwhile, aside from the baby-bottle ban, the FDA has changed nothing about the safety status of BPA and other bisphenols—zero, zip, nada. Unbelievable as it may seem, industry interests were directly involved in the agency's tracking and evaluation of BPA research, and the safety assessment relied heavily on industry-funded studies.[36]

DÉJÀ VU ALL OVER AGAIN—AND AGAIN, AND AGAIN . . .

If you just felt your head about to explode and have some serious flashbacks kicking in right about now, perhaps that's because there are more than a few uncanny parallels between the BPA rigmarole and some of the sinister shenanigans deployed by—believe it—the tobacco industry. It's pretty much the same drill, from the industry lobby wielding influence within the EPA to the use of straight-up staged scientific debate as a way to manipulate public opinion and delay regulatory action. This treacherous tactic is known as "manufacturing doubt." It is an all-too-well-worn page directly from Big Tobacco's dirty and deadly playbook, and it is being used to keep BPA and other harmful EDCs (pesticides, plasticizers, fragrances, flame retardants) on the market long after scientific inquiry has identified their potential to cause harm. In a leaked memo from the bowels of the chemical industry, it was revealed that industry was going to look for a pregnant woman to become their BPA spokesperson.[37]

Bottom line: The safety system is fundamentally corrupt. When testing is paid for by the companies and industries that will profit from the chemicals being deemed safe,

> *The public interest is not being served if there is no firewall separating the research from the companies.*

WHY I JUST SAY *NO* TO GMOS

When you consider how egregiously flawed the regulatory system is and how clearly corporate profits take precedence over public interest, it's no surprise that GMO technology is a huge concern. GMOs (a.k.a. genetically engineered products) are monkeyed with at the molecular level to insert genes from one species into another as a means of obtaining desired traits. There is raging debate over GMO safety and whether labels should be required for products containing them.

Look, here's the truth: Technology is neutral. It can be used for good or for evil, but when the guys running the show are money-grubbing dudes who value profits over people, you are likely to find yourself in trouble. Deep trouble.

You can guess where I stand on this one, so pardon me while I set aside my composure and unleash a tirade about the axis of evil, a.k.a. Monsanto, Syngenta, and Dow Chemical. Why do I call them that (and so many other nasty names)? Well, here are just a few of the dastardly crimes that win them that special distinction:

- They have poisoned communities by dumping their shit everywhere, causing miscarriages, birth defects, and a big ol' cancer buffet.[38]
- They have harassed legit scientists who discovered how toxic that shit was and sent people to intimidate them and their families.[39]
- GMO crops were supposed to mean less pesticide use but have ended up increasing the amount of the weed killer glyphosate being used. Yeah: So much of this probably-endocrine-disrupting and carcinogenic shit is being sprayed on GMO crops that it's raining glyphosate in the Midwest.[40]
- According to an estimate from the Center for Food Safety—a non-profit organization that works to protect human health and the environment—upward of 75 percent of the processed foods lining supermarket aisles contain genetically engineered ingredients (which include corn, soy, cottonseed oil, canola, sugar beets, potatoes, and apples, so we're talking pretty much all processed foods).[41]
- Many breakfast cereals and other standard-issue packaged products are testing positive for glyphosate.[42]
- We aren't even given the courtesy of having a say in whether we consume GMOs in conventional food produce, unlike the 14 countries of the European Union as well as the United Kingdom, Japan, Brazil, Australia, New Zealand, South Korea, and China, where labeling on foods containing genetically engineered ingredients is mandatory.[43]

This crew has a *very* bad track record that stretches back decades (a few fave tunes from their greatest hits album: Agent Orange, asbestos, PCBs, and DDT), and it casts a long shadow far into our future because this is environmentally persistent shit that will be with us for generations to come.[44] I don't trust them. And from working in politics for years and knowing how powerful lobbying groups operate, I've got to tell you that you shouldn't trust them either. Whatever they tell you, the fact remains that they are spraying a ton of probable endocrine disruptors and carcinogens on our food—and that shit is also poisoning us via the environment because it is permeating the air, water, soil, and food chain.[45]

That means organic as much as possible because while I love seeing that little Non-GMO Verified Project butterfly logo on things (it's on lots of labels nowadays), if you don't see the USDA Organic seal next to it, then there's a good chance the product has still been doused with pesticides. USDA Organic is, by definition, both non-GMO and free of toxic-persistent pesticides.[46]

Of course, it's not always possible to get organic everything, but before long you might start seeing a new certification label designed to help you sort out what's what: DetoxProject.org's "Glyphosate-Residue Free." This tag will tell you that the product or piece of produce you're looking at is certified to be free of glyphosate, the herbicide that is heavily applied to many GMO crops. Thank heaven for independent scientists!

MEANWHILE, BACK AT THE BOYS' CLUB

It is difficult to be optimistic that things regulation-wise will improve because, well, *politics*. Depending on who's holding sway in Congress, efforts to strengthen regulation can be obstructed, weakened, or even perverted—which is how the measures taken to control toxic substances have ended up making it *even easier* for manufacturers to skirt around safety. And depending on who's in the White House, regulatory agencies can be led by people drawn straight from the industries that profit from lax safety regulations. Recent real-world examples of what goes down on the regular include:

- Just when the highly toxic and heavily used synthetic pesticide chlorpyrifos was on the verge of being banned—like, literally days away—the new head of the EPA announced that no changes would be made.[47]
- Within weeks of *finally* beginning to analyze certain foods for residues of glyphosate—a weed killer that is used by the metric ton (you know it as Roundup) and has been identified as a probable carcinogen by the World Health Organization—the FDA pulled the plug on testing.[48]
- Also cut: the EPA's Endocrine Disruptor Screening Program.[49]

> *Bottom line: Human health is not a priority. Test no evil, find no evil.*

BREAKING BULLSHIT

There are some good things happening out there. Kraft finally got the artificial food coloring out of their mac and cheese.[50] General Mills is removing artificial additives and preservatives from some of their cereals.[51] Dannon's gone GMO-free on animal feed.[52] Perdue went antibiotic-free on their chicken,[53] Tyson is working on doing the same—and so is McDonald's![54] Meanwhile, SC Johnson now discloses the ingredients in its cleaning products,[55] Target is pushing brands to get rid of phthalates in personal care products and cleaning products,[56] and CVS is removing from its store-brand lines 500-some beauty products containing phthalates, parabens, and ingredients that most commonly contain formaldehyde.[57]

Is this enough? Hell, no. But is it progress? Absolutely.

Why are these companies taking steps beyond what any rules or regulations require them to do? Because, as their PR reps are known to phrase it, "there's a business benefit." Translation: because *we are demanding it.* More and more of us are refusing to buy their bullshit—literally. And that, sister of mine, is an effective way to make changes happen.

A FEW MORE THINGS TO KNOW ABOUT ME

CHILDHOOD

- Constantly put in the corner/sent to principal's office on account of sassy mouth and inability to sit still/keep quiet
- New town + new school = lonely Solace = McDonald's Happy Meals = my new best frenemies and beginning of my fast-food obsession
- Chunky by second grade, obese by fourth
- Athletic as a teenager, but can't outrun that eating disorder

TWENTIES

- Master's degree: check. Kick-ass career: check. Happily married: check. Subsisting on prefab packaged food: check.
- Seriously ill and morbidly obese— can't fit in an airplane seat
- Epiphany in early motherhood inspires giving up fast food, diet soda, etc., discovering real food, and ultimately losing more than 100 pounds
- Several family members die of cancer or complications from pharmaceutical drugs
- Create Mamavation, a social media community that ultimately morphs into a huge mom-focused blogger network and source of health infor-mation that millions of moms rely on every year
- Have one child
- Lose my father to mesothelioma (cancer caused by asbestos exposure)

THIRTIES

- Have two more children (for a total of three; all boys!)
- Shape magazine names me Mother of the Year; Cision Media ranks me in their "Top 10 Mom Bloggers"
- Become more focused on pesticides and EDCs
- Organize bloggers to communicate the importance of labeling GMOs in the United States; work on California, Oregon, and Washington State initiative campaigns from 2014 to 2016
- Revise blogging network to be the first non-GMO blogging network in the US, meaning we no longer promote products containing GMOs
- Monsanto recruits bloggers through a blogger network and publicly calls out Mamavation as enemy No. 1 in questionnaire of application process
- Host annual eco-wellness blogger conference with hundreds of bloggers, brands, and nonprofits
- Gain some weight back to become a more comfortable size
- American Academy of Pediatrics takes my advice and cuts ties with Monsanto

Your dollars are *yours*. How you choose to spend your money matters. A lot. Each and every one of those greenbacks is another way to speak—in a loud and clear voice that will be heard and heeded. And each and every buck is another way to cast your vote and be sure it is counted. So wield that cash. It is powerful. *You* are powerful.

ABOUT THE SCIENCE IN THIS BOOK

I don't have a degree in science, and I make no bones about that. What I do have is an advanced degree in communications and extensive experience in politics, public relations, social media, public health, and organizing large groups of people to accomplish amazing things. People with my professional background are used far and wide to communicate scientific information. Corporate conglomerates, universities, and governmental agencies task people like me with explaining complicated things to everyday folks. And professionals like me are deployed by manufacturers like Monsanto and big industry lobbies like the American Chemical Association to convince you that chemicals are completely safe and you should slather them all over your children. In addition to my advocacy work, I consult for the independent guys, helping to communicate emerging truths in science to everyday folks about things that are disgustingly toxic, endocrine-disrupting, and otherwise hazardous to our health.

Can I debate chemicals with a scientist? No. That isn't my superpower. But I *am* able to break this down for you in an understandable way that empowers you to slay the chemicals contaminating your home.

BUT DON'T JUST TAKE MY WORD FOR IT!

Everything I say in this book has passed muster with two highly regarded experts, one of them an environmental scientist of great renown, the other a leading pediatrician. Both are also parents, so they understand what we're all up against in trying to raise healthy, happy kids. And both have dedicated their professional lives to making the world a safer and healthier place. Basically, they've got our backs. You will see that they chime in from time to time throughout the book to offer further details on the science, an extra dose of expert advice, and sometimes even just their own two cents. It's an honor to introduce you to my crew:

JOHN PETERSON MYERS

Pete is founder, CEO, and chief scientist of Environmental Health Sciences (EHS), a biologist specializing in endocrine disruption, and a parent of two grown children. I call him "the Godfather." EHS is an independent, foundation-funded news organization that reports, publishes, and contextualizes news stories on environmental health topics at EnvironmentalHealthNews.org and DailyClimate.org. Pete publishes regularly in the scientific literature on EDCs, including as a coauthor of that study I mention on page 34. He is also coauthor of *Our Stolen Future: Are We Threatening Our Fertility, Intelligence, and Survival? A Scientific Detective Story,* which first revealed to the world how endocrine disruption was discovered, how it works, what it means, and how families can protect themselves and their communities. He's been working on EDCs for so long, he literally invented the term *endocrine disruption* in 1991.

TANYA ALTMANN, MD, FAAP

A forward-thinking pediatrician with an integrative medicine and nutrition focus, Dr. Tanya is founder of Calabasas Pediatrics, an assistant clinical professor at UCLA Mattel Children's Hospital, a spokesperson for the American Academy of Pediatrics, and the mother of three young boys. She is also the author of *What to Feed Your Baby: A Pediatrician's Guide to the 11 Essential Foods to Guarantee Veggie-Loving, No-Fuss, Healthy-Eating Kids* and *Baby and Toddler Basics* and is the editor in chief of the American Academy of Pediatrics' *Caring for Your Baby and Young Child: Birth to Age 5.* Dr. Tanya is a child health and wellness expert for numerous news programs and talk shows; basically, if you see an expert pediatrician on television, chances are it's her.

THE COMMON TONGUE VS. PERFECTION POLICE

As a communication professional, I can tell you that if you want to be understood you need to keep it simple and use language that people understand. Using the familiar tongue grants you access to doors and minds. Technical scientific terms are used in this book, but there are a couple that I have taken liberties with and will define those terms for you here so you understand. When I refer to the word "chemicals" I'm referring to synthetic, nasty, toxic or endocrine-disrupting shit you don't want around your family. I'm not referring to water, which is also technically a chemical. And when I refer to the word "pesticides" in some contexts it's used as a catchall phrase for pesticides, herbicides, fungicides and all the other cides. Linguistics and the understanding of words is also a science that evolves faster than we can keep up. This book is a reflection of those two worlds crashing together.

ONE
START WITH FOOD

SO YOU WANT TO clean up the way you feed yourself and your family? Start with the processed foods in your house.

Reckon with the reality that there is a *chemical shitstorm* in many of the packaged products in your fridge and pantry cupboard. And that's okay because you are normal. Unless you are living in a yurt in the middle of the Mojave Desert, you are probably eating at least some highly processed food.

But I can help you figure out how to clean up your act and make the whole situation *not* suck.

REALITY CHECK

Crack your fridge wide open and take a good look around. Scope out the contents of your freezer. Throw open the cupboards and check them out. Focus on the front row in each of these places—that top tier of go-to grub you and your dearly beloveds plow through on the regular. That

PETE DROPS SCIENCE:

If you want to take a deep-dive into this learning process, read Joanna Blythman's book *Swallow This*. It's *all* about processed food.

is where we are going to concentrate our efforts—where it counts.

How many of those mainstay items are packaged? Be literal about this; count every single thing that came home from the store in a container and/or wrapping—and, yes, that includes milk in a carton and prewashed salad in a bag. Pull it all out and line it up on the counter to get the full panoramic view. Remember to stick strictly with the stuff that's in daily rotation. Also, unless you notice an overdue sell-by date or a Petri dish situation, *don't throw anything out.* This is *so* not a pantry purge or a refrigerator rehab. Look, don't toss. (A little later I'll explain why you are only looking.)

Now here's the thing, sister: Every single one of these items on your counter is a processed food. Yes ma'am. That is the hard truth. All these foods have undergone some degree of processing. For some, it's minimal; for others, it's another story. But remember, right now you are amazing enough to take this journey, so you do *not* have permission to beat yourself up about anything here. We live and we learn, and right now you are learning.

ZONE OUT

Processed food spans a massive spectrum, from minimally modified natural ingredients (like bagged salad mix, page 25) to 100 percent synthetic crap (like diet and nondiet soda, page 41). On the minimal end of the spectrum is a safe and happy place I call the Green Zone, where plenty of packaged items consist of very few individual ingredients—all readily identifiable, nothing significantly modified, and nothing artificial. To know for sure that a packaged item is in the Green Zone, you need to take at least a passing glance at the ingredient label, and I'm going to tell you exactly how to do that.

FIRST CUT: FRIDGE

Swivel back to your countertop lineup and pull aside everything you'd figure belongs in the Green Zone. Single-ingredient products and simple combos are a good place to start, beginning with the fridge items so you can get them back in the cold where they can stay fresh.

To help get you started, here's how I'd go about evaluating a few of the basics commonly found in the family kitchen.

PACKAGED PRODUCE

Who doesn't routinely rely on packaged salad mix or some form pre-prepped produce? Washing lettuce doesn't really take all that much time, but it's enough of a pain that I, for one, jumped at the chance to establish an amicable separation from the salad spinner.

My bottom line on pre-prepped produce: Whole is ideal, but convenience can be a real blessing. Just be sure to scan the ingredients list on the label so you're certain there's nothing funky going on, like syrup or sweetener added to a container of mixed fruit salad. And you might want to be on the lookout for citric acid, which is used to preserve freshness and prevent browning and may or may not come from a citrus fruit. Whether or not you're as skeeved as I am by a mystery additive like that, be aware that it indicates the item sat around for quite a while after it was cut, and fresher produce is always better.

YOGURT

If the yogurt in your fridge is plain, then you are looking good right out of the gate. If it's organic and/or from the milk of grass-fed cows, even better (see page 122). And if it's Greek yogurt, major health points for being packed with protein. However, an ingredient label listing anything other than milk, live cultures, and maybe pectin (a plant-derived thickener that's used in some organic yogurts to prevent separation) means that once you've finished up whatever you have on hand, it is time to find a brand of yogurt that doesn't have unnecessary and potentially unhealthy additives.

DR. TANYA'S PRESCRIPTION:

For kids, I recommend staying under 4 teaspoons a day of added sugar (that's about 16 grams). Of course, even less is better! Until recently, it's been hard to figure out what is added, versus what is natural sugar from the food, but new labeling requirements have recently been adopted that require food companies to list grams of added sugar clearly and prominently on the label.

If it's nonorganic, the cow could have been fed a steady diet of growth hormones and antibiotics (page 122) as well as genetically engineered feed.[58, 59, 60] Some companies have cleaned up their act in recent years, but watch out for artificial food dye and/or caramel color,[61] plus preservatives.

The news does not get better if your flavored yogurt is "light," "reduced-calorie," or, God forbid, sugar-free or fat-free because the sugar and/or fat has been replaced with über-unhealthy artificial sweeteners (page 43) and/or other bogus additives.

Bottom line: yogurt = two ingredients: milk and live cultures. Flavoring plain yogurt yourself is easy and hella delicious. Try it. You'll see. Some sliced fresh fruit. Maybe some nuts or granola and a dribbling of maple syrup. Put out a selection of toppings and the whole family will be bellying up to the yogurt bar and knocking back the good stuff by the bodacious bowlful.

FIRST CUT: PANTRY

Now sift through your lineup of pantry products. Here's a quick rundown on a few typical cupboard items.

JARRED SALSA

This is a pretty easy one. All of the ingredients on the label should be very familiar produce items—tomatoes, onions, peppers, garlic, chilies, herbs—plus citrus juice and spices. But hold up! Do you see "natural flavor" or some such on there? That could be a code word for monosodium glutamate[62] (MSG) (page 35), a notoriously noxious flavor enhancer that is beyond unnecessary in a product that's essentially a straight-up combo

of a few things packed with, well, actual
natural flavor. Y'know, as in flavor that's
actually occurring naturally, right there
in the food? Granted, not all companies
do this, but some sneaky ones do. (See
page 35 for the lowdown on MSG.)

> **PETE DROPS SCIENCE:**
>
> Professor Robert Lustig considers one sugar, fructose, to be an endocrine-disrupting compound.

You might also see sugar in the ingredients, probably not in very large amounts, but still totally unnecessary. Ditto thickeners like xanthan. Lastly, if a lot of the ingredients are recognizable but listed as juice, extract, powder, dehydrated, etc., that means a whole lot of processing's gone down. A much better product is supereasy to find and mucho tasty and it's also easy to make yourself.

And P.S. "fresh" salsa that comes in a plastic tub from the refrigerated section could be—surprisingly—worse than the jarred variety from the supermarket shelf. Just because the label says "fresh" doesn't mean it doesn't contain artificial preservatives. For instance, your jar of Pace Picante sauce lists suspiciously vague "natural flavoring," but it's a better way to go than something like La Mexicana, which is sold from a refrigerated case and comes in a plastic tub emblazoned with "perishable" and "keep refrigerated"—a look at the ingredients will tell you that it is loaded with artificial preservatives like sodium benzoate and potassium sorbate. It's easy to be tricked by products that are packaged and placed to seem fresh when they really only have the *appearance* of being fresh. Preservatives are added to keep the food looking that way, and it's especially easy to be fooled by plastic containers in the refrigeration section. Again, pick up some tomatoes and jalapeños instead, and throw together a salsa that *is* fresh instead of just looking like it.

PASTA/NOODLES

A few iffy additives occasionally crop up in basic pastas and noodles, such as potassium bromate (a synthetic "flour bulking agent"), diglycerides (which can add trans fat), and tapioca and other starches (which constitute added sugars). Rice flour, either in rice noodles or added to other kinds of pasta, can mean trace amounts of arsenic[63] (yes, really; see page 156). But

PETE DROPS SCIENCE:

All I need to know about potassium bromate is that it has been banned from use in food products in countries as diverse as Brazil, Argentina, Peru, South Korea, and the European Union. This speaks to the weakness of the US regulatory agencies.

most plain pasta and other dry noodles are likely to pass Green Zone inspection.

Ramen and Cup O' Noodles? Not so much. That flavor packet is pure unadulterated evil (MSG and sodium out the wazoo) and even the noodles are a chemical nightmare. Ramen and other products processed to infinity and beyond are on the polar opposite end of the packaged-foods spectrum, a world away from the simple foods of the Green Zone.

But before we head over yonder and climb aboard a fun-house ride deep into the Red Zone, I want you to cull the rest of the solidly Green Zone items out of your countertop lineup and stow them away where they belong. Also, put back any items you've already flagged as not so good. Again, we're not in the business of purging here—steady as she goes, sister—just make a note to start looking for good replacements the next few times you go food shopping, and get back to sorting through the rest of your lineup.

CHEMICAL CRAP

Time to deal with the Red Zone. Some of what's in the Red Zone is screamingly obvious: mass-produced candy, breakfast cereal riddled with marshmallows, greasy and salty snack foods, fake cheese in an unrefrigerated brick or can, nondairy creamer, mystery toppings (*nothing* about that Whip is a Miracle or remotely Cool at all), and other hellishly hydrogenated, high-fructosed, monosodium-glutamated crap. P.S.: Bonus bullshit points for anything brightly aglow with artificial color.

Got anything like this in your countertop lineup? Chances are you have at least a few Red Zoners in the mix, give or take a less blatant baddie here and there. Scan through the ingredient labels. It doesn't take a deep dive to sniff out the wackness. Clue No. 1: honkin' huge ingredient list. Clue No. 2: one or more (and there's usually more) chemically engineered constituents (pages 48–51).

Prime suspects include any and all ready-mades, from canned soup to frozen dinners and pizzas. Same goes for shortcuts in a box (or pouch). And packaged baked goods are also treacherous territory—not just cookies and cakes, but also rolls and sandwich bread. Just because it's got "multigrain" in the name doesn't mean it's not chock-full of chemicals. Actually, if it has the words "added fiber" or "made with whole grains" on the packaging, those are red flags and you gotta give it a good once-over and count up the ingredients (page 37).

Worst of all, in their own special and sinister way (for those of us who've logged some mileage on the weight-loss hamster wheel), are the diet food products—as in anything labeled fat-free, sugar free, reduced calorie, etc. The yummy stuff's been sucked out of those products and replaced with chemical crap, which—surprise!—isn't good for you but—get this—makes you more likely to add pounds than lose them.

FINAL ROUNDUP

Back to the counter lineup. By now you've got the idea here. We've skimmed the good Green Zone stuff off the top, then we reckoned with the Red Zone stuff at the bottom. Now it's time to deal with everything left: the in-between products that aren't perfect, but aren't bad either. This is likely your largest zone.

Now let's take a final lap through the counter lineup, dealing with everything that's left: the stuff that's in between Green Zone goodness and Red Zone badness.

TAKE STOCK

Your countertop is now populated with products that didn't make the cut for the Green Zone. Welcome to the Yellow Zone, a vast stretch of nutritionally nebulous middle ground. The terrain here can be tricky to navigate because it's thick with seemingly innocuous products, many of which, upon closer

PETE DROPS SCIENCE:

FDA scientists have confirmed that glyphosate is in the US food supply. Getting a fast-food burger with all the trappings? Glyphosate is in the meat because of the GMO soy filler added to the beef and the fact that the cows were fed GMO soy and corn. It's in the bun because the flour was made from wheat that was dried, possibly right before harvest, with glyphosate. The French fries are from potatoes also dried right before harvest. By the way, that drying, called "pre-harvest desiccation," guarantees high levels of contamination. And the oil used to fry those fries? GMO canola oil. It's in the soft drink because it contains high-fructose GMO corn syrup.

Other scientists also report that glyphosate is widespread in the American food chain. For example, the Alliance for Natural Health has published a devastating report on glyphosate (Roundup) levels in breakfast foods.

inspection, turn out to be full of crap. Here are the rap sheets on a few likely suspects.

CEREAL

Cornflakes may seem like a decent way to start the day, but many iconic breakfast cereals contain the highly suspect preservative BHT (page 46), as well as undisclosed flavor agents. Many of the cereals marketed as super healthy/high in fiber are very heavy on grains that, if conventionally grown, more than likely contain GMOs (page 47); and that often also means the presence of the pesticide glyphosate (especially wheat and oats, as well as soy, corn, and sugar beets). Bottom line: In my view, cereal should be organic whenever possible because that means no toxic persistent pesticides and genetically engineered ingredients (page 16). You may want to improve on some of this stuff as you get further along.

SPREADS

Be sure to give a thorough once-over to the various things you routinely schmear on sandwiches, from ketchup and mayo (real and faux) to peanut butter and jelly. There's often some mighty nasty ingredients in these jars, like high-fructose corn syrup and/or other sweeteners (page 43), artificial and/or undisclosed flavorings, hydrogenated oils, and chemical preservatives.

SALAD DRESSING

That Wish-Bone Italian may have zing, but it also has a long list of highly processed ingredients, a base of unhealthy, GMO-laden soybean oil, "natural flavor" (which can mean a lot of things, some not good—see page 35), and caramel color (a suspected carcinogen). And if it's fat-free—ugh—don't even get me started. Be choosy about bottled dressings. Better yet, make your own—way cheaper and way tastier (recipes, page 138). I'm serious. It's not hard.

NO SUDDEN MOVES

I want you to finish this marathon, not get stuck within the first half mile because the whole family decided to ditch you and go home. So avoid freaking the fuck out right now, and don't go rushing into anything at a dead sprint. Pace yourself.

That means that however bummed out you might be feeling about how much crap you've just found lurking in your food supply, fend off the urge to flip out and start pitching a lot of stuff straight in the trash. **A much more practical and navigable route is to use up whatever you've got there in your kitchen and, meanwhile, stock up on various other options so you're not left scrambling when supplies run out.**

Even if you do get all fired up to go ahead and kick some of the worst food to the curb, my advice remains the same. First get an array of appealing alternatives on hand so you don't make yourself crazy figuring out what the hell to put on the table and in the lunchboxes—and so you don't set yourself up for a mutiny. Because that is exactly what you'll get if a favorite standby snack goes AWOL and there's nothing appealing in its place.

It is very important to keep in mind that this isn't just about you, it's about other people too. And if you are making these decisions *for* them, you need to keep it as painless as possible. Remember, slow and steady wins the race. That's the idea here. Too much, too quick, and you'll just piss everyone off. For some people, one thing at a time works best, while other people can do two to four switch-ups at once. You'll have to adjust based on what you know about your own family and how you find they respond.

PETE DROPS SCIENCE:

I would avoid BHT whenever possible. The US National Toxicology Program has found that a close chemical relative, BHA, is likely to be a human carcinogen, and BHT itself may be an animal carcinogen. While the evidence is somewhat ambiguous, who needs this, especially for their kids.

SHOULD IT STAY OR SHOULD IT GO NOW?

Once you've made your way through that initial list (and the next few chapters, which will help you the rest of the way along) and comfortably integrated an array of new foods into your everyday routine, then you can dig deeper into your food supplies, create lists, rank your priorities, and gradually deal with whatever items need replacing.

Ferreting out all that processed crap is a humongous first step. I know how hard it is to face up to how much of it turns out to be in the food you've been relying upon to nourish yourself and your family. And it is no small task to get savvy about bogus ingredients, deceptive labeling, and misleading marketing. So congrats, lady, on an excellent kickoff.

WHY I BUY ORGANIC

I buy organic packaged food for a lot of reasons, but I can boil them all down to just one.

BUYING ORGANIC TAKES THE CRAZY OUT OF GROCERY SHOPPING

What puts the crazy in grocery shopping? For starters, having to spend an eternity standing in the supermarket aisle scrutinizing labels, trying to suss out the suck, and basically turning every product choice into an ordeal on par with TSA airport screening. That is crazy. Who has time for that? I sure don't, with three young boys and a business to run.

But it would also be crazy to let a lot of label gibberish and deceptive marketing get in the way of protecting my family from what I know full well to be the main route of exposure to toxic chemicals: contaminated food.

Buying organic is a beautiful twofer. Looking for that trusty green seal liberates me from overly laborious label reading and it keeps the crap out of my family's food. I do check sugar levels and I pay attention to nutritional values, but I don't have to be on the lookout for high-fructose corn syrup, artificial flavors, artificial preservatives, or anything industrially or chemically produced. If dairy, eggs, or meat products of any kind were involved in

PETE DROPS SCIENCE:

If it has soybean oil and it's not explicitly organic, it's highly likely to contain glyphosate, the main ingredient in Monsanto's Roundup. The World Health Organization's International Agency for Research on Cancer concluded glyphosate is a probable human carcinogen.

making the product, I make sure they were raised without hormones, antibiotics, and steroids. Any produce or agricultural crop I buy has to be grown without toxic, persistent pesticides; sewage sludge and GMOs (page 47).

If you go with organic when you buy packaged foods, and you get to keep your precious time *and* eat healthier. That's a win-win in my book.

NEED MORE CONVINCING?

Recent studies yield a bumper crop of even more reasons to eat organic:

- Prenatal or early-childhood exposure to pesticides may lower IQ, cause neurological damage and behavioral problems like ADHD, and play a role in obesity and metabolic disorders later in life (see page 9).[64]
- Eating *even a little* organic can reduce your exposure to pesticides.[65]
- Organic meat and dairy is richer in heart- and brain-healthy omega-3 fatty acids.[66]
- Organic farming and feeding practices reduce the emergence of antimicrobial resistance in poultry and dairy farming.[67]
- If the package says "Organic" or "Made with organic ingredients," it's better than straight conventional, but not all of the ingredients are organic so you could be purchasing something that has GMOs and pesticides in it. Look for the seal!

WHY BUY ORGANIC

A recent scientific analysis calculated the annual costs of various EDCs
in terms of both dollars and IQ points and added cases of intellectual
disability. The finding? The researchers estimated that, in the United
States, exposure to a class of flame retardants called PBDEs accounts for
11 million lost IQ points in children, 43,000 more cases of disability, and
total health costs of $266 billion.[68] **The tab for pesticide exposure: 1.8
million lost IQ points, an additional 7,500 intellectual disability
cases, and health costs of $44.7 billion.[69]**

Therefore, buying organic takes the crazy out of grocery shopping.

WHEN YOU SEE "ARTIFICIAL COLORS," THINK "CHEMICAL SHITSTORM"

Artificial food dyes are found in beverages, ice cream and various frozen
desserts, cake and candy, macaroni and cheese, and medicines (I'm pointing at you, Pedialyte Powder in Fruit Punch flavor). Bear in mind that
artificial color can crop up where you wouldn't tend to expect it. For
example, in a chocolate cake with white frosting, the cake will often contain a combination of dyes used to create a nice chocolaty brown (especially if the ingredients don't involve much in the way of real chocolate
or cocoa in), and blue dye can be used to make white icing appear bright.

Here are the food dyes to look out for:

- Yellows 5 & 6: linked to ADHD in children; may contain PCB-11, a
  substance banned in high doses.[70]

◢ Red 40: a carcinogenic dye that the FDA has banned in cosmetics and certain drugs.[71]

◢ Blue 1: of special concern because it crosses the blood-brain barrier.[72]

All of these dyes trigger allergic reactions, such as hives, in some people.[73] Numerous studies have found that various amounts of artificial food dyes triggered hyperactivity or other adverse behavior in some children;[74] there is particular concern that there may be a link between the behavioral effect and the combination of food dye and certain preservatives, so it's yet another reason to keep kids away from processed foods.[75]

WHEN YOU SEE "FLAVORING," THINK CHEMICAL SHITSTORM

MSG (monosodium glutamate, a chemically manufactured form of an amino acid found in the body) is added to many, many processed foods. It makes bland shit taste yummy. It is a known excitotoxin/neurotoxin.[76]

"NOT FROM CONCENTRATE," THINK CHEMICAL SHITSTORM

When your OJ carton says "not from concentrate," that makes you think it hasn't been reconstituted, but it totally has. Here's what goes down: Because orange juice has to be available year-round and harvests are seasonal, it is stored in large containers that sometimes alter the taste. And in order to make the flavor of the juice more consistent, "flavor packets" are added—and companies aren't required to disclose this on the label.[77] Cold-pressed oil is made and fractionated into single isolated compounds that exhibit orange flavor nodes. This sounds technical because, well, it is. No additives are listed on the label because super loose regulation of the citrus industry dating back to the 1940s allows them to present something that is manufactured from the fruit's constituent ingredients as juice. Also note, by the way, that the orange oils can be made from the rind, which has been sprayed with pesticides—so those are going into the juice. How ridiculous is that?

So go organic, but go the extra mile and be really particular about it. Even some organic OJs have been known to use a version of flavor packets that's less bad (no pesticides, for one thing), but still not what you're after when you shell out for "fresh" organic juice. Unless what you want is a carton of the juice formerly known as orange—with a shitload of massively processed

DR. TANYA'S PRESCRIPTION:

I (and the American Academy of Pediatrics) recommend that babies and toddlers do not drink juice. At all. Even watered down juice just gets them used to wanting to drink sweet tasting beverages. Plain water (and milk) is all they need. For older kids, juice is a dessert so if that's what they want for dessert at a party, then that's fine. However, kids who don't get used to juice when they are young tend not to choose it and instead drink plain water.

Getting babies used to the taste of plain water is one of the best things you can do. Offer it daily starting around 6 months of age, when you start solid food. Infants who drink water turn into young children and adults who like plain water. What could be healthier than that!

ingredients (plus, it's been pasteurized, which means any bacteria have been cooked out along with any remaining innate flavor). Unlike conventional OJ, organic and packet-free won't taste *exactly the same* from carton to carton and from brand to brand. Ever noticed that? Now you know why—eww!

Make the occasional glass of juice a sweet treat (page 36), not a crappy sugar bomb. And beware the kiddie-size boxes and pouches! Don't let "no added sugar," "100% juice," "all natural" fool you—check the nutritional analysis for total grams of sugar (page 42) and the ingredients list for lots of fruit concentrates. Better yet, if you're going to have OJ, it's so much easier and cheaper to just make your own—and it tastes way, *way* better! In some grocery stores they even have a juice-squeezing station where you can just make your own right there—no home equipment required!

BAIT AND SWITCH

Along with the various red-alert additives to look out for, if the package says anything about being "healthy" or "natural"—anything about being rich in vitamins, fiber, protein, or anything boosting your immune system or helping you fight heart disease or other health problems—slow down and proceed with caution. As someone who works with foods brands, it pains me to say it, but it's probably even *more* important to be wary of foods billing themselves as healthy and/or natural. I've found this is hit or miss. Sometimes it's a good buy, but most of the time, it isn't. You are not being told the full story, since your attention is directed

PETE DROPS SCIENCE:

The burden of funding tests of safety should rest on the manufacturers, but they should not conduct the research. It should be undertaken by independent scientists free of conflicts of interest. Moreover, all too often people assume that the absence of evidence of harm is proof of safety. For most chemicals in the market, including those added to food, absence of evidence of harm is an indication that no one has performed appropriate tests.

DR. TANYA'S PRESCRIPTION:

Marketing junk food to kids is a serious problem. As a pediatrician and mom of three, I see it every day. Kids are exposed to advertising everywhere they go—on the Internet, on TV, in movies, and even sometimes at school! I agree with the American Academy of Pediatrics that marketing of unhealthy foods to kids may contribute significantly to childhood and adolescent obesity and poor nutrition (not to mention use of tobacco, alcohol, and drugs). Children under 8 can't tell the difference between fantasy and reality, and therefore they are uniquely vulnerable. It should not be standard business practice for fast-food and other conglomerates to bombard children with billions of dollars of advertising every year. European countries have put in place restrictions that ban or limit advertising aimed at children. The US should too.

toward certain particular attributes. It's a ruse that advertising and marketing create that then plays into your expectations—often falsely. For example, if you were to buy a jug of Kool-Aid or a bag of Cheetos, you'd know those weren't healthy. But what about a loaf of Arnold Whole Grains Healthy Multi-Grain Bread? Take a closer look—past the package boasting high fiber, no high-fructose corn syrup, artificial flavors or colors—at the ingredient list and you'll find a string of chemicals that certainly aren't healthy, including emulsifiers such as monoglycerides, which keep the bread squishy and can also be a hidden source of trace amounts of trans fat.[78]

Bottom line: The labeling can be confusing. The government oversees the use of these terms:

⬧ 100 percent organic: All the ingredients are certified organic.

⬧ Organic: At least 95% of the ingredients are certified organic.

⬧ Made with organic ingredients: At least 70 percent of the ingredients are certified organic.

Two others that are legit and useful:

⬧ Non-GMO verified (with the butterfly logo) means no GMOs—but there can still be pesticide residue)

⬧ Certified Glyphosate Residue Free by DetoxProject.com

Other than these, any and all other labels, such as "all-natural" and "farm-raised," aren't regulated, so they don't mean much. Buyer beware!

SUGAR SHENANIGANS

There are lots of different kinds of sugars, and some of them are naturally occurring in whole foods—even in food that we don't experience as sweet, for example, like the lactose in plain milk and yogurt, or the fructose, sucrose, and glucose in an onion. Too much sugar of any kind is a problem, but it is less of a concern when it's coming from a whole food surrounded by high fiber and other nutrients.

Then there is a whole array of sugars that are added to processed foods. Some of these sugars are derived from natural high-sugar sources, like beets, corn, rice, and grapes. You name it, they've figured out how to hybridize it and manufacture it into sweetener—and synthesize it into syrups and other concentrates to load by the ton into packaged foods.

There are massive quantities of added sugar in all sorts of foods we don't think of as sweets, like bread, processed meat, salad dressing, condiments, crackers, etc. (And fast food? Fuggedaboutit.)

And try this on for supersize. Do you think you're avoiding grotesque amounts of added sugar by not buying items that don't list sugar or high-fructose corn

DR. TANYA'S PRESCRIPTION:

If my patients really want sugary cereal, I suggest that they choose it as dessert. Definitely not before noon. Sugary fake-colored cereal isn't breakfast after all; it really belongs in the dessert category. Energy drinks are only useful in very specific situations, such as vigorous outdoor exercise in the heat lasting more than an hour. In most cases of kids' exercising or being outdoors, water and a healthy snack is all they need. The same goes for flavored yogurt with too much added sugar or treat toppings. Honestly, I just don't buy that stuff for my house, but when I see families that already do buy it, the first thing I do is move it to later in the day, then slowly wean down the times of week they can have it, or mix it with healthier versions to slowly retrain their palate and brain.

syrup in the ingredients? Wrong. They just put in multiple forms of sugar and use a whole slew of sly aliases—from fruit juice concentrate and evaporated cane juice to maltose and dextrose, from tapioca syrup to rice bran, barley malt, and sorghum (page 51).

Sometimes labels don't say sugar: there are 6l other names used, like syrup and barley malt

Percent of food items in US grocery stores that contain added sugar: 68%

Cereal is sweet—too sweet: the average cereal packs more than the 5% recommended daily sugar limit for kids

Put down the soda! 74% of all added sugars consumed in the US are in soft drinks

THE SCARY TRUTH: ON AVERAGE, A PERSON CONSUMES 66 LBS OF HIDDEN ADDED SUGAR PER YEAR

So it takes some sugar Sherlocking. The less packaged food you buy, the less sleuthing you need to do.

My advice, in all seriousness, is to consider things like sweet cereal, granola bars, energy drinks, juice, and fruit rollups (to name just a few) to be *candy* because that's how much sugar (and other crap) they contain. Not to mention that routinely eating this stuff is keeping America's sugar intake crazy high.[79]

SODA SUCKS

NOT SO SWEET

There is no shortage of research showing that going beyond the recommended daily limit on sugar intake is bad for you. Evidence that sugar is addictive is also adding up.

Among the lengthy list of health harms that refined sugar has been linked to:

Tooth decay
Acne
Impaired immune system
Obesity
High blood pressure
Insulin resistance
Type 2 diabetes

DR. TANYA'S PRESCRIPTION:

I agree that artificial sweeteners aren't healthy for kids (or adults) as they simply teach your brain to want super sweet-tasting things and throw off your perception of what natural sweet foods should taste like.

The one exception would be for a diabetic child that really can't have any sugar. Then a little artificial sweetener in a dessert could occasionally be considered okay.

Polycystic ovary syndrome

Vision problems

Liver damage

Memory/cognitive decline

Heart disease

Cancer

Meanwhile, high-fructose corn syrup has recently been racking up an equally charming array of adverse associations:

- Alterations in the brain that may lead to a wide range of diseases, such as Alzheimer's disease, depression, and attention deficit hyperactivity disorder (ADHD)[80]
- Damage to the female reproductive system (another good reason to avoid high-fructose corn syrup if you have young girls)[81]
- And, no surprise here—obesity, diabetes, heart disease, and various cancers.[82]

SUGAR SHOCK—HOW MUCH SHOULD YOU *REALLY* BE EATING?

CHILDREN 4 TO 8

American Heart Association (AHA) recommended daily limit for added sugar: about 3 teaspoons (13 grams)

Average daily intake: around 21 teaspoons (88 grams)

PRETEENS TO TEENS

AHA recommended daily limit for added sugar: 5 to 8 teaspoons (21 to 34 grams)

Average daily intake for 14- to 18-year-olds: around 34 teaspoons (144 grams)

ADULTS

AHA recommended daily limit for added sugar: 6 teaspoons (25 grams) for women, 9 teaspoons (38 grams) for men

Average daily intake: around 22 teaspoons (93 grams)[83]

"Sugar arithmetic is tricky." But here's a visual to keep in mind: For every 4 grams listed on the label, picture a teaspoonful (if you want to be precise, multiply each teaspoon by 4.2 to get the number of grams).

So, say you're looking at a bottle of Snapple that has 26 grams per serving. That translates to more than 6 teaspoons of sugar. Imagine heaping that much sugar into a glass of unsweetened iced tea or a cup of black coffee and then knocking that shit back. It's enough to make me shudder just thinking about it.

WHEN YOU SEE "SUGAR FREE," THINK CHEMICAL SHITSTORM

Artificial sweeteners are chemical concoctions that make it possible for products to taste sweet without calories. While there is no definitive

PETE DROPS SCIENCE:

In 2015, researchers discovered that two common chemicals added as "emulsifiers" to low-fat and nonfat foods harm the gut microbiota and induce colitis, obesity, and metabolic syndrome. http://go.nature.com/29BTD3a

proof yet that these substances cause health problems, evidence is strong, caution is warranted, and more research is needed. And the burden of proof that they are truly safe should rest not on the public, but on the manufacturers raking in the profits.

Risks associated with artificial sweeteners include:

Weight gain /obesity

Cancer

Preterm labor

Headaches/dizziness

Increased risk of diabetes and related illnesses

Increased risk of heart attack or stroke[84]

A NOT-SO-TASTY SAMPLER OF FOOD INGREDIENTS BANNED IN OTHER PARTS OF THE WORLD—BUT NOT HERE IN THE UNITED STATES

ARTIFICIAL COLORS/DYES: Often derived from coal tar, artificial dyes and colors are linked to hyperactivity in children, allergic reactions, and cancer. Blue 1, Blue 2, Yellow 5, and Yellow 6 are some of the specific colors that are banned abroad.[85]

AZODICARBONAMIDE: This is the "yoga mat" chemical that Subway was compelled by public outcry to remove from its bread. Azodicarbonamide is both a bleaching agent and dough conditioner, but not a necessary one. It's banned in Europe, the U.K., Singapore, and Australia. Why the concern? Inhalation of azodicarbonamide is linked to asthma.[86]

MOTT'S APPLESAUCE

—because your most popular version has high-fructose corn syrup but there is a Box Tops for Education logo on your package, encouraging moms to feed their kids high-fructose corn syrup. I guess you also like diabetes in children.

BEST FOODS MAYO

—because you make almost every sandwich in America a preservative concoction more suited to embalming a corpse than nourishing a live human.

WEIGHT WATCHERS

—because you tout yourself as a healthy company and yet sell the most atrocious food products on the market, full of nasty preservatives, GMOs, and artificial sweeteners.

LUNCHABLES

—because you put nitrates, additives, preservatives, and other hazmat shit in your crappy boxes and target young children in their own living rooms.

GO-GURT

—Does yogurt have to be blue? Really?

HEINZ KETCHUP

—for putting high-fructose corn syrup in America's refrigerators from sea to shining sea.

DR. TANYA'S PRESCRIPTION:

I'm not an applesauce person, but Mott's has a natural applesauce line that is fine and has no added sugar at all, for those who want applesauce. Again, compared to lots of junk kids eat, natural applesauce isn't that bad when they want something that tastes sweet.

GOLDFISH

—because you seductively smiley, cheesy little fuckers are the most popular toddler snack food and you are made of 100 percent crap.

BHA AND BHT: You'll find these preservatives in nuts, beer, and cereal, to name a just a few foods. They're derived from petroleum and keep oils in foods from going rancid. Research has shown that BHA and BHT are harmful to the blood and the circulatory system. Lab rats also developed tumors when given the chemical, leading to concerns that it could cause cancer.[87]

BROMINATED VEGETABLE OIL (BVO): BVO is used in sports drinks and other beverages to preserve flavor. This vegetable oil's main ingredient, bromine, is used as a fire retardant for sofas and carpets—not exactly something you want to be drinking.[88]

DIPHENYLAMINE (DPA): Have you ever seen an apple that looked perfect and blemish-free? Maybe it wasn't nature, but rather diphenylamine that made the apple look that way. The chemical is banned in Europe, but here in the US, conventional apples are often soaked in DPA to prevent brown spots from forming on the skin during storage. The European Commission banned DPA partly because of the presence of nitrosamines, which caused cancer in lab rats and elevated certain cancers in humans. Ultimately, there was not enough evidence to prove that diphenylamine wasn't harmful, so it was banned.[89]

FARM-RAISED SALMON: Farm-raised salmon is currently banned in New Zealand and Australia due to the use of antibiotics, which can lead to antibiotic resistance in both the animal and those consuming it.[90, 91] In addition, farm-raised salmon is pumped full of chemicals to speed up growth and increase size. PCBs are a major concern in salmon, and they are 16x more prev-

PETE DROPS SCIENCE:

I avoid MSG because it's just stupid to use the most important excitatory neurotransmitter in the brain in food. The FDA says MSG is safe, but all too many times we've had official agencies declare something safe and later turn out to be wrong, and all too often these agencies have cozy relationships with the industries they regulate. Many aspects of the MSG story smell like that. So I say play it safe and take a reasonable precautionary step: Don't eat food to which a powerful excitatory neurotransmitter has been added. If you want to know more about potential risks posed by MSG, you can tune in to the YouTube channel of Dr. Russel Blaylock, a neurosurgeon, researcher, and author of *Excitotoxins: The Taste That Kills*.

alent in farmed salmon than wild salmon, according to research. This banned chemical is found in things like asbestos, and is still present in the environment *despite* it being banned.

GENETICALLY MODIFIED ORGANISMS (GMOS): As of 2017, 38 countries have banned or restricted GMO cultivation and/or imports. The United States has yet to adopt similar guidelines and instead passed an embarrassingly weak labeling bill in 2016.[92] See page 15 for more concerns.

OLESTRA (OLEAN): Although Olestra was hailed as a breakthrough in low-fat food, it turned out to be too good to be true. Cramps, gas, and irritable bowel–type symptoms are a common side effect of this chemical. And if the reports of anal leakage after consuming olestra weren't bad enough, it has also been found in some cases to deplete the body of essential vitamins and nutrients by inhibiting their absorption. Both Canada and the U.K. have banned this ingredient.[93]

POTASSIUM BROMINATE (BROMINATED FLOUR): Bromine is problematic because it has the ability to displace iodine in the human body. It can also cause nervous system and kidney disorders, as well as gastrointestinal discomfort. Oh, and it was found to be carcinogenic in lab rats so there's that.[94]

SYNTHETIC HORMONES (RECOMBINANT BOVINE GROWTH HORMONE OR RECOMBINANT BOVINE SOMATOTROPIN): Cows are often treated with hormones to boost their milk supply. The end result is dairy tainted with synthetic hormones, and a high level of insulin-like growth factor 1 hormones, which are linked to breast, prostate, lung, colon, and other cancers.[95] Cows treated with hormones also experience mastitis and other infections, which then require antibiotics, which can contribute to antibiotic resistant bacteria.

WHY "VEGETABLE OILS" ARE AN INGREDIENT TO AVOID

Vegetable oils often contain high levels of polyunsaturated fats. Why is that a problem? They are highly unstable and quick to oxidize, which leads to free radical formation, chronic inflammation, and even DNA damage.[96] Two of the worst offenders, soybean oil and canola oil, are likely genetically modified and are the most often found vegetable oils in pasta sauce, as well as in countless other processed foods.

50 SHADES OF MESSED UP

MSG

MSG masquerades as:
*E indicates a known excitotoxin, but this may not appear on the label.

ALWAYS INDICATES MSG:

1. Calcium glutamate (E 623)
2. Glutamate (E 620)
3. Glutamic acid (E 620)
4. Magnesium diglutamate (E 625)
5. Magnesium glutamate (E 625)
6. Monoammonium glutamate (E 624)
7. Monopotassium glutamate (E 622)
8. Monosodium glutamate (E 621)
9. Ajinomoto
10. Autolyzed anything
11. Calcium caseinate
12. Gelatin
13. Anything hydrolyzed
14. Hydrolyzed whey protein concentrate
15. Natrium glutamate
16. Anything protein
17. Pectin soy protein
18. Plant protein
19. Soy protein
20. Soy protein concentrate
21. Soy protein isolate
22. Textured protein
23. Textured vegetable protein
24. Whey protein
25. Whey protein isolate
26. Whey protein protease
27. Sodium caseinate
28. Sodium cocoyl glutamate
29. Umami
30. Vetsin
31. Xanthum gum E415
32. Yeast extract/Yeast food/ Yeast nutrient

ADDITIVES THAT ARE ONLY USED IN CONJUNCTION WITH MSG

33. Disodium 5`-guanylate (E 627) or Disodium Guanylate E627
34. Disodium 5`-inosinate (E-631) or Disodium Inosinate E631
35. Disodium 5`-ribonucleotides (E 635)

36. Anything containing enzymes
37. Anything fermented
38. Any flavors or flavoring
39. Malted barley
40. Malt extract/maltodextrin
41. Nutritional yeast
42. Oligodextrin
43. Pectin (E 440)
44. Protease
45. Seasonings
46. Soy sauce/Soy sauce extract
47. Stock
48. Torula yeast
49. Anything ultra-pasteurized
50. Whey protein concentrate

GMOS (100 SHADES OF MESSED UP!)

GMO crops include soy, cotton, canola, corn, sugar beets, Hawaiian papaya, alfalfa, potatoes, apples, zucchini, and yellow squash. In addition to those crops, these 100 ingredients, usually indicate the presence of hidden GMOs unless the product is certified organic or non-GMO project verified.

1. Corn flour
2. Corn masa
3. Cornmeal
4. Corn oil
5. Corn sugar
6. Corn syrup
7. Cornstarch
8. Starch
9. Food starch
10. Modified food starch
11. Modified starch
12. Hydrogenated starch
13. Milo starch
14. High-fructose corn syrup
15. Dextrin
16. Cyclodextrin
17. Maltodextrin
18. Dextrose
19. Malt
20. Malt syrup
21. Malt extract
22. Hydrolyzed vegetable protein
23. Baking powder
24. Caramel color
25. Sugar (unless specified as cane sugar)
26. E951
27. Nutrasweet
28. Aspartame
29. Aminosweet
30. Canderel
31. Benevia
32. Phenylalanine
33. Equal
34. Confectioners' sugar
35. Invert sugar
36. Inverse syrup
37. Fructose (any form)

38. Glucose
39. Condensed milk
40. Milk powder
41. Glycerides
42. Glycerin
43. Glycerol
44. Glycerol monooleate
45. Diglyceride
46. Mono and diglycerides
47. Triglyceride
48. Teriyaki marinades
49. Tofu
50. Tamari
51. Tempeh
52. Textured vegetable protein
53. Soy flour
54. Soy isolates
55. Soy milk
56. Soy oil
57. Soy sauce
58. Soy protein
59. Soy protein concentrate
60. Soy protein isolate
61. Protein isolate
62. Soy lecithin
63. Lecithin
64. Whey
65. Whey powder
66. Xanthan gum
67. Canola oil (rapeseed oil)
68. Cottonseed oil
69. Vegetable oil
70. Vegetable fat
71. Shoyu

72. Monosodium glutamate
73. Glutamate
74. Glutamic acid
75. Citric acid
76. Lactic acid
77. Phytic acid
78. Oleic acid
79. Stearic acid
80. Erythritol
81. Inositol
82. Mannitol
83. Sorbitol
84. Cellulose
85. Hemicellulose
86. Methylcellulose
87. Trehalose
88. Colorose
89. Malitolmaltose
90. Cobalamin (vitamin B12)
91. Vitamin B12
92. Vitamin E
93. Diacetyl
94. Isoflavones
95. Tocopherols (vitamin E)
96. Threonine
97. Glycine
98. Leucine
99. Lysine
100. Cystine

SUGAR

Sugar is sneaked in as:
1. Agave nectar

2. Barbados sugar
3. Barley malt/barley malt syrup
4. Beet sugar
5. Buttered syrup
6. Cane juice/cane juice crystals/cane sugar
7. Caramel
8. Carob syrup
9. Castor sugar
10. Coconut palm sugar/coconut sugar
11. Confectioners' sugar
12. Corn sweetener/corn syrup/corn syrup solids
13. Date sugar
14. Dehydrated cane juice
15. Demerara sugar
16. Dextrin
17. Dextrose
18. Evaporated cane juice
19. Free-flowing brown sugars
20. Fructose
21. Fruit juice/fruit juice concentrate
22. Glucose/glucose solids
23. Golden sugar
24. Golden syrup
25. Grape sugar
26. High-fructose corn syrup)
27. Honey
28. Icing sugar
29. Invert sugar
30. Malt syrup
31. Maltodextrin
32. Maltol
33. Maltose
34. Mannose
35. Maple syrup
36. Molasses
37. Muscovado
38. Palm sugar
39. Panocha
40. Raw sugar
41. Refiner's syrup
42. Rice syrup
43. Saccharose
44. Sorghum syrup
45. Sucrose
46. Sweet sorghum
47. Syrup
48. Treacle
49. Turbinado sugar
50. Yellow sugar

NAMING NAMES:

FROZEN FOODS

Many frozen, ready-to-eat meals are hiding a minefield of hazardous ingredients, including toxic preservatives. The following list covers 70 brands of frozen foods commonly found in grocery stores around the country. The ranking represents tendencies across each brand's various product lines, not the contents of each and every individual product. Some brands are much more ingredient-aware than others and make efforts to provide better options; others—not so much. Generally, the longer the ingredients list, the more likely its contents are problematic. And no matter what the label says, never *ever* microwave anything in the package.

BAD

These brands frequently use ingredients like high-fructose corn syrup, artificial and "natural" flavors, MSG, toxic preservatives, plus modified starches, and other highly processed and potentially harmful ingredients.

505 Southwestern
Arturo's of Chicago
Atkins
Bagel Bites
Banquet
Bar-S
Beast Burger
Boca
Boston Market
Bird's Eye Voila!
Delimex
DiGiorno
Doritos
El Charrito
Farm Rich
Gorton's
Hot Pockets
Hungry-Man
InnovAsian
Jimmy Dean
José Olé
Kid Cuisine
Marie Callender's
Michelina's
Morningstar Farms
On-Cor
Pierre Drive Thru
P.F. Chang's Home Menu
Sam's Choice
Smucker's
Stouffer's
State Fair
Tai Pei
Tina's Quesarito
Totino's
White Castle
Zatarain's

BETTER

These brands are in the middle—they may contain some semi-undesirable ingredients, but very overtly hazardous substances. Some of them may contain ingredients you prefer to avoid, so give the labels a good close look.

Aqua Star

Bertolli

Better Bakery

Chili's

Gorton's Simply Bake

Great Value

El Monterey

Healthy Choice

Kahiki

Kim & Scott's Pretzels

Lean Cuisine

Sandwich Bros

SeaPak

Smart Ones

Stouffer's Fit Kitchen

Tyson Gluten-Free

Van de Kamp's

Welch's

BEST

Here's where the good brands live, and they're becoming more and more available in our local stores. There's still some minimal use of iffy substances like soy ingredients, natural flavors, and vegetable oils, but they're very minimal. Again, it's important to always check your labels.

365 Everyday Value

Alexia

Amy's Kitchen

Annie Chun's

Annie's Homegrown

Applegate Naturals

Artisan Bistro

Blake's

Cascadian Farms Organic

Dr. Praeger's Sensible Foods

Healthy Choice Simply

Hip Chick Farms

Kashi

Love

Luvo

Michael Angelo's

Udi's

CONDIMENTS

BAD

These brands are best left on the shelf. They contain high-fructose corn syrup made from GMO corn, sugar from GMO sugar beets, GMO soybean oil, "natural flavorings" and "natural smoke flavor," which can indicate all MSG, preservatives, and additives. Note that no mustards landed on this list.

Best Foods Real Mayonnaise

Heinz BBQ Sauce

Heinz Tomato Ketchup

Hunt's BBQ Sauce

Hunt's Tomato Ketchup

Kraft Mayo with Olive Oil

Kraft Real Mayo

Sweet Baby Ray's Barbecue Sauce

BETTER

These condiments are better choices, although some contain preservatives like calcium disodium EDTA or the vague "natural flavors."

Bull's-Eye BBQ Sauce

French's Classic Yellow Mustard

French's Spicy Brown Mustard

French's Dijon

Grey Poupon Dijon Mustard

Heinz Yellow Mustard

Hunt's 100% Natural Tomato Ketchup

Just Mayo

Simply Heinz Tomato Ketchup

BEST

These organic and natural condiments are free from GMOs, artificial preservatives, and MSG. You can accessorize that sandwich as saucily as you please, just make sure you've read up on which meat you should be buying (pages 121–122, 125–127). *However*, it's important to note that ketchups and barbecue sauces tend to have high sugar content, and mayonnaise is high in fat.

Annie's Naturals Organic BBQ Sauce

Annie's Naturals Organic Dijon Mustard

Annie's Naturals Organic Ketchup

Annie's Naturals Organic Yellow Mustard

Bill's Best Organic BBQ Sauce

Cucina Antica Organic Tomato Ketchup

Gulden's Spicy Brown Mustard

Heinz Organic Tomato Ketchup

Heinz Organic Yellow Mustard

O Organics Tomato Ketchup

Primal Kitchen Mayo with Avocado Oil

Sir Kensington's Classic Ketchup

Sir Kensington's Mustard

Spectrum Organic Mayonnaise

Spectrum Organic Mayonnaise with Olive Oil

PASTA SAUCE

A surprising number of questionable ingredients can be found in store-bought spaghetti sauce. Organic sauces are generally your best bet because they ensure you're avoiding 99 percent of the ingredients of concern. But as you can see below, there are some great nonorganics out there. Beware of sauces in a can.

BAD

These contain things we want to avoid: GMOs, high sugar, toxic preservatives, vegetable oils, caramel color, animal fat, *and* a couple are packaged in BPA-lined cans.

Barilla
Bertolli
Del Monte
Gaetano's
Great Value
Hunt's
Luigi Bonura's
Prego (thanks for the label disclosure: "Partially produced with genetic engineering," but no thanks!)
Ragu
Scimeca's
Taste of the Hill

BETTER

Although they have higher sugar content and/or semi-questionable ingredients, like soybean oil and the mysterious "natural flavoring," these sauces are okay choices. Most are widely available.

Always Save
Amy's Organic
Best Choice
Cascone's

Classico
Emeril's
Francesco Rinaldi
Muir Glen Organic
Newman's Own
Walnut Acres

BEST

There are plenty of good choices with acceptable ingredients and relatively low sugar content—phew!

Cadia Organic
Lidia's
Mezzetta
Mom's
Monte Bene
Organico Bello
Organicville
Superior Selections
The Silver Palate
Thrive Market
Victoria Trading Company

BREAD, HOT DOG ROLLS, AND HAMBURGER BUNS

TO BE AVOIDED

These are brands to avoid because they contain various questionable ingredients such as dough conditioners (mono- and diglycerides, ethoxylated mono- and diglycerides, calcium peroxide, diacetyl tartaric acid ester of mono- and diglycerides (DATEM), azodicarbonamide, enzymes), yeast nutrients (monocalcium phosphate, calcium sulfate, ammonium sulfate), calcium propionate, high-fructose corn syrup, soy lecithin, coloring, and artificial flavor.

Arnold
Bunny
Great Value Wheat
Holsum
Kroger
Martin's
Stroehmann Sunbeam
Sara Lee
Wonder Bread

THE HEALTHIEST CHOICES

These brands stick with healthier grains, organic and/or non-GMO products, sprouted and ancient grains, and generally avoid added sugar.

Alvarado St. Bakery Sprouted Buns
Canyon Bakehouse (gluten-free)
Ezekiel/Food for Life
Silver Hills Sprouted Bakery
Rudi's Bakery (gluten-free)
Dave's Killer Bread
Manna Organics

Legit Bread (gluten-free)
Open Nature
Whole Foods Market Organic Wheat
Vermont Bread Company

SALAD DRESSING

BAD

These brands contain multiple ingredients to avoid, such as MSG, high-fructose corn syrup, natural and artificial flavors, GMOs, and artificial preservatives or stabilizers.

Bob's Famous Salad Dressing
Bolthouse Farms
Cains
Girard's
Hidden Valley
Ken's Steakhouse
Kraft
Kroger
Litehouse
Makoto
Marie's
Olive Garden
Red Shell
Signature Kitchens (Safeway)
Virginia Brand
Walden Farms
Wishbone
Wishbone EVOO

BETTER

These dressings may still contain some of the ingredients to avoid, such as canola oil or GMOs.

Briannas
Cardini's
DeLallo
Good Seasons
Lucini
Maple Grove Farms
Marzetti
Naturally Fresh
Newman's Own
Oak Hill Farms
Simple Girl
Stonewall Kitchen
Trader Joe's

BEST

These dressing do not contain GMOs, artificial flavors, MSG, or most of the ingredients to be avoided.

Annie's
Bragg
Follow Your Heart
Newman's Own Organic
Organicville
Primal Kitchen

CRACKERS

BAD

Brands listed here use at least some of the following: toxic preservatives (TBHQ, BHT), GMOs (soy lecithin, modified starches, corn products), leavening agents (sodium acid pyrophosphate, monocalcium phosphate), MSG ingredients (MSG, autolyzed yeast extract, disodium inosinate, disodium guanylate), sulfites, high sugar, and artificial colors and flavors.

Austin
Breton Original Crackers
Great Value
Keebler
Kellogg
Cheez-It Cheddar Jack crackers
Cheez-It White Cheddar crackers
Lance Captain's Wafers Jalapeño
    Cheddar Crackers
Lance Toast Chee Peanut Butter
    Sandwich Crackers
Munchies Peanut Butter Sandwich
    Crackers
Nabisco
Chicken in a Biskit
Honey Maid Graham Crackers
Honey Maid Low Fat Cinnamon
    Graham Crackers
Wheat Thins

BETTER

Less bad stuff here, but there might be very small amounts of leavening agents, MSG, preservatives, artificial flavors, and colors.

Back to Nature Crispy Cheddar
Crackers

Cabaret Crisp and Buttery
Crackers

Dare Grains First Whole Grain
Crackers

Funley's Delicious Super Crackers

Geraldine's All-Natural Chipotle
Cheddar Cheese Straws

Glutino Original Gluten Free
Crackers

Gratify Gluten Free Original Baked
Bites Crackers

Great Value Buttery Smooth
Crackers

JFC Rice Cracker Mix

Kashi Original 7 Grain Crackers

Kellogg's Cheez-It Original
Crackers

Lance Gluten Free Peanut Butter
Sandwich Crackers

Late July Organic Mini Cheddar
Sandwich Crackers

Milton's

Nabisco

Barnum's Animal Crackers

Good Thins Original

Grahams

Ritz Crackers

Premium Rounds with Whole
Grain Saltines

Premium Original Saltine Crackers

Pepperidge Farm Goldfish
Crackers

Sesmark Rice Minis Crackers

Smoreables GF Graham Style
Crackers

Stauffer's Original Animal
Crackers

Van's Gluten Free Say Cheese!
Crispy Whole Grain Baked
Crackers

BEST

Almost no questionable ingredients here (exceptions noted).

34 Degrees Natural Crisps

Absolutely Gluten Free Original
Crackers

Annie's

Blue Diamond Almond Nut-Thins

Carr's Table Water Crackers

Crunchmaster Multi-Seed Original Crackers (Maltodextrin)

Crunchmaster Toasted Sesame
Rice Crackers

Diamond Original Hawaiian Soda
Crackers

Doctor Kracker

Firehook Mediterranean Garlic
Thyme Baked Crackers

Flackers

Food Should Taste Good Sea Salt
Brown Rice Crackers

Glutino Gluten Free Original Animal Crackers (Soy lecithin, natural flavor)

La Panzanella Mini Croccantini
Cracked Pepper Crackers

Late July Organic Classic Saltine
Crackers

Manischewitz Unsalted Matzo
Crackers

Mary's Gone Crackers Original
Crackers

Mediterranean Snacks Rosemary
Herb Lentil Crackers

Nabisco Triscuit Original

OTC Original Wine All Natural
Crackers (natural flavors)

Bell Plantation PB Thins Peanut
Butter Crackers

Saffron Road Lentil Crackers

Schar Gluten-Free Honeygrams
(modified tapioca starch)

Sensible Portions Pita Crackers

Tam Tams Rye Snack Crackers
(monocalcium phosphate as a
leavening agent)

Wasa Light Rye Crispbread

Wellington Traditional Water
Crackers

PEANUT BUTTER

BAD

These brands use bad stuff, such as sugars and sweeteners from GMO sugar beets and GMO corn; vegetable oils derived from GMO crops; unsavory emulsifiers like mono- and diglycerides; processed soy, which is a GMO and can possibly wreak havoc with estrogen levels; and soy protein concentrate (which can mean MSG).

Better'n Peanut Butter

Great Value

Jif

Peter Pan

Planters

Reese's

Skippy

Smucker's

Smucker's Reduced Fat

BETTER

These have few to no questionable ingredients, but may not be non-GMO or organic.

CB's Nuts

Justin's

Smart Balance

BEST

These are healthier, organic, and use better choices for sweeteners and salt.

Artisana Organics

Barney Butter Crunchy Nut Butters

Betsy's Best Nut & Seed Butters

Crazy Richard's Peanut Butter
Co.

Earth Balance
Essential Living Foods Organic Nut Butters
NuttZo Peanut Butter
Once Again Organic Nut Butter
Sneaky Chef (peanut butter alternative)
Santa Cruz Organic
Thrive Market Organic
Woodstock Foods
Yumbutter

Fiber One
Fit & Active (Aldi)
Herbalife
Isanagix
MET-Rx
OhYeah!/ OhYeah! One
PowerBar
Power Crunch
Special K
ThinkThin
Tiger's Milk
ZonePerfect

PROTEIN/ NUTRITION BARS

When you need a snack, it's nice to be able to reach for a bar, but it can be difficult to find one that gives you lasting energy and a full feeling, not a sugar jolt followed by a hard crash. Here's how some of the most common brands rank.

BAD

This category is for bars that contain artificial and "natural" flavors, energy blends, and carbohydrates created from sugar products, non-GMO soy, and poor ratios of protein to carbohydrates.

Balance Bar
Detour
Extend

BETTER

These are decent options. They have organic ingredients, but a lot of sugar; or maybe a great ratio of protein to complex carbs, but possibly GMO ingredients.

Atkins
Avalanche
Caveman
CLIF Bar
Exo
FitJoy Nutrition
Kashi
Lenny & Larry's
LUNA Bar
Nature's Path
Nature Valley
Odwalla
SimplyProtein
Square Organics

BEST

The cream of the nutrition bar crop includes whole nuts, chia seeds, organic ingredients, and a touch of sweetness using dried fruit, agave, or brown rice syrup. They have a good protein-to-carbohydrates ratios and use whole foods for fiber to keep you full.

18 Rabbits
Bounce
Epic
GoMacro
Go Raw
Health Warrior
Julian Bakery's Paleo ProteinKind
LaraBar/LaraBar Organic
Mamma Chia
Mission1
No Cow Bar
NuGo Organic
Oatmega
Orgain
Pro Bar
Pure Organic
Raw Rev
Rise Bar
RxBar
SimplyProtein
Two Moms in the Raw
Usana
Vega Snack Bar
Zing Bars

HUMMUS

Ingredients to keep an eye out for when you're selecting a premade hummus include objectionable oils, such as canola, which is not only likely derived from GMOs but produced using solvents that leave toxic residues behind in the oil that we then ingest. See pages 46–48 for why it's a good idea to avoid canola and other vegetable oils even when organic/non-GMO verified, and why you should steer away from problematic preservatives such as sodium benzoate, phosphoric acid, and potassium sorbate.

BAD

Athenos
Cedar's
Good Neighbors
Nasoya Super Hummus
Otria
Sonny & Joe's
Sunflower Kitchen
Trader Joe's

BETTER

More natural ingredients and less additives, but not organic or GMO-free.

Abraham's
Lantana Embrace Life

Garden Fresh Gourmet
Sabra (transitioning to non-GMO)
Tribe

BEST

These brands are organic or non-GMO verified.

Boar's Head
Cedar's Organic
Engine 2
Hannah
Hope
Joseph's
Oasis
Pita Pal Organic
Roots
Tribe Organic
Wildwood
Yorgo's (organic)

CHIPS AND SALSA

TORTILLA CHIPS

BAD

These tortilla chips contain GMOs, hidden MSG, artificial colors, natural flavors, and more ingredients it's best to avoid.

Calidad
Casa Sanchez
Doritos

El Ranchero
El Sabroso
Manomasa
Mission Brown Bag
On the Border
Santitas
The Snack Artist
Tostitos
Tyrrell's
Utz
Xochitl

BETTER

These items use some, but not all, organic or GMO-free ingredients, but may still contain flavors or seasonings.

Beanfields
Chirps
Cornitos
Frontera
Late July Clásico
Paqui
The Good Bean

BEST

These options are organic or GMO-free and contain no natural or artificial flavors.

365 Everyday Value
Beanitos
Bearitos

Food Should Taste Good
Garden of Eatin'
Green Mountain Gringo
Jackson's Honest Organic
Kirkland Signature Organic
Late July
Mission Organics
O Organics
Que Pasa
RW Garcia
Terra
Way Better Snacks
Wickedly Prime Organic (Amazon)

Pace
Rojo's
Sabra
Signature Select (Safeway)
Tapatío
Tostitos
Valentina

BETTER

Salsas on the better list are free from artificial and natural flavors and the worst offending ingredients, but are not organic.

SALSAS

BAD

These salsas contain artificial and natural flavors, sodium benzoate, GMOs, and other ingredients to avoid.

Bobby Salazar's
Casa Martinez
Concord Foods
El Pato
Goya
Herdez Guacamole Salsa
Jardines
La Mexicana
La Victoria
Mrs. Renfro's
Old El Paso

Desert Pepper
Frontera
Green Mountain Gringo
Herdez
Mission
Newman's Own

BEST

Here at the top are organic salsas that are free of GMOs and artificial ingredients.

505 Southwestern
Emerald Valley Kitchen
Muir Glen Organic
O Organics
Que Pasa

TWO

FOOD PACKAGING, COOKWARE, AND STORAGE CONTAINERS

THIS CHAPTER IS ABOUT even more ways heinously toxic chemicals can get into your food without a label. I know you're wondering right now: What the heck is she talking about? Didn't we deal with a bunch of pesky food additives already? Well, yes—we did, but I have more to pile on your endocrine-disrupting plate.

If what I'm saying already makes you want to roll your eyes, I get it. But *listen up,* you goddess, you. You need to get with me and stay with me here because you are about to make your home a whole lot safer. I'm bringing it to you now because it's *important.* Keep reading and you'll get why. I'll make it as entertaining as possible, m'kay?

The chemicals that sneak into your food while you aren't looking could be causing you serious problems. Welcome to the cornucopia of chemical craziness! This is my favorite chapter because this is where you can make the biggest dent in your toxic load—and fast.

Let me explain.

PETE DROPS SCIENCE:

Leah is not exaggerating here. Food-packaging material is probably the biggest source of chemical contamination in your food, and almost certainly the least-known.

DR. TANYA'S PRESCRIPTION:

Food additives that come from your packaging are referred to as "indirect food additives" and they are not labeled. Indirect food additives enter your body through the manufacturing, packing, packaging, transporting, holding, or other handling of your food. There are more than 3,000 substances that are recognized by the FDA as indirect food additives. Substances like PFCs, pesticides, BPA, phthalates, mycotoxins, dioxins, PCBs, and melamine are all concerning.

Picture this: Your 4-year-old has a runny nose. You give him a kiss and the snot from his face is all over your mouth. Gross, but such is life with little kids. You wipe it off and go on with your day. But what if, unbeknownst to you, he takes a bite of your hamburger, leaving that same slime trail. Then you take a bite. And swallow. You just got even more thoroughly slimed by that 4-year-old. But that's not the point . . .

Would you consider his mucus an ingredient in your food?

You should. You are eating it.

Now, let's say the burger came from a certain fast-food establishment, so it has been wrapped in special paper; there's good a chance that paper is treated with fluorinated chemicals. This stuff makes the paper grease-resistant, but the chemical can migrate from the paper onto the food. And the longer the food stays in that wrapper, the more likely that happens.[97] Which means that when you eat the burger, you eat the fluorinated chemicals from the wrapping.

Would you consider that chemical an ingredient in your food?

You should. If that shit's on the paper, you're eating it.

And that's just for starters. There are all kinds of substances like this that show up in your food, but are not on any labels. And they are most definitely *not* okay to ingest.

What we have here is a shady alphabet soup of abbreviations that includes the fluori-licious fiends, perfluorinated chemicals. They're linked to development and immune-system problems, low birth weights, and decreased fertility and cancer.[98] A few more headliners: diethyl phthalate and DEHP, a.k.a. phthalate plasticizers, a.k.a. endocrine disruptors extraordinaire (page 5); PVC, in which the "VC" stands for vinyl chloride, a known carcinogen, but that's just one of the hazardous components up in there; plus, of course, estrogen-imitating bisphenol A (BPA) (page 14) and the bevy of even worse chemicals that "BPA-free" has come to mean. And that's just to name a few.

> **PETE DROPS SCIENCE:**
>
> Theo Colborn, Dianne Dumanoski, and I first started writing about this in 1996, in *Our Stolen Future.*

> **PETE DROPS SCIENCE:**
>
> Studies link food-packaging material to a wide array of human maladies, including ADHD, infertility, weakened immune system, diabetes, obesity, inflammatory disorders, and several types of cancer.

And here you thought it was just the French fries making you fat.

Plus, much as I hate to break it to you, even if you were perfectly angelic and never ever got anywhere near fast food of any kind, there are *lots* of ways these hazmats can get into your grub—not just from the materials used to package your food before you buy it, but also from the gear you use to cook it and serve it, the dishware you eat off of, and the wraps and storageware you use—even the supercute containers you use to pack your kid's lunch!

So here's the ultimate upshot in a gnarly little nutshell: These added chemicals that you will never see on an ingredient list can have a cumulative effect on your health.

It's enough to make you freak all the way out, I know.

But listen up! I also have *good* news: You can minimize the impact of these chemical interlopers by making some simple changes to the way you shop, cook, and store your food. We're talking about taking small steps that get big results.

Now I'm going to hook you up with some easy ways to cook, serve, and store your food. First, we're going to bust out a few easy ways to make the biggest difference.

Get ready to say sayonara to a whole slew of nasty chemicals.

3 CHANGES TO MAKE IN YOUR KITCHEN RIGHT NOW

Getting a handle on the number of chemicals creeping into your food supply may sound like a daunting task, but trust me—it doesn't need to be. I've streamlined things for you and broken it up into stages. Start out by making just the following three changes and you will have taken a *huge* step in safeguarding your family's health.

I. NIX THE NONSTICK

Let's kick things off by slaying one big, fat, foul-breathed dragon that has just got to go: nonstick cookware.

You may have caught wind of the controversy swirling around Teflon over the past decade or so.

The FDA and Environmental Protection Agency (EPA) took steps to ensure that the chemical perfluorooctanoic acid (PFOA), used to manufacture Teflon, would not be released into the environment. Problem solved? Hardly. The replacement chemicals don't appear to be any safer. Years after the phaseout was supposed to be complete, you can hop online and buy yourself a great big sheet o' Teflon, right now if you want to, and Teflon *still* contains chemical variations on PFOA that are still based on fluorine and are still—at the very least—obscenely persistent.[99] Scientists have almost no information about the toxicity of these chemicals. (Bonus: Fast-food packag-

DR. TANYA'S PRESCRIPTION:

The widespread use of PFCs has led to substantial human exposure and potential harm. In fact, data from the National Health and Nutrition Examination Survey (NHANES) found PFC levels highest in children; 98 percent of 12-year-olds tested had it in their blood. Although human exposure to these chemicals occurs primarily via food, it can also occur through inhalation of outdoor air and indoor air dust. Although there is still much research to be done and much to learn, the best way to avoid exposure is to avoid microwave popcorn and cooking with nonstick pans if you want to avoid these chemicals inside your home.

ing materials continue to test positive for traces of these harmful chemicals; see page 66).

Asshats.

Coatings made with these fluorinated chemicals effortlessly latch onto your food, contaminating your body as well as the environment. That means, despite what you may have heard, you don't need to overheat the pan for nonstick to be a very serious problem. The science on this stuff has been around a while, and there are lawsuits and hefty settlements galore, but the companies that profit from the sale of nonstick products continue to claim they're safe. Multiple independent studies establish that using them is hazardous.[100]

And nonstick isn't limited to your pots and pans—this stuff is all over small appliances (slow cookers and rice cookers, especially) and bakeware.

Of course, with all the negative press about nonstick, the market now abounds with new alternatives that are being advertised as free of fluorinated chemicals and super-duper safe. But why take the chance? Cast iron and ceramic cookware are safe, and usually cheaper too.

Bottom line: Although I almost always advocate phasing things out gradually, sometimes the stakes are high enough—and the change is easy enough—that you can just kick it to the curb. This, my friend, is one of those times. The nonstick cookware (and anything else with a nonstick coating) has got to go.

> ## PETE DROPS SCIENCE:
>
> When research reveals that a chemical needs to be eliminated from use, a repeating pattern is that little is known about the toxicity of its replacement. This happens so often, there's even a technical term for the process: regrettable substitution.

HOW TO DEAL: CAST IRON ALL THE WAY, BABY

Cast iron cookware is undeniably a good deal—inexpensive, indestructible, and infinitely versatile. With a little seasoning and basic care, they form a smooth surface that beats the hell out of any synthetic because not only are they safe, and not only can they go in the oven, they do a better job cooking your food.

2. BANISH THE CANS

I hate to break it to you, but that can of lovely organic tomatoes you nabbed on sale last week probably wasn't such a good deal at all—even if it sports a cute little "I'm BPA-Free!" label.

Here's the real deal. To protect cans from rusting, manufacturers line them with secret concoctions that more often than not involve chemicals called bisphenols—these are the nasty buggers that put the *B* in BPA, which leach from the lining into the food.[101] Once in the body, BPA mimics the hormone estrogen; it has been linked to a host of health problems, including obesity, early puberty, cognitive and behavioral issues, heart disease, and breast cancer (page 257).[102]

And, of course, if you have little girls, *listen up*! BPA and her bitchy sisters have plans to shove your daughter down the stairs in junior high. Don't invite them to the party.

After more than a decade of public outcry about BPA, the food industry finally vowed to replace the coatings in many cans. But it's not happening quickly, and it's not even clear that the replacement coatings are any less toxic. In fact, evidence indicates some might even be worse.[103] And here's the icing on the cake: Many manufacturers won't confirm which of their products have truly made the transition to BPA-free, nor will they say what is going into their replacement linings. You'd have to test the cans yourself to find out.

Well, that's exactly what an independent study did (collaborators included Safer Chemicals, Healthy Families' Mind the Store campaign and the Breast Cancer Fund). The researchers collected a broad sampling of national brands as well as private-label products (the stuff that is sold as a store brand from grocery stores like Kroger, Publix, and Albertsons).

The results were enough to make any reasonably sane person go crazy. It's an example of when an industry vows to change and then just hopes we forget all about it. Eighty-eight percent of those cans came back positive for BPA, Albertsons had 36%, Kroger had 33%, Dollar Tree had 33%, and 99 Cents Store had 52% BPA. BPA tends to leach more easily into foods that are fatty and/or acidic, so the fact that they showed up so consistently in the lining for these products is, ahem, less than ideal.[104]

And, much as data about bisphenols might make your head spin, it also opens up a can of worms on all the things we don't yet know—and may never know—about the replacement liners. In that arena, we have far less published science on how chemicals like acrylic and polyester resins, oleoresin, and PVC copolymers (which are a known carcinogen) affect our food supply. Manufacturers rely on liner "recipes" based on the type of food a can must hold, and the formulas are considered trade secrets (a.k.a. we don't have to tell you anything we don't want to tell you!). Right now I'm not holding my breath on this one. It doesn't seem like most canned foods are going be much safer anytime soon.

> ## DR. TANYA'S PRESCRIPTION:
>
> Human exposure to BPA via the linings used for canned food, even at low levels, could still potentially pose a risk. A recent study has linked perinatal exposure to minuscule amounts of BPA (1/100th of the dose considered safe by the FDA/EPA) with food intolerances/allergies. I recommend avoiding BPA exposure whenever possible.

So what about that no artificial flavorings, cane sugar–sweetened soda you are drinking from an aluminum can? Where do you draw the line? Don't get me wrong: I love when brands like Zevia come along making organic soda, but they are still using primarily BPA-coated aluminum cans to deliver your liquid sugar rush. Glass bottle, please. I had a conversation with the CEO of Zevia at an event and he basically told me the BPA stays until his consumers demand it be gone. So get demanding, ladies! And don't just demand BPA-free—demand bisphenol-free!

HOW TO DEAL: GO WITH FRESH OR FROZEN

Of course, canned foods are good for emergencies and those "OMG, there is nothing in this house to cook" days, but giving them a routine role your diet is just not a good idea. So phase them out as best you can and try cooking with safer options.

PETE DROPS SCIENCE:

If being a grandmother is on your bucket list, try to avoid BPA even before you are pregnant (and make sure you keep your growing daughter away from it too). Too many animal experiments demonstrate severe effects on female fertility to claim that human exposure won't cause problems.

The list of potential effects revealed by animal experiments is quite long, beginning with setting the stage for aneuploidy, which is the largest known cause of miscarriage in people. Aneuploidy is when you wind up with the wrong number of chromosomes in your eggs (or sperm) and hence, the fertilized egg has the wrong number too. Most of the time that fertilized egg dies. A few special cases of aneuploidy survive through birth. One of those causes Down syndrome. BPA's impacts don't stop there, however. They alter crucial hormone signals that in people are needed for ovulation and affect the timing of puberty.

BPA also causes mice to stop producing viable eggs at an abnormally young age. And it is toxic to ovaries, as experiments with monkeys have shown.

START OUT SLOW: A good first step in scaling back your reliance on canned goods is to seek out similar products in safer packaging. Cooking staples like broth, beans, and tomatoes are increasingly available in cartons. I'm talking about those containers that look like oversized juice boxes; they are made from cardboard and aluminum with a thin layer of polyethylene terephthalate (PET) (resin code #1) lining the interior. Also keep an eye out for tomatoes and beans in jars (page 74).

Up for going full domestic goddess with home canning? Right on, sister. (I'm all about my backyard chicken coop and vegetable garden, but canning has never been my jam. *Snort.*) Please just be sure to use bisphenol-free lids.

UP YOUR GAME: Finding better shelf-stable stuff will help, but the overall gist here is that it's time to start cooking with fresh or frozen produce and meats whenever possible.

In Chapter 5, I'll hook you up with a bunch of delicious, easy ways to get more good-for-you foods into your family meals. Once you're on good terms with cooking up a big batch of basic beans now and then, relying on the canned stuff will hardly seem worthwhile. And once you've transformed your end-of-season tomato crop into an easily bankable supply of Slow Roasted Tomatoes (page 165), you'll never find yourself reaching for a standard 28-ounce can again.

3. PURGE THE PLASTIC

Time to get totally real about the kitchen plastics, my friend. As in, bite the bullet and conduct a full appraisal of *all* the plastic containers, cups, bottles, and dishware in your kitchen. I'm talking everything from sippy cups to Tupperware. But remember: Pace yourself! You don't have to do it all at once—just one majorly manageable step at a time.

FIRST CUT: REPURPOSED PLASTIC

First off, we're going to start with any and all plastic containers you may have repurposed from food packaging. I know diligently reusing the many plastics that come through our kitchens—disposable water bottles, yogurt containers, deli tubs, zip-top bags—seems like the earth-friendliest thing to do. But you need to stop.

That repurposed plastic? It's is a freaking superhighway of hazmats.

First and foremost, refilling and reusing disposable bottles from water or other beverages is *not okay*. Same goes for clear plastic jars/bottles from products like peanut butter and salad dressing as well as all manner of squeezable bottles and the bags from bread and frozen foods. These plastics, often bearing recycling codes #1, #2, or #4 (page 80), are widely considered safe—for *single* use, as in one and done. When you reuse, some bacteria can get in there and take hold. So there's that. But know this: Those plastics are made using toxic chemicals that are increasingly likely to leach into whatever liquid or food they contain the longer that stuff is in the container—so they're not completely safe the first time around, anyway—and exposure to warm temperatures (like in your car or garage, or even a warehouse or loading dock the product spent time in before it came home with you) makes migration even

DR. TANYA'S PRESCRIPTION:

Baby bottles in the United States are prohibited from containing BPA. That should alert you to a bigger problem: There are no such laws on the books to protect small children, so watch out for plastic cups that could contain BPA or some of the regrettable substitutions Pete talks about.

BETTER THAN CANNED

Here are some of the brands offering safer packaging options for some of the things that are super convenient to have on hand in the cupboard. If your supermarket doesn't already stock them, it's worth asking if they'll start!

TETRA PAK

BETTER

Truitt Bros. beans
Kitchen Basics stocks
Campbell's soups
Victor beans
Swanson broths
Dr. McDougall soups
Hunt's tomatoes
Vegeta broths
Progresso Artisan soups
Kissan tomatoes
Santa Teresa soups
Pomi tomatoes
Original Soupman soups

BEST

365 Everyday Value organic beans
Farmer's Market organic vegetables
Daily Chef organic soups
Fig Food Co. organic beans
Imagine Organic broths
Dr. Fuhrman soups
Jack's Quality organic beans
Kettle & Fire broths
Imagine Organic soups
Sainsbury's Organic beans

Pacific Foods organic stocks
Pacific Foods organic soups
Simply Balanced organic beans
Trader Joe's soups
Dei Fratelli Truly tomatoes
Pomi organic tomatoes

GLASS JARS

BETTER

Cento beans
Cento tomatoes
Contorno tomato paste
Randall Beans
Cipriani tomatoes
Cosi Come tomatoes
La Valle tomatoes

BEST

Biona organic beans
Alce Nero organic tomatoes
Biona organic vegetables
Jovial beans
Bella Terra organic tomatoes
Eden organic sauerkraut
Bionaturae organic tomatoes
R.W. Knudsen organic tomato juice
Central Market Organics tomatoes
Cipriani organic tomatoes
Eden Organic tomatoes
Honest to Goodness organic tomatoes
Jovial organic tomatoes
Lucini organic tomatoes
Muir Glen organic tomatoes
Prunotto organic tomatoes
Yellow Barn organic tomatoes

more likely.[105] So just straight-up avoid these plastics as much as possible. It's the most commonsensical thing to do.

I really hope you don't come across any #3s, #6s, or #7s. If you do see a #3, that means it's made out of polyvinyl chloride, a known carcinogen.[106] As for the last two? These numbers represent the true Frankenstein end of the spectrum, which includes foam plastics and other harmful blends that don't fit neatly into other categories. (Note: The #7 category is a catchall for all plastics developed since the 1980s, so some newfangled good inventions like compostable plastic are jumbled in there with the bad. All the more reason the recycling code system needs reworking—see box, page 81.)

BOTTOM LINE: Get all those repurposed plastic containers and bags *out* of the house. Now. Recycle what you can, trash the rest, and do your very best to avoid the 1's, 3's, and 4's in the future.

SECOND CUT: SCRUFFY CONTAINERS, CUPS, AND DISHWARE

Now it's time to get a grip on the situation with all those store-bought bowls, boxes, bottles, and cups you use for storing leftovers, packing lunches, dispensing beverages, feeding kiddos, and so on.

Step one is to inspect each piece for signs of wear, by which I mean etching, scratches, or nicks, or any cloudiness or discoloration. Subject the items you

PETE DROPS SCIENCE:

Migration from plastic into food speeds up the higher the temperature. And more makes it into food the longer the food is in contact with the plastic. What migrates? Sometimes it is the basic building block—the monomer—of the plastic, which has been chemically strung together to make the plastic. Sometimes it's one or more additives that's added to the plastic soup to affect its physical characteristics (like taking a rigid polymer and making it flexible). Sometimes it's what's left from the synthesis process, when some fraction of the original ingredients remains without having chemically converted to the plastic. And sometimes it's stuff that entered inadvertently—for example, via air pollution in the manufacturing facility. Think about where a lot of plastic is made. In China. That means the same type of plastic can differ from batch to batch with regard to these inadvertent additives.

use most often to close scrutiny, especially any you've been putting through the dishwasher. Why? Because these are all signs that the plastic is degrading, and when plastic degrades the chemicals are more likely to migrate out of the plastic and into your food/beverages. So any and all pieces that show signs of wear and tear are destined for the dustbin (or recycling can). Any plastic that's gone in the microwave does not even get a glance: trash it, girl.

BOTTOM LINE: Say your goodbyes and be done with all that chemical-shedding crap. Your cupboards should be starting to look nicely uncluttered at this point. If you're already down to too few containers to get by, treat yourself to a few new ones—glass or stainless only (see page 77).

DR. TANYA'S PRESCRIPTION:

Here are the official recommendations from the American Academy of Pediatrics regarding plastics:

1. Avoid plastics with recycling code 3 (phthalates), 6 (styrenes) and 7 (BPA) unless plastics are marked "biobased" or "greenware."
2. Do not microwave food and beverages (including baby bottles) in plastic.
3. Do not microwave or heat plastic wraps.
4. Use alternatives such as glass and stainless steel and ceramic.
5. Buy phthalate-free toys or those approved by the European Union.

Source: *Pediatric Environmental Health, 3rd edition.* Published by the American Academy of Pediatrics.

FINAL ROUND: THE FLIP TEST

Whatever you have left in the way of plastics should look pretty much brand spankin' new. Here's what you're going to do now: Flip each item over and look for the recycling code on the bottom (see page 80 for a quick guide to what those numbers mean). These numbers are optional; manufacturers are not required to use them, so you will probably find some that have no number at all (in my experience, go cups and black plastic items are almost always unmarked)—those flunk the flip test for sure. Chuck 'em.

Now the process becomes very simple: 1) Pull out and set aside the pieces that are clearly marked as #5 plastic. 2) Bid farewell to everything else. In the kitchen, I simply cannot in good conscience recommend that you use any plastic other than #5. And I also have two big caveats. First, as Pete would say, it's not rocket science: heat and plastic do not mix, so even those #5's do not go in the dishwasher. Second, for the love of all things holy, never ever put *any* plastic in the microwave. (Seriously. See page 82 for more about microwaving.)

Bottom line: Did you just get rid of most of your plastic storage containers? Congratulations—you've just put a stop to a literal ton of toxic chemicals making their way into your family's food supply!

HOW TO DEAL: GO FOR (MOSTLY) GLASS

You'll only have to shell out maybe $20 for a good set of containers to get you started (see page 91 for a list of brands). Try it for a while and see how it goes; take it further if that suits you. In general, the plastic lids that keep glass containers spillproof aren't a serious issue as long as they aren't in direct contact with food. I still play it safe and hand-wash them rather than put them through the dishwasher. That's because this little chemical migration problem isn't a problem just when food is present. When you put plastic in the dishwasher, you're actually bathe the whole load in whatever chemicals the hot water, soap, etc. might cause to migrate out of the plastic. Terrifying.

BOTTLED WATER??

USE THIS	NOT THAT
Glass water bottles	Plastic bottled water

Enough already with the bottled water! We all know full well that plastic water bottles are really, really bad for the planet. And there is strong evidence that they might also present leaching problems that seriously affect our health. For example, the BPA levels in a case of reusable water bottles increase when left in a hot place (like the trunk of your car). So please, just reach for the refillable glass or unlined stainless-steel water bottle whenever possible.

DR. TANYA'S PRESCRIPTION:

Whenever humanly possible, transfer all kid food to glass or unlined stainless-steel containers. There are plenty of cute, safe, washable, reusable ones available that your kids will love to display their lunch and snacks in. For other containers, carefully inspect them and toss them if they show *any* signs of wear and tear or if you've had them since your older kids were young. Time to upgrade!

PETE DROPS SCIENCE:

Many tea bags are now made with plastic fibers. Use loose tea instead and make sure it's organic. The amount of pesticide used on some chamomile tea plantations in India forces importers of conventional tea to Europe to purchase organic chamomile so they can dilute the pesticides to a level the meets European safety standards (which themselves are probably insufficiently protective).

A convenient bonus: Glass *is* safe to use in the microwave—just be sure to use an inverted plate rather than the plastic lid.

It's totally okay if you want to keep some of the most pristine pieces from the #5 pile (I've kept a few of these around, but only for cold foods, like cereal)—on one condition: I implore you, don't *ever* use it in the microwave. And please, for the love of God, *no warm food* in them either.

WHAT ELSE CAN YOU DO? PLENTY.

Once you've started to knock out the first few things that lower your family's exposure to the toxic crap hitchhiking its way into your body via your food, you'll realize how much *power* you really have. And I'm willing to bet you'll be ready to kick even more synthetic chemical ass. That's good, because those noxious hitchhikers are lurking everywhere, from convenient prepackaged pouches of ready-to-eat food to microwave popcorn bags and pizza boxes. There's no shortage of other ways to make a difference. Here's what you need to do and when.

PETE DROPS SCIENCE:

Phthalates are so notorious, there's even a term in environmental health science for their effects in rats: the phthalate syndrome in males. It includes undescended testes and reduced sperm viability. The counterpart in people is called testicular dysgenesis syndrome (TDS), and many studies link this to chemicals, like phthalates, that work against testosterone. The main components of TDS are undescended testes, sperm maladies, hypospadias (birth defect of the penis), and testicular cancer.

AT THE GROCERY STORE

Do your best to avoid Styrofoam and shrink-wrap. Those Styrofoam trays (commonly known as butcher's trays) are made from polystyrene, the main chemical component of which (styrene) is classified as a human carcinogen by the EPA. Linked to leukemia, lymphoma, and other cancers, polystyrene contains toxins that can leach into your food, especially when subjected to heat.[107]

> ### DR. TANYA'S PRESCRIPTION:
>
> I second that! Never microwave *anything* in plastic, including frozen-food containers.

As for the shrink-wrap? The products you probably use at home are safe-*ish* (it's resin code #4; see page 80), but supermarkets need to rely on the heavy-duty commercial-grade shrink-wrap that is typically made from PVC (a.k.a. resin #3, see chart page 80). That belongs at the top of your *"hell* no" list because it contains phthalates (see page 5), kingpins in the endocrine-disruption realm. So as soon as you get home, peel off that plastic and, if feasible, wash whatever was wrapped in it.

"MICROWAVE S̶A̶F̶E̶," MY ASS

When a label claims that a cooking container is microwave safe, what that really means is that the manufacturer has taken steps to assure their dish doesn't contain chemicals that will explode in your oven. It does *not* mean that there aren't any toxic chemicals that could leach into your food. So don't take chances with plastic products that claim they're made for microwaving. Just don't. Stick to glass, sister.

P.S. I've said it before and I'll say it again: No matter what it says on the package, *never microwave anything in a plastic bag, pouch, or plate!*

STYROFOAM *SUUUCKS*

So just how bad is polystyrene? Consider its record in the environment (after all, what's bad for us is also usually bad for the world around us). As far back as 1986, the EPA listed polystyrene as the "fifth largest creator of hazardous waste," although they do not list is it as unsafe in cups and utensils. The manufacturing process pollutes the air, and the product itself poses serious risk to wildlife that might digest it.[108] New York City recently banned Styrofoam. America, take note!

BREAKING THE CODE

Here's a quick-reference rundown on those teeny tiny numbers on plastics.

■ safe to use, but avoid heat
■ reasonably safe, but don't reuse
■ avoid like the plague

#1: PET or PETE (polyethylene teraphthalate). Bottled water comes in this plastic, which is designed for single use so it's not especially strong. As with all plastics, heat is a problem. When you leave a plastic bottle sitting in the sun or your hot car, you're effectively helping all those chemicals leach into your water. Plus, bacteria can accumulate with repeated refills, so don't reuse—recycle.[109]

#2: HDPE (high-density polyethylene). Typically opaque with a lower risk of leaching, so many consider it safe. Best to avoid reusing; most curbside recycling programs will pick it up.

#3: V or PVC (vinyl). Used to make detergent bottles and some food wraps. Never cook with or burn this plastic. May contain phthalates, which are linked to numerous health issues, and DEHA, which can be carcinogenic with long-term exposure. Most curbside recycling programs do not accept PVC.[110]

#4: LDPE (low-density polyethylene). It's found in squeezable bottles, frozen food and bread bags, and some food wraps. Curbside recycling programs typically do not accept it. Considered safer, but concern about endocrine-disrupting chemicals is mounting, particularly when it comes to use with fatty foods like cheese and ham.

#5: Polypropylene. Used to make yogurt containers and bottles for ketchup and syrup, this plastic is becoming more accepted by curbside recycle programs. It's safe to reuse if it's in good condition and you avoid exposing it to heat.

#6: Polystyrene. Used to make meat trays and those squeaky egg cartons. It's bad for the environment because it is notoriously difficult to recycle, and it's bad for us because it leaches potentially toxic chemicals (especially when heated). Most recycling programs won't accept it.[111]

#7: Other, Miscellaneous. All of the plastics that don't fit into the other categories are placed in the 7 category. It's a mixed bag of plastics that includes polycarbonate, which contains the toxic bisphenol-A (BPA) and plant based alternatives. The best and the worst are here. Use caution.

WHEN YOU GET HOME

Here's a new rule that's super simple: Anything that came home from the store encased in heavy-duty plastic wrap and/or sitting on a Styrofoam tray does not go into your fridge until you've liberated it from that putridly poisonous packaging. Period! It can be tough to avoid bringing at least a few food items packaged with this stuff, from meats and cheeses to bell peppers and snap peas, so make putting your food in safer storage

NUMBERS RACKET?

One of the reasons it's simply commonsensical to approach any and all plastics with caution is that those little recycling numbers (a.k.a. resin codes) are *not* put there as part of a consumer safety program. It isn't even a regulatory program. Get this: It is a voluntary program that was created and continues to be operated by a trade association within the plastics industry, and its primary purpose has always been to help sort trash for recycling facilities (another industry). As concerns about the safety of various plastics have escalated, the recycling-number system has ended up serving the additional purpose of telling us at a quick glance (or squint—those numbers can be minuscule) if a plastic container is made of hazardous materials.

Ever since I found this out, I have had a very big question: Can a system set up by the plastics industry to serve the waste management industry also do double duty as a consumer protection program?

Since I have yet to get a definitive answer on this, my own response is "Umm, *no*.

containers part of your grocery-stowing ritual (see pages 91–93 for some good storage-container options and a list of better choices than plastic wrap).

WHEN YOU MICROWAVE

Never *ever* microwave food in the manufacturers' packages, no matter what it says on that package of frozen green beans or organic enchiladas or perfectly seasoned precooked rice. The science behind this advice is simple. Most of the toxic chemicals in food packaging just get excited *waaay* too easily. Expose them to a little heat and they'll start jumping onto your food like college kids at a spring break pool party.

I'm not saying don't use the microwave. And I'm not saying don't ever nuke a few ready-made meals from time to time. Trust me, I too live in the real world, where keeping your family well fed means you need to have quick backup options. So here's how I make the balancing act eas-

STICKERS SUCK

Here's yet another insidious way chemicals could be getting into your food. You know those scanning labels and stickers slapped onto your meat and cheese packages? Those stickers are stuck on with toxin-laced glue, chemicals so strong they can, according to at least one study, seep through packages and into food. Even worse— sometimes those stickers label individual pieces of produce, so take 'em off! If necessary, give your food a good scrape and a scrub (see page 106 for produce-washing instructions).

BUY THIS	NOT THAT
Unlined stainless steel/glass reuseable water bottle	Bottled water/plastic water bottles
Tetra Pak or glass	Canned anything
Loose fruits and veggies	Shrink-wrapped anything
Meat wrapped in butcher paper	Shrink-wrapped anything
Popcorn in a jar/from the bulk foods section	Popcorn in a pouch

ier: Take it out of the package first. Simply put those frozen organic enchiladas (or whatever you need to feed the crowd) in a glass dish, cover with a plate, and zap it in the microwave according to the manufacturer's instructions . . . Boom. Mealtime dilemma solved.

WHEN YOU CHOP, BLEND, MIX, OR BREW

Take a moment to think about all the synthetic materials tucked away in your kitchen. From the hard, shiny plastic to the flexible rubbery stuff—much, if not all of it, is made from God-only-knows-what diabolical potion of recycled plastic. In Europe, the plastic in some kitchen utensils has been found to come from recycled computer parts.[112] *Egads!* So I do strongly recommend phasing out plastic gadgets, utensils, cutting boards (see sidebar on page 73), and small appliances (see "Kitchen Gadgets That Make the Grade," page 88), starting with the items you most often use with hot food, and replacing them with stainless or wood.

As far as small appliances are concerned, if there's one thing I want you to pay attention to, it's this: When I use (insert name of that can't-live-without appliance here), will any plastic come in contact with my food? And, most importantly, will heat be involved?

Many plastic-based small kitchen appliances contain toxic chemicals such as BPA, PVC, and mysterious #7 plastics. Plus there's the question of polybrominated diphenyl ethers—flame retardants that are added to all sorts of products. And because manufacturers aren't required to label their products with the materials/chemicals used during production, I have yet to discover a single one that discloses that information. So this is tricky territory. (See "Kitchen Gadgets That Make the Grade" on page 88.)

By and large, in the realm of small kitchen appliances, polycarbonate plastic (that hard, clear, shiny shit) is very often the bad material to be reckoned with. And, of course, it is not realistic to expect to replace all your gear in one fell swoop. Whenever you do have occasion to trade up on one of your most-used gadgets, remember to check for areas of food

DR. TANYA'S PRESCRIPTION:

There is no safe level of lead exposure. Even low levels can permanently affect kids' brains and cause behavioral and learning problems, including inattention, impulsivity, aggression, and hyperactivity.

Prevention by eliminating sources of lead before exposure occurs is the best way to avoid childhood lead toxicity. I also check kids' lead levels in my office at 9 months and at 2 and 5 years of age because often there are surprising sources that affect our kids.

I had a doctor friend whose child had a very high lead level caught at the 9-month checkup. After surveying their entire house twice, it was found that the main source was a china cup they were using to heat up baby food. Lead was also found in a rug in their home and decorative buttons on their daughter's sweaters and other clothing items.

An important ingredient in some pottery glazes, lead from improperly fired earthenware can leach into food. Unfortunately, there's still reason to be concerned about some pottery even if it's labeled lead-free. Researchers at the FDA tested samples of pottery made in Mexico that had been labeled lead-free, and while the glazes used were safe, the researchers suspect that the pottery had been fired in kilns contaminated with lead from prior firings.

To play it safe, pick up lead-testing kits (sold in hardware stores and online) to ensure your earthenware is safe. These kits come with swabs and easy-to-follow instructions. In most of the tests, the swab will change colors if lead is present. If you get a positive result for leachable lead, relegate the pottery to your "doesn't that look pretty" shelf and never use it for cooking, serving, or storing food or drinks.

contact, both inside and out. Because there is very little transparency, it's nearly impossible to know what these things are actually made of—but you can be sure that an assortment of plastics might be involved. Whenever possible, seek out glass and stainless steel. Contrary to what you might expect, these are not always more expensive than plastic. (Example: My brand-new Oster blender—all glass and stainless, for the deliciously low price of $29.99!) See page 88 for a roundup of good options for whenever you're ready to pony up for a new, safer appliance.

THE WORD ON WOODEN CUTTING BOARDS

Good news here! You don't need to ditch your old wooden cutting board. Turns out using a plastic one may not protect you from foodborne bacteria as much. When researchers slathered the surface of both types of cutting boards with salmonella and then cleaned them with plain old soap and water, they found that the wooden boards had less bacteria than the plastic.[113] The wood sucks the bacteria beneath the surface, where it can't replicate and eventually dies off. Also worth noting: Putting a plastic board in the dishwasher only redeposited the bacteria on other surfaces.

WHEN YOU COOK

Use stainless steel pans to supplement the cast iron pans we already discussed. A quality deep-sided sauté pan is a worthy investment for several reasons. First, stainless is lighter than cast iron, so you'll have an easier time moving that hot skillet from place to place. It also heats evenly, can be slid into the oven (as long as the handle is heatproof), and doesn't react with acidic foods (like tomato sauce). See page 90 for some cookware recommendations.

THE LOWDOWN ON LEAD-SAFE CERAMICS

For the most part, we've been talking about how toxic chemicals in various plastics and synthetic cooking equipment can get into your food. However, let's not leave lead poisoning by the wayside—this heavy metal has been making people sick for millennia.

WHEN YOU BAKE

Personally, I found nonstick bakeware hard to part with, but it's a really good move to make if you can.

For brownies and other one-pan treats, you can use heatproof glass or lead-free baking dishes; for cupcakes, use steel muffin tins. Cookie sheets and other bakeware should be uncoated aluminum (lined with parchment paper) or steel. Bundt cake? Well, our great-grandmas knew the trick did it—a good slathering of butter followed by a light dusting of flour.

I've been amazed to find how often I can just use parchment paper in all kinds of baking dishes (except that curvaceous Bundt pan). If I'm especially worried about something sticking, I butter or oil the paper. Parchment is easy to cut to fit most cake pans. And for cupcake/ muffin tins, there are liners made of unbleached parchment—carried at most stores that sell cooking supplies and at craft stores that have a baking section—in the full range of sizes, from teensy-weensy to jumbo.

WHEN YOU GET TAKEOUT

I'm not here to judge. Fast food happens. Just do yourself a favor and *immediately* ditch the packaging those fries (doughnuts, tacos, whatever) came in. Same goes for pizza. It's likely loaded with fluorinated chemicals or something Styrofoamy.

Fluorinated chemicals are a true invention of modern technology. They can repel oil and moisture, so they make fast food wrappers and pizza boxes better for holding greasy foods. Oh, yeah—and they've been linked to cancer and obesity.[114] These are chemicals that, invented in the 1950s, have been piling up in our environment ever since. Great.

Along the same lines, steer clear of disposable cups designed to hold hot beverages. They're lined with heat-resistant chemicals, too.[115] Who wants to slurp down a side of toxic chemicals? Instead, do yourself a favor and bring your own to-go cup to the coffee shop. Stainless steel, of course.

Also, you know those horrible Styrofoam clamshell containers that never seem to stay closed anyway? When you get takeout food that's packed in those, at the very least get it out of there and off those toxic surfaces as soon as you get home. And there is another, even better option: Bring your own containers. If this is something you can do, I salute you.

NONTOXIC DISPOSABLE DINNERWARE

Just like those nasty fast-food wrappings, most mainstream brands of disposable dinnerware are rife with chemicals. Luckily, there are tons of good products to use instead. You won't necessarily find these brands in your supermarket—and they cost a bit more than you might be accustomed to paying for paper plates and such—but with a little extra time and investment, you'll be keeping your family safe.

JOJOGREENS DISPOSABLE WOODEN CUTLERY: 100 percent biodegradable and compostable, these untreated birch utensils are meant for single use only.

EARTHEASY BIODEGRADABLE BAMBOO PLATES: Chemical and pesticide-free, no bleaches or dye and made of 100 percent certified organic bamboo, these disposable plates are compostable. Plus, they are made from sustainable bamboo and are USDA Certified Biobased.

REPURPOSE PRODUCTS: Repurpose provides compostable, BPA-free paper products, including hot and cold cups, lids, plates, bowls, and utensils. Their products are 100 percent made from plants—no petroleum or chlorine. They do use soy-based inks, though, so be aware if you have soy sensitivities.

> ### DR. TANYA'S PRESCRIPTION:
>
> Regarding melamine dishware for kids—it's so hard to part with these unbreakable kitchen items when you have little ones at home who may drop and throw their dishes, even accidentally. Although melamine and other types of plastic items are labeled as safe when used as directed, further investigation will show that they really shouldn't be heated for cooking or washing or even have hot or warm food touch them. Whenever possible, choose glass (many cute options available for babies and toddlers), even those with silicone liners that you put on just for dropping purposes, but that don't touch the food or liquid your child is ingesting.

VERTERRA: Dinnerware made from fallen leaves? Love it! VerTerra offers a fairly affordable solution for single-use, biodegradable dinnerware using only leaves and water in the process.

GLASS DHARMA STRAWS: Naturally, these are reusable and harmless to the environment, but they also come with a lifetime guarantee against breakage. And, of course, it's easy to see when they are clean. They're not practical for large parties, but will serve you well for every day family use or as a substitute for straws at your local restaurant to help reduce waste.

ECO AT HEART STAINLESS STEEL STRAWS: If glass worries you, this alternative is another good answer to disposable straws. BPA-free; guaranteed not to bend, break, or rust; and dishwasher safe, these straws will not leave a metallic taste in your drink.

NAMING NAMES

KITCHEN GADGETS THAT MAKE THE GRADE

FOOD PROCESSORS

Braun TributeCollection (stainless steel; polypropylene lid)

FOOD MILLS AND CHOPPERS	BLENDERS (STANDARD)	BLENDERS (IMMERSION)
These are made of stainless steel.	These have an all-glass carafe.	
Maxam chopper	Oster	Stainless steel food contact parts.
GEFU food mill	Hamilton Beach	KitchenAid
Graniteware food mill	KitchenAid	Breville
Winco food mill		The Sharper Image
Norpro food mill		Chefman
RSVP Endurance food mill		Bamix
Weston food mill		Waring Quik Stik Plus
Mirro Foley food mill		All-Clad
Stainless steel or glass bowl.		
KitchenAid		
Sunbeam		
Hamilton Beach		
Kenwood		

COFFEE MAKERS

Most conventional automatic drip-style coffee makers are basically multiple layers of plastic designed to withstand heat and heavy use, so they don't make the cut here. The water is heated in the plastic, transported through plastic tubes (usually made of PVC), and most often filtered through plastic down into the pot. Ugh! So, here I've only listed models made of glass and/or stainless steel. Those with small amounts of plastic (free of BPA, PVC, and phthalates and mostly on nonfood contact areas) are relegated to Better. Stronger recommendation is reserved for those entirely free of plastic.

BETTER

Breville One-Touch tea maker (glass/ stainless steel; polypropylene)

Bodum Pebo Vacuum coffee maker (glass; polypropylene)

Bodum Travel French Press coffee mug (stainless steel; polypropylene)

Hamilton Beach coffee urn (stainless steel; polypropylene spout)

BEST
STAINLESS STEEL

Bialetti Venus stovetop percolator (stainless steel)

Copco stovetop percolator (stainless steel)

Ilsa stovetop espresso maker (stainless steel)

Presto coffee maker (stainless steel)

Thermos coffee press (stainless steel)

West Bend percolator (stainless steel)

GLASS

Bodum Santos stovetop coffee maker (glass)

Chemex coffee maker (glass)

OTHER/COMBO SAFE MATERIALS

SterlingPro coffee and espresso maker (glass/stainless steel)

Le Creuset French press (stoneware)

Nee coffee dripper (porcelain)

FORLIFE coffee and tea press (ceramic/stainless steel)

Hario drip coffee pot (glass/ fabric)

BETTER BAKEWARE

No nonstick here, of course (see page 68). And no silicone, either, because it's unknown whether or not silicone remains inert when heated. Not on this list: brands that don't clearly disclose what their products are made of.

GLASS

Pyrex

Anchor Hocking

Glasslock

Libbey

Creo SmartGlass

Simax

STONEWARE

Le Creuset

Corningware

Revol Belle Cuisine

ENAMELED

CasaWare

Graniteware Better Browning

CERAMIC

Chantal

CAST IRON COOKWARE FAVES

Hands down, cast iron cookware will see you through most any cooking situation. Here are the most reliable brands.

CAST IRON

Lodge

Calphalon

All-Clad

Universal Housewares

King Kooker

California Home Goods

ENAMELED CAST IRON

Lodge

Le Creuset

INVESTMENT-WORTHY STEEL PANS

Steel cookware is generally more expensive than cast iron, so it's important to know your investment is worth it. Here are brands that deliver the goods.

CARBON STEEL

Lodge preseasoned

Joyce Chen uncoated

Paderno unseasoned

UNCOATED STAINLESS STEEL

Gibson

Le Creuset

All-Clad

Cuisinart

T-fal

Viking

ENAMELED STAINLESS STEEL

The enamel on these brands is verified heavy-metal safe.

Magma

Chantal

Graniteware

STAINLESS STEEL–LINED COPPER

The following brands are safe to use because the copper is fully covered by stainless steel.

ExcelSteel

Lagostina

Cuisinart

KitchenAid

Mauviel M'Heritage

Falk USA

FOOD STORAGE CONTAINERS

Here's a rundown of some of the brands and types of containers out there. Remember: Only the glass is okay for warm food or putting in the dishwasher or microwave. End of story.

BAD

These products are made of plastics that are questionable at best.

Kinetic
Komax container set
Lock & Lock container set
OXO
Rubbermaid Brilliance; Premier
Schoeneck Containers

BETTER

These products are made of comparatively safer plastics (#2 and #5), except where noted.

Ikea food saver
Kinderville (silicone)
Preserve
Rubbermaid Lock-Its; Easy Find; TakeAlongs; Fasten+ Go
Sistema
Tupperware

BEST

Calphalon Pantryware (stainless steel)
Glasslock (glass; polypropylene lid)
Innate MC2 (stainless steel; silicone lid)
Libbey (glass; polypropylene lid)
Pyrex Snapware (glass with a PET polyethylene teraphtalate]/ polypropylene lid)
Wean Green (glass; polypropylene lid)

FOOD-SAFE LUNCH BOXES

These products have nonplastic food-contact surfaces. Note: Silicone is an inert material that is safe as long as it is not heated because, you guessed it, of the possibility of leaching.[116]

Beatrix New York
Dabbawalla
EcoLunchbox

DR. TANYA'S PRESCRIPTION:

I recommend investing in a good lunch box that is durable and will keep your child's lunch healthy and safe. Also, it's important to remember that lunch boxes can heat up when left in lockers and backpacks, but ice packs are key.

Greentainers

Kids Konserve

LunchBots

Onyx sandwich box

PlanetBox

Smart Planet Pure Glass

Thermos food jar

Thinkbaby

PLASTIC WRAPS AND ZIP-TOP BAGS

You know, I'm a realist—not all foods will fit neatly into a glass container, so plastic wrap and bag are needed sometimes. But do evaluate your options carefully—when you're talking plastics, "better" is just that: It's *better,* but it ain't great (or risk-free).

PLASTIC WRAPS

BAD

These products are made of toxic PVC.

Boardwalk

PolyVinyl Films

Reynolds

Saran Wrap Premium

BETTER

These products are made of low-density polyethylene (LDPE),

which is considered a safe plastic for single use. But please for the love of GAWD nothing hot inside.

Glad

Great Value

Natural Value

Saran Wrap Cling Plus

BEST

These food wrap alternatives are made of safe materials (no plastics here!).

Abeego wraps (beeswax)

Bee's Wrap (beeswax)

Beyond Gourmet unbleached parchment paper

EcoCraft natural freezer paper

EcoCraft soy wax deli paper

Green Wacks unbleached food wrap (soy wax)

ZIP-TOP BAGS/SMALL BAGS

Because baggies don't have to be stretchy, like plastic wrap, there's no need for PVC and phthalates (plasticizers) so, in general, they are considered safe.

BETTER

These bags are made with LDPE, which is considered safe for single use.

Ziploc

Great Value

Glad

Full Circle (reusable EVA [ethylene vinyl acetate])

BEST

These alternatives are made of safe, nonplastic materials.

If You Care unbleached paper sandwich bags

2 Red Hens (reusable fabric)

Itzy Ritzy (reusable fabric)

SnackTaxi (reusable fabric)

Lunchskins paper sandwich bags

Wrap-N-Mat(reusable fabric)

Planet Wise zipper bags (reusable fabric)

Fluf snack packs (reusable organic cotton)

Kinderville sandwich pouch (silicone—don't heat!)

Stasher storage bags (silicone—don't heat!)

STARBUCKS

I really don't want to bash Starbucks. It's an oasis. I like their comfy chairs, the organic milk for my kids, and the selection of whole foods and non-GMO options. They have tons of fair-trade coffee and dark chocolate. Those are all pluses in my book. But those coffee cups they use? Lab results are testing positive for phthalates in coffee. And that's not all. They stack those cups inside one another, so the ink used on the outside transfers chemicals to the inside, and when the hot coffee goes in, what you've got there is a toxic brew. Delicious, right? Always, always ask for a ceramic cup when you buy coffee.

WATER BOTTLE MANUFACTURERS

—for not having a viable bioplastic solution yet. You asshats have had plenty of time to solve this problem..

SODA COMPANIES

You already suck, but you suck even harder for abandoning glass bottles and putting your product in toxin-lined aluminum cans.

BITE ME, HEFTY, RUBBERMAID, AND ALL YOU OTHER PLASTICS MANUFACTURERS

—for claiming your product is dishwasher-safe, microwave-safe, or both.

K-CUP (AND OTHER PURVEYORS OF COFFEE IN PLASTIC PODS)

—for heating hot liquid in plastic and then turning around and saying it's safe and it doesn't leach into coffee.

PANERA, CHIPOTLE, AND ALL Y'ALL "HEALTHIER FAST-FOOD" COMPANIES

—for making a big show of improving your ingredients—but ignoring the ones that are leaching into the food from the packaging you continue to use.

ZEVIA

—for selling organic soda in a BPA-lined can.

ALL YOU FROZEN-FOOD-FOR-WEIGHT-LOSS MANUFACTURERS

—for encouraging people to put those plastic pouches and trays in the microwave? Really? That can result in chemicals leaching into your customers' food that cause endocrine disruption—which can lead to more weight gain.

THREE

CLEANER PRODUCE—HOW TO FEED YOUR FAMILY MORE FRUITS AND VEGGIES, LESS PESTICIDE

AS LOADED AS CHAPTER ONE might be with smart swap-outs for processed foods, I am by no means suggesting that you simply replace all those packages with *more* packages. Especially now that Chapter 2 has filled you in on how much the packaging itself can be hazardous to your health.

That is so *not* the point.

Finding some better alternatives to keep in the mix is important, but the crucial shift you are gearing up to make here is toward eating some *real food*—and that means, first and foremost, fresh produce. The more fruits and veggies your family consumes, the healthier y'all will be.

That, sister, is a proven fact. Eating more fruits and vegetables and less processed foods is good for you. This part isn't rocket science.

One caveat, and it's a hefty one (this is the part that can feel like rocket science): A serious ton of toxic synthetic pesticides are used in conventional agriculture (page 104—myriad sprays, dips, and other treatments begin on the plant and continue into the grocery store).

PETE DROPS SCIENCE:

Pesticides used in agriculture generally fall into five overlapping classes: herbicides (kill plants), insecticides (kill insects), fungicides (kill fungi), fumigants (kill soil organisms), nematicides (kill nematodes).

The herbicidal agent glyphosate is the most widely used pesticide in the world. It is commonly sold as Monsanto's Roundup. Other abundantly used herbicides include 2,4-D, atrazine, and metolachlor.

Commonly used insecticides include chlorpyrifos, metam sodium, a collection of chemicals known as neonicotinoids, methyl bromide, malathion, and permethrin.

Commonly used fungicides include metam-sodium, metam potassium, chlorothalonil, mancozeb.

Commonly used fumigants include 2,3-dichloropropene, chloropicrin, metam-sodium, methyl bromide, and sulfuryl fluoride.

These chemicals combat rot, pests, fungus, and more, but they also disrupt our endocrine and nervous systems and can cause cancer.[117] Data out the wazoo shows that a cocktail of these chemicals makes its way into our bodies via certain conventionally grown produce items because the chemical residue doesn't come off with a good scrubbing or peeling. Bottom line: This is bad stuff and we're eating it.

But know this: Produce does *not* have to be risky. You don't even have to go 100 percent organic to steer clear of a potential chemical cluster bomb on your plate, and more and more studies are proving that even small adjustments to your diet can make a huge difference in the amount of chemicals inside.[118] I know you have a grocery budget to stick to, and I'm here to help you create and maintain your very own zone of Zen.

TAKING STOCK

Produce inventory time!

Chances are, in your kitchen at this very moment there's a bunch of bananas and a tomato or two on the counter and a stash of onions and/or potatoes tucked away in a drawer or cupboard. In the fridge, you've probably got a few apples and/or a grapefruit, a head of lettuce or bag of greens, some carrots, and maybe a head of broccoli or a couple zucchinis. Even if it's the dead of winter, it's also possible you picked up a pint of strawberries—nowadays they're available year-round, coast to coast.

THE NOT-SO-GOOD NEWS

Wah-wah-wah (sad trombone sound): Several of those 11 produce items have been found to have seriously worrisome amounts of synthetic pesticide residue.[119] This isn't woo-woo hysteria from an organic fangirl. This is data from the USDA, and that data is public. So thanks to Environmental Working Group (EWG) and Consumer Reports (CR), we know that this is a problem. Both groups are independent nonprofits that analyze pesticide contamination data from testing conducted by the USDA.

However, there are plenty of produce items that are reasonably safe to buy conventional, so you can be selective about what you buy organic. This is where you need to pay close attention if you're buying on a budget.

Meet the Dirty Dozen and the Clean 15! These indispensible lists deliver a straight-up rundown of the most and least pesticide-contaminated produce items—thank God for the superheroes at EWG, who use USDA testing data to compile these lists and update them annually.

The Dirty Dozen is my grocery-shopping copilot, and the items on it are the only ones I'm super strict about. This keeps things simple and it keeps me feeling like I am doing due diligence safeguarding my health and that of my family. For me, that's the ticket. And general consensus among experts (from the wary, but reasonable, all the way over to the still skeptical) is that this is a sensible way to go. Not everyone can afford organic food all the time. So this is how you pick your battles. You buy organic when it counts a lot and conventional when it counts much less. This is a sanity saver.

Major props also to CR for creating their own online tool for buying produce with the least pesticide residue. I love that CR drills down into specifics

PETE DROPS SCIENCE:

While the data is patchy, around the world farmers use as much as 5.2 billion pounds of pesticides each year. Of that, roughly 1 billion pounds are used in the United States, according to the EPA.

DR. TANYA'S PRESCRIPTION:

People who eat more fresh fruit and veggies have lower disease and illness rates and healthier weights overall.

PETE DROPS SCIENCE:

Phytonutrients are chemicals made by plants and present in plant foods. There are more than 25,000 known to science. They can help protect your health, in several different ways. Carotenoids come with fruits and vegetables that are yellow, red, or orange in color. They act as antioxidants, rendering compounds known as free radicals (think Russell Brand) less harmful. Flavonoids are another class of phytonutrients that also act as antioxidants. They are found in a variety of different food types, including fruits, vegetables herbs, and teas.

Cruciferous vegetables like Brussels sprouts, cabbage, kale, and broccoli contain a third type of phytonutrient: glucosinolates.

Resveratrol is found in grapes, purple grape juice, and red wine. It, too, is an antioxitdant and it also flights inflammation.

Phytoestrogens have estrogenic properties. Sometimes they cause estrogenic-like effects. Whether that's good depends upon the stage of life you are in. Sometimes they can block the effects of natural estrogen.

Pomegranates, blackberries, cranberries, raspberries, strawberries, and peaches contain yet another type of phytonutrient called ellagic acid, which is also an antioxidant. Some studies indicate ellagic acid can block certain carcinogens from binding with DNA.

when countries of origin can make a difference for pesticide residue on particular produce items. For instance, did you know that if you were careful enough to always buy apples imported from New Zealand, conventional would be just fine; it's the ones from everywhere else, US included, that are mad contaminated? Or buying US- or Mexican-grown asparagus is typically safe, but Peruvian-grown, not so much? And CR wins my eternal gratitude for basing its risk assessment not on an adult, but on a so-much-more-vulnerable $3^1/_2$-year-old child.

Let me break it down for you . . .

BANANAS

◢ **GOOD NEWS** Potassium party! With more than 400 milligrams per single banana, this fruit is a stellar source of potassium, a mineral important for digestive and muscle function. Studies have also demonstrated that potassium-rich foods can lower blood pressure and protect against cardiovascular disease. Also worth noting: Bananas taste sweet, but are relatively low in sugar and are a solid source of digestion-regulating fiber.

◢**NOT-SO-GOOD NEWS** At No. 31 on EWG's most recent list of 50, conventionally grown bananas don't make it into the Clean 15, but they are pretty darn close. If my household didn't eat so many, I'd regard them as organic-optional.

- *𝌀* **BOTTOM LINE** A toss-up. I go organic, but this one's middle of the road, so you decide.

ONIONS

- *𝌀* **GOOD NEWS** Along with the savory flavor that's a must-have for so many dishes, onions deliver a nice bundle of heart-healthy sulfur compounds and antioxidant flavonoids, plus vitamin C, folate, potassium, calcium, and fiber.
- *𝌀* **NOT-SO-GOOD NEWS** None! EWG consistently ranks onions toward the top of their Clean 15, and in 2017 they reported that more than 80 percent of conventionally grown onions tested had *no* pesticide residue.
- *𝌀* **BOTTOM LINE** Conventional A-okay by me. You can save money here.

TOMATOES

- *𝌀* **GOOD NEWS** Fruity, juicy, and (in summer anyway) sweet and fragrantly flavorful, tomatoes pony up a killer combo of phytonutrients that help protect against cancers and cardiovascular disease.
- *𝌀* **NOT-SO-GOOD NEWS** Consistent member of EWG's Dirty Dozen.
- *𝌀* **BOTTOM LINE** Hello, organic!

POTATOES

- *𝌀* **GOOD NEWS** The carb-bomb bad rap is largely undeserved if you're leaving the skins on and not deep-frying: Potatoes are a vitamin B6 bonanza and a good source of potassium.
- *𝌀* **NOT-SO-GOOD NEWS** EWG has found that the average potato has more pesticides by weight than any other produce.[120] This is

PETE DROPS SCIENCE:

If you're buying at a market where you can talk to the farmer and they are Certified Naturally Grown, ask them what they mean and why they aren't certified organic. Most likely it's the cost, but the practices are fine.

particularly worrisome considering that Americans consume more potatoes than any other vegetable.

🌿 **BOTTOM LINE** I'm all-organic on taters, but only at home; it's impossible in the outside world, so on the home front is where you can make a difference.

LETTUCE

- 🌿 **GOOD NEWS** All varieties of lettuce show up to the party with plenty of bone-healthy vitamin K. But romaine kicks some serious vitamin A butt, and serves up the K and folate, too. All hail Caesar (salad)!
- 🌿 **NOT-SO-GOOD NEWS** Along with cucumbers and cherry tomatoes, lettuce is on the verge of making it into the Dirty Dozen.
- 🌿 **BOTTOM LINE** I feel better about organic greens in my salad bowl, and when you go for dark green leafies like spinach and chard, bear in mind that those guys are more than Dirty enough to merit going organic.

CARROTS

- 🌿 **GOOD NEWS** Root veggies bring the fiber and phytonutrients like a boss, and with blockbuster levels of immunity-boosting A, they're no slouch in the vitamin department either.
- 🌿 **NOT-SO-GOOD NEWS** At No. 25, carrots are smack-dab in the middle of the EWG batting order; could be better, could be worse, but well outside the Clean 15.
- 🌿 **BOTTOM LINE** Organic tends to be sweetest tastewise, and riskwise they're low enough on the EWG list that you'd be reasonable to go either way—or just go with organic when the price is right.

APPLES

- 🌿 **GOOD NEWS** Full of fiber and protective antioxidants, apples are true to their wholesome reputation.

PETE DROPS SCIENCE:

Multiple lines of scientific evidence indicate that eating organic produce will both lower children's exposure to agricultural pesticides and provide health benefits in the form of better cognitive function. The data are less clear for other types of health risks, at least from human studies, but they suggest that eating organic may reduce exposure to a range of pesticides that have been implicated in risk of certain cancers, infertility, obesity, diabetes, and a variety of developmental problems.

The available data do not prove causation. Why? It is virtually impossible to achieve this level of certainty in studies of people because of the complexity of the scientific challenge. Consider that exposures may occur years before a cancer is detectable or diabetes develops. This makes it very hard for an epidemiologist to link an exposure from long ago to a specific disease outcome. Consider that no two people eat exactly the same thing or are exposed to precisely the same pesticides. This impairs the ability of epidemiologists to reach firm conclusions. Consider that each of us is exposed to a complex mixture of pesticides simultaneously, where all the testing to determine what a "safe" level of exposure might be is done one pesticide at a time.

Moreover, scientists have learned over the past three decades that many pesticides interfere with hormone action: They are "endocrine disruptors" or "hormone hackers." Many studies show, in animals, how EDC chemicals, including pesticides, can contribute to the diseases listed above. And one of the hallmarks of EDCs is that they can have adverse effects at extremely low doses, well within the range of what can be found on conventional produce.

I am a scientist with two now-grown children. Fortunately, they are both healthy: no asthma, no allergies, no ADHD, no diabetes, no obesity, and with good, intellectually demanding jobs. As these scientific discoveries unfolded over the last three decades, I understood both the uncertainty of the science but the potential magnitude of harm. As a parent, I made the choice to switch my family from conventional food to an organic diet. It was a precautionary decision that I have never regretted. And over the course of the ensuing decades, the science supporting that decision has only gotten stronger.

◢ **NOT-SO-GOOD NEWS** Near the top of the Dirty Dozen and among produce items that, according to EWG, came up positive for lots of pesticide residue tested by the USDA.[121]

◢ **BOTTOM LINE** For me, organic *fo sho.*

GRAPEFRUIT

- **GOOD NEWS** As low in calorie content as it is high in vitamin C and antioxidant phytonutrients, grapefruit is renowned in some quarters for weight-loss benefits. And how can you not love the ruby red ones for their color?
- **NOT-SO-GOOD NEWS** None; No. 15 on the most recent Clean 15.
- **BOTTOM LINE** Anything goes, so do some commonsense economizing.

BROCCOLI

- **GOOD NEWS** Eat 1 cup cooked of broccoli and you are downing a whole orange's worth of vitamin C—even more when you eat it raw—plus cancer-fighting phytonutrients vitamin K, beta-carotene, fiber, and assorted vitamins, minerals, phytonutrients.
- **NOT-SO-GOOD NEWS** Broccoli is ranked No. 36 on EWG's most recent list of pesticides in produce, far enough down to be way below the über-contaminated Dirty Dozen, but just shy of the relatively worry-free Clean 15.
- **BOTTOM LINE** Broccoli is one of the veggies I buy organic when that's convenient and affordable, but don't sweat going with conventional.

ZUCCHINI

- **GOOD NEWS** High in vitamin C, wicked low in calories—who knew?
- **NOT-SO-GOOD NEWS** More or less halfway between the dirtiest and the cleanest on the EWG list.
- **BOTTOM LINE** This is another one where I consistently go organic because I eat so freaking many of them. If it's not on your table all that much, I'd call it a coin-flipper.

STRAWBERRIES

- **GOOD NEWS** Supercharged with vitamin C, 1 cup delivers more than 100 percent recommended daily allowance, plus

fiber and potent antioxidant flavonoids that may have special protective effects for the cardiovascular system.

- ◢ **NOT-SO-GOOD NEWS** Strawberries have recently overtaken
apples as the No. 1 most toxic pes-
ticide-laden produce item—rated
worst of the worst by both EWG
and CR.[122] There is no shortage of
data on this, but I have a few cents
to add. I happen to live near a massive facility growing conventional
strawberries, so between my natural inclination and the high incidence of asthma and *major* behavioral problems in our area's
elementary schools, you can bet
I've researched the situation.
Between anecdotal information
I've gathered from people working
with local schoolchildren and
investigations by the state of California into the hazards of living so
close to such farms, I can tell you
for certain that conventional
strawberry production is a seriously toxic business.
- ◢ **BOTTOM LINE** I only buy organic;
if they're too pricey, I go with
a different fruit. In general, I'm
only purchasing these guys in
season because organic isn't
available year-round.

DR. TANYA'S PRESCRIPTION:

When fresh organic berries aren't available or aren't in season, buy frozen! Frozen berries can be thrown into smoothies and pancakes. And take this opportunity to explore other colorful fruit with your children. Cut any fruit up into small pieces or make a fruit kabob. You may learn that your child likes a new fruit. Strawberries also grow like wildflowers, so consider planting a pot in your own yard!

PETE DROPS SCIENCE:

Take a look at why EWG ranks strawberries as the worst of the conventional produce: Analyzing USDA data, they find that not only do 98 percent of conventional strawberries have residues of at least one pesticide, 40 percent had 10 or more and the dirtiest had 17. Why is that important? Science now clearly shows that mixtures add up. Yet regulatory testing establishes safety standards examining just one chemical at a time!

A fungicide banned in Europe was detected on 30 percent of samples. And an insecticide determined by California regulators to be a possible human carcinogen was on 40 percent. Conventional strawberries might better be called PDDs: pesticide delivery device.

EWG'S DIRTY DOZEN (2017)

Buy organic whenever possible:

Strawberries	Cherries
Spinach	Grapes
Nectarines	Celery
Apples	Tomatoes
Peaches	Sweet bell peppers
Pears	Potatoes

Source: EWG's 2017 Shopper's Guide to Pesticides in Produce™

PESTICIDES IN ORGANIC FARMING?

Strict EPA regulations apply to any use of synthetic and persistent pesticides in organic farming. A very limited range of mostly naturally derived pesticides can be used, but only as a last resort after a stringent set of other preventative and alternative practices have been implemented. Also, all pesticides used in organic farming have been EPA-approved after extensive scientific review far beyond that which is conducted on chemicals used in conventional agriculture.[123] Furthermore, in addition to being safe, pesticides occasionally used in organic are neither environmentally nor biologically persistent—they don't take up residence in soil or water or spread through the air, so they don't sneak into the food chain.[124] And they don't penetrate or cling tenaciously to the produce they're applied to—meaning they wash off! Because they are not persistent, larger quantities of these pesticides quantities are necessary. But, also because they are not persistent, they wash away with the rain and the wind. Not so with the synthetic stuff. For me, the better choice is clear.

PETE DROPS SCIENCE:

And when thinking about cost, consider this: When you buy organic, you often have to pay more than buying conventional. But would you rather pay a little more now to the store (or the farmer) or a lot more later to your doctor?

PRODUCE CLEANING TIPS

Because organics are not sprayed with antibacterial chemicals, bacteria can build up on organic fruit and vegetables and cause them to spoil faster. Organic produce can also get contaminated by the chemicals on conventional produce during transport and storage.

Before peeling or trimming, clean produce with a vinegar-water solution to clear off any bacteria, spores, or pesticides. For leafy greens and berries, I recommend soaking in a mix of one part vinegar to three parts water. For harder produce, such as apples, spray with the same solution and scrub with your hands or a brush. Follow both options with a rinse of cold water.

WAX ON, WAX OFF

Did you know that wax coatings protect fruit—but can also trap chemicals? Both conventional and organic produce can be covered in a protective coating for transport and even sometimes during the growing process. Americans are used to seeing a shiny finish as their proof of a healthy fruit, but many produce items such as apples, plums, and pears produce their own protective coating to prevent moisture loss and protect themselves. When picking the fruit straight off of the tree, an apple or plum may show its natural wax coating as a dull white "bloom." This coating is removed in the handling process.

For organic produce, the USDA allows carnauba wax (made from carnauba leaves) and beeswax. Unbleached shellac, which is kind of like beeswax but made by a different insect (a lac bug), is also approved. Wash your organic produce using the solutions described above.

EWG'S CLEAN 15 (2017)

These are the least pesticide-contaminated of all crops tested, so it's okay to buy conventionally grown:

Sweet corn*
Avocados
Pineapples
Cabbage
Onions
Sweet peas (frozen)
Papayas*
Asparagus
Mangos (CR notes that mangoes from Brazil should be avoided)
Eggplant (CR specifies that conventional eggplants from Mexico and Peru are okay, but recommends organic if grown in the US)
Honeydew melon
Kiwi
Cantaloupe
Cauliflower
Grapefruit

*EWG notes that a small amount of sweet corn and papayas sold in US are genetically modified.
Source: EWG's 2017 Shopper's Guide to Pesticides in Produce™

On conventional produce, it is permitted to use a greater variety of coatings to protect fruit from bruising, pests, and fungus; this is in addition to farming practices that rely upon toxic and persistent pesticides to grow them. It's a double whammy. Wax isn't a good thing when it's holding the bad stuff inside.

If you want to avoid coatings, buy at a farmers' market, where—whether it's organic or conventional—the produce is less likely to be coated with wax. Take more care in handling local produce from the farmers' market because lack of wax can mean additional risk of bruising or damage (see washing instructions, page 105). Wash store-bought conventionally grown fruit well with a fruit wash or vinegar solution (page 105) to remove the coating and at least some of the chemicals trapped underneath.

WHEN YOU CAN'T BUY ORGANIC

Washing (see page 105) and/or peeling won't cleanse produce of *all* pesticide residue, but it can remove some of it. Here are some recommendations on reasonable measures from the always-sensible pros at Consumer Reports:

- Produce with firm edible skin can be scrubbed with a clean produce brush. Wash produce brushes regularly with hot soapy water and dry completely. Nutrients can be found in peels, too, so consider keeping the peel.
- Wash produce before removing inedible peels to prevent pesticide residue contamination on your hands and on the edible parts.
- Remove the outer leaves of heads of lettuce or cabbage because the outer leaves are likely to have higher levels of pesticide residues.
- If you use citrus peel (such as for zesting), consider buying organic.

Source: *From Crop to Table: Pesticide Report*, Consumer Reports © Food Safety and Sustainability Center, March 2016.

FOUR
HEALTHIER MEAT AND DAIRY

NEWS FLASH: THE SAME industry biggies who have trashed our planet with pesticides, heavy metals, and endocrine disruptors have *also* messed with our hamburgers. Pollution = polluted animals. But what to do about it in your day-to-day? Well, here's the part where I drop the bomb and say you gotta go vegan.

Just kidding!

Although it is true that going vegan is the one and only way to avoid the inevitable bacterial and chemical grossness involved in all animal products, the thing is, well, I once saw a bumper sticker that says it all:

> *I* ♥ *ANIMALS*
> *They're delicious.*

So, yeah, veganism is cool and can be überhealthy (if you stay on top of the vitamins and protein), but is it a route I'm able or even willing to go? Nope. It's not for me, and even if it were, I could never drag the carnivorous foursome I live with along on that ride. No way.

But we all have to seriously recalibrate our diets to focus more on plants and less on animal products. In the next chapter, we'll take a deliciously deep-dive into exactly how to go about doing just that. In the meantime, let's up the quality and safety of the meat and animal products you consume at home. (All bets are pretty much off when you eat out. And that's okay.)

So: Meat and animal products . . . and hormones and antibiotics and *E. coli,* oh, my! What's a health-conscious mom to do about the raging shitstorm in the meat, poultry, and dairy departments?

It's a tough question, for sure, because these refrigerated cases are stacked high with 'em. And I hate to break it to you, but when it comes to animal products, organic isn't a perfect solution. Nothing really is.

But have no fear—simple solutions and reasonable compromises *do* exist, and I'll steer you toward the ones that are right for you. I'm going to tell you the truth about what is out there *and* the truth about what I do for my own family, which is not perfect. You'll be equipped to make your own choices about where you want to be. You got this, my friend.

THE MEAT OF THE MATTER

As with processed food and produce, you gotta be aware of the noxious ingredients in animal products and get smart about how to minimize—as best as you can—your family's exposure. The hazmats we're most concerned about avoiding here are antibiotics, growth hormones, synthetic pesticides and fertilizers, genetically modified organisms (GMOs), polychlorinated biphenyls (PCBs), phthalates, and dangerous pathogens.

Now, I am going to spare you the gory details on factory farming (seriously, you can't unknow this shit). I am also not going to subject you to another altogether different horror show: Trying to make *any* sense of the regulatory situation. Right now, that won't help you get down to the business of choosing cleaner meat and dairy. To do that, you need to be able to sort through the hodgepodge of labels plastered on the packages.

LABEL-PALOOZA

Until a lot of regulatory loopholes get sewn up (not holding my breath!) or someone invents a decoder ~~ring~~ app for animal-product packaging, translating meat and dairy labels is going to take a lot of know-how. Again, that's what you've got me for—to help you get past the labels that are just marketing fluff, and zero in on those that actually identify what level of clean and safe comes in that package.

And I wouldn't be keeping it real if I weren't also helping you figure out how to contain cost, because—CHA-*ching!*—good meat and dairy, poultry, and eggs can be pricey. Which is all the more reason to make sure the products we're shelling out for really are cleaner, safer, and healthier.

> ## BEWARE OF BOGUS LABELS
>
> When I was in the middle of writing this book, I was invited to an industry breakfast where a lady who was part of one of the fake humane-animal-labeling organizations got up to tell the retailers and brands in the room that her organization wasn't like those "animal-rights activist groups." What she meant was they weren't going to hold anyone's feet to the fire when it came to what qualified as humane treatment of farm animals. Shocking, but not really. This specific certification was like a rubber stamp for factory farms. Some of these guys are just here to make money, and I'll show you how to weed them out.

HOW TO DEAL

All US food-labeling standards are a bewildering jumble, but the rules governing labeling of animal products really take the cake. And the problem is compounded even further by lax regulatory enforcement. But are we going to let that stand in our way? Hell, no! I've come up with a guide that simplifies the job of selecting better beef, dairy, poultry, and eggs.

I've assembled the marketing claims and certifications you're most likely to encounter into a ranking from rock bottom to top-notch. Three important things to note:

1. The top category is a utopian ideal, so don't let it drive you crazy. In the meadows those animals are roaming, you'll also find rainbow unicorns that poop organic Tootsie Rolls. Bottom line: Things are getting better, but the best category is not available at your typical grocery store. Think local, or online and delivered to you frozen.

2. You'll see top rankings in both categories include labels that refer to animal welfare or eco-friendliness. While it's true that some claims and certifications regarding humane/sustainable practices are pretty bogus, some provide essential information about how a product was produced. Comprehensive, stringent, and strictly enforced humanity and sustainability standards yield high-quality food products.

3. With only a few exceptions, there is no single certification that, on its own, tells you everything you need to know. In most cases, at least one additional certification is needed to make a label legit enough to elevate it to utopia unicorn land. That's why the top level of each category is mostly occupied by combos—because you'll need to look for certain labels and seals that appear together.

KEY

Wherever your starting place may be, use this guide to determine what level works for you in each category: beef and dairy, chicken and eggs, and pork.

Keep in mind that each phrase or certification is listed by its stand-alone value until you get to the upper levels, where a few of the most valuable combinations are what will get you the best products.

UGH!

This is essentially the factory-farm zone. Give it a hard pass. There are two ways a label lands at this rock-bottom level: 1) either it indicates the presence of serious amounts of noxious contaminants; or 2) it's a bogus/meaningless marketing claim.

BOTTOM LINE: I have made peace with the fact that my family and I will ingest products from this level when we're not at home, but the buck stops there. This level is rarely in my kitchen.

MEH

Better, but not great. This rank is for labels that may not be totally meaningless, but just don't mean enough—they imply the product isn't as bad as it could be, but don't tell you it's substantially better either. Also firmly lodged at this level: labels making claims that are not credibly verified, and certifications with significant gaps in their standards or enforcement practices (see page 109).

BOTTOM LINE: I would rather wing a work-around—better quality or a different protein altogether—but, in a pinch, I'd go with something from this category rather than the bottom one.

BETTER

Okay, this is pretty darn good. To make it to this level, a certification must have meaningful and solidly verified claims that go a good long way toward making the product as safe as possible—even if they don't quite make the full distance.

BOTTOM LINE: Go this route to avoid some of the worst toxic contaminants without putting too much wear and tear on your wallet. This level is a compromise that falls just shy of perfect; it's also where I land most of the time.

BEST

Yaaasss! This is nirvana, complete with those organic-Tootsie-Roll-pooping unicorns, pixies frolicking in the golden grass, the whole nine. This is the utmost animal deliciousness in the world, where you're getting the highest existing standards across the board.

DR. TANYA'S PRESCRIPTION:

I am a big believer in dairy for children, as it is simple (milk in the store looks pretty much like it did coming out of the cow) and provides nine important nutrients for growth. My family drinks milk and I recommend that my patients drink milk (I can give alternatives if they cannot or choose not to drink it). Generally I recommend whole or 2 percent milk for children ages 1 to 2. Then, after age 3, I recommend switching to low-fat or skim milk. Most small children benefit from the calories, protein, and fat that milk provides.

Yes, ideally, I want them to buy organic. However, the reality is that sometimes organic milk is more than twice the price. For yogurt, I just recommend the simplest yogurts without added colors or too much added sugar.

When it comes to meat, I don't necessarily recommend adding red meat if someone isn't already eating it. There are so many meat choices, it is mind-boggling. How do you rank organic versus grass-fed versus kosher versus lean, and then, of course, the cost consideration. In general, I think it's a good policy to buy a higher quality of meat but have less of it, rather than buying more of the lowest quality. Fast-food meat, for example, isn't the highest quality.

Of course, I prefer grass-fed if it is available, but it is not always widely available or in the cut that you want. For ground meats, definitely drain the fat and cook it until it reaches 160°F, because ground meat is more prone to food safety problems.

BOTTOM LINE: This is the top-of-the-line. Depending on where you live and which tax bracket you occupy, it can be a challenge to find and/or afford this much of the time.

PETE DROPS SCIENCE:

In the two largest studies of their kind, a team of scientists from multiple European countries conclude that organic meat and milk are more nutritious than conventional.

BEEF & DAIRY

These unicorns are *very* hard to find in a grocery store. So talk to your local farmer and visit the farmers' market to ask them about how they treat their animals. You can also use AmericanGrassfed.org and PCO 100% Grassfed sites, as well as others such as EatWild.com to tap into networks of small, local family farms focused on pasture-raising. Most American Grassfed Association Certified ranches are superior. The Cornucopia Institute's Organic Dairy Scorecard[125] is super handy for finding the organic brands with the best possible farming practices. And you can purchase meat online from companies like Butcher Box and EatWild.com, or through the American Grassfed Association, where they hook you up with local certified farms.

POULTRY & EGGS

For the very best chicken and eggs, find family farms that have pastured birds, either through local farmers markets or resources like EatWild. com, ButcherBox.com, BuyingPoultry. com (a project of Farm Forward, a nonprofit animal welfare organization [also the listings at AWA.org, AGA. org.]) Or, if you have enough space and zoning latitude, you could jump on the backyard chicken-coop bandwagon and have fresh eggs (see "Backyard Eggs," page 117).

PETE DROPS SCIENCE:

Organic free-range chickens are one of my last refuges in the meat-centric world. Comfort food. I love scrambled eggs also, but, in the spirit of moderation, limit my consumption to a batch perhaps twice a month. With organic salsa picante and GMO-free tortillas. Tasty!

EAT SMARTER!

So . . . about the whole sticker-shock scenario. When I got serious about cleaning up the whole animal-product situation in my household, I knew it was going to cost me, but holy cow, organic or grass-fed beef and pastured pork cost a prettier penny than I'd bargained for. The

DR. TANYA'S PRESCRIPTION:

I buy organic chicken and eggs for my family and recommend both as foundation foods for infants and children to eat regularly for protein, iron and other nutrients. If I could raise my own chickens and serve my family fresh eggs from our own backyard I would (but we are not zoned for that, not to mention I don't have time to clean a chicken coop.)

PETE DROPS SCIENCE

What I know as a scientist has made a near-vegetarian of me. The contortions and manipulations industrial feedlots puts animals through is too much to stomach (literally). And they create too many opportunities for health hazards for you and your children. There is so much great tasting organic and meatless food out there! Why not give it a try! And don't forget the salsa picante, avocado and black beans with organic rice.

first phase of my action plan was cutting back on red meat, strictly as a fiscal measure. And although the prices on organic chicken, eggs, milk, and whatever other organic dairy I could find were not as jaw-dropping as the ones I'd encountered in the meat department, I did do a bit of gasping.

There's no way around it—in this department, better quality means ponying up more cash.

The sensible solution here is, again, to eat less meat. It's also way healthier for you and your family to nudge the animal products out of their former, diva-like position at the center of your diet. I'm not saying turn everything inside out and upside down. (And, yes indeed, my husband does what he can to compensate for this by ordering meat *every* time we eat out.) I'm suggesting slow, gradual change here. Think of it like flexitarian, but less regimented—more *flex,* less *tarian.*

MORE AND MORE TO LOVE ABOUT ORGANIC

In 2016 and 2017, research studies were published showing that:

1. Eating organic reduces pesticide exposure, especially in young children.[126]
2. Eating organic reduces certain birth defects for babies of pregnant women.[127]

3. Organic farming reduces the spread of antibiotic-resistant bacteria.[128]

4. Organic pork has less antibiotic-resistant bacteria present.[129]

5. Antibiotic use in livestock increases methane emissions from cows ... so climate change, yo![130]

6. Organic milk and meat both have a healthier nutritional profile, with more omega-3 fatty acids than conventional.[131]

YET ANOTHER THING TO LOVE ABOUT THAT ORGANIC BURGER

A recent Consumer Reports investigation found less bacteria on organic beef than on conventionally produced ground beef, which had twice as many samples contaminated with antibiotic-resistant superbugs.[132]

Bear in mind that bacteria levels can affect how well meat keeps in the fridge, as well as how safe it is to eat after it is cooked.

PETE DROPS SCIENCE:

Here's the problem. The philosophy of "better living through chemistry" has us buggered this way and that. Free-range chickens and their eggs can have high levels of dioxins—really nasty stuff—because of pervasive soil contamination. It's not everywhere, but it's in a lot of places. Do we choose free-range organic or conventional that's fed crap and is dosed with antibiotics and arsenic? This is why moderation is so key. Don't become one of those people who develop mercury poisoning because they eat tuna every day. Vary your diet. Choose organic if you can. Eat low on the food chain.

BACKYARD EGGS

I'm a city girl through and through, and I never had any interest in farming until, a couple of years ago, a homesteader friend of mine (Angela England, who wrote *Backyard Farming on an Acre or Less*) decided that I had to get myself some laying hens. "They are *so* easy to maintain and fresh-laid eggs are *so* amazing," said she.

She talked me into it, and she was right. I love my three hens and they love me right back. When I let them out of the coop, they follow me around the backyard. Getting them back in the coop is as easy as walking back over to it—for me. Not so for the men in the house; the birds run away from them, and fast. (I'm not gonna lie, it's entertaining to watch my husband and the kids chasing them around the yard. But I do intervene because you don't want to upset the birds. Stress = fewer eggs. And it's just not nice.)

In the most perfect of worlds, you too would have chicken coop with a few of your very own fine-feathered babes laying delicious eggs for you daily. It can be done in the city, suburbs, or countryside, depending on local ordinances. You feed them non-GMO feed, vegan scraps from the table, wilted vegetables from the drawer of good intentions, and they peck away at bugs and tiny rocks in your backyard. If you get the eggs right after they've been laid—OMG. The yolks are a golden orange and have the most beautiful taste.

Chickens are easy, affectionate backyard friends. Just make sure they are fed, let out when the sun comes up, put away when the sun goes down, and clean their cage as often as you can. And wash your hands after you handle them. That's important.

Not everyone can do the backyard chicken thing, but if you can, go for it.

CHEEP TRICK

Be on the lookout for misleading labels on poultry and eggs.

If the carton of eggs or package of chicken says it's "hormone-free" or "raised without hormones" that's what you're getting—right? Well, yeah, but there are no eggs or chicken in the United States raised with hormones. It's strictly verboten. So don't get played: If "no hormones" or something to that effect is the primary selling point, I say put it right back and just buy whatever's cheapest because you're getting the same freakin' thing either way.

> ### DR. TANYA'S PRESCRIPTION:
>
> That's right. I think it's important for buyers to know that *all* chicken sold in the United States is hormone-free by law, so "hormone-free" on the package is sort of false advertising.

OTHER MISLEADING LABEL LANGUAGE

Cage-Free: Without certain additional certifications, this claim does *not* mean the bird didn't spend its entire life in confinement,[133] packed tighter than a New York City subway car—minus the windows and plus lots of excrement.

Free-Range: Without certain additional certifications, this claim doesn't mean more than a few feet of outdoor space, max, and that space could be a metal platform.[134]

PIG TALES

If you're hankering to put any pork on your fork, third-party labels are every bit as essential as with beef and chicken. Once again, "pasture-raised" sounds great, but it only means anything if it's accompanied by particular certifications.

The USDA forbids hormones in pork production, but not antibiotics—and they are used in massive quantities not only for disease prevention, but for growth promotion, as is ractopamine and other drugs called beta-agonists.[135]

One problem is that there is very little organic pork in the United States; in 2015 there was an actual shortage. Organic

PETE DROPS SCIENCE:

In the United States, raising livestock consumes more antibiotics than treating people. The bottom-line threat is that this abundant use is creating strains of microbes that are resistant to drugs essential for treating people. Indeed, in 2016 the first US case was discovered of a person sickened by a strain of *E. coli* bacteria resistant to the antibiotic colistin, the last remaining medicinal antibiotic to which, until then, no resistance had yet arisen. Now, cases are popping up around the world.

PETE DROPS SCIENCE:

While ractopamine is used in the United States to make pigs grow up lean, it is banned in more than 180 countries, including the European Union, Russia, and China. What do their scientists know that the FDA refuses to acknowledge? Canada and Japan also allow its use. It is a the equivalent of a synthetic hormone that increases the pace of growth and leanness in pigs. Ractopamine binds to the same receptor in muscles to which the hormone adrenaline binds. Veterinarians have observed several types of impacts on treated animals, including hyperactivity, broken limbs, and lost feet. Health risks in people include high blood pressure, tremors, and heart-rate increases.

PETE DROPS SCIENCE:

I don't take chances here. I don't eat farmed salmon. In significant part that's because their levels of persistent organic pollutants are higher than Alaska wild salmon. But it's also because of the environmental damage caused by typical salmon farms, particularly their use of antibiotics, made necessary by the high density of salmon in the pens.

PETE DROPS SCIENCE:

I loved tuna, but I don't eat it anymore. First because of the high levels of mercury in many types of tuna. Read Jane Hightower's book Diagnosis: Mercury [http://bit.ly/29IIfnn] about her experience of treating tuna eaters for mercury poisoning. Second, because the tuna fishing industry is rapaciously destroying tuna fishing stocks around the world. Avoid canned tuna packed in oil. Most of this product is packed in soy oil. In the US, 95% of soy is likely to be contaminated with RoundUp's active ingredient, glyphosate.

pork can often be found at stores like Whole Foods or bought directly from local farmers (see EatWild.com for listings), but it's harder to come by than organic chicken and beef.

Surprise, surprise: You can get the best meat at your local farmers market or directly from the farm. And if you aren't able to do that all the time, see page 121 for help making better selections.

FISH ON YOUR DISH

As important as it is to eat plenty of fish, it's also crucial to know how to avoid excessive exposure to dangerous contaminants occurring in particular types of seafood.

Wild salmon, especially Alaskan, is an ideal candidate for your diet because it is delivers lots of omega-3 and has very low levels of mercury. It's also delicious, easy to cook, and wicked versatile. That's what makes it one of my "Foods That Rock" (page 129).

Farmed salmon can be contaminated with PCBs, so you either need to steer clear altogether or know for sure that it comes from a farm with credible third-party auditor certification (Whole Foods has created its own stringent certification program). Plus, the USDA has okayed genetically engineered farmed salmon—without any labeling!—so beware of farmed Frankenfishy.

Other top choices for high omega-3s and low mercury include rainbow trout, Atlantic mackerel, sardines, and mussels. Other on-the-safe-side seafood options that provide plenty of protein but less omega-3s include scallops, clams, and shrimp (look for wild; be very choosy about farmed).

Slow down and proceed with caution when you're contemplating the big, mercury-laden kahunas like shark, swordfish, king mackerel, tilefish, and, of course (as you surely know unless you've spent the past 25 years living in a cave on Mars)—*tuna*.[136] As top-of-the-food-chain marine predator fish, these bad boys harbor high concentrations of mercury, an environmental hazmat that is toxic to the human brain, kidney, liver, heart, and nervous system—and all the more hazardous to developing fetuses, infants, and young children.[137]

If you love tuna and yellowtail sushi—which I do—you need to be conscientious about how often you chow down on it (again, salmon's much better, so keep that in the mix). If you're someone who eats tuna sushi, fresh cooked tuna, or canned tuna on a regular basis (see page 65), you'd be well advised to get in the habit of using a tool like EWG's mercury calculator (ewg.org/research/ewg-s-consumer-guide-seafood/seafood-calculator).

NAMING NAMES:

PORK

BAD

These are the brands that use antibiotics for growth promotion, steroids, or other drugs.

Hatfield (Clemens)
Hormel Foods
Smithfield Foods
Swift (JBS)
Tyson

BETTER

American Homestead Natural Pork (soon to be Non-GMO Project verified)
Coleman Natural
Nature's Place
Nature's Rancher
Niman Ranch
Simple Truth (Kroger)
Sugar Mountain Farm
Sweet Stem Farm
Wellshire Farms

BEST

American Homestead Organic
Applegate Organic
Becker Lane Organic
McDowell Farms
Organic Prairie
White Oak Pastures

PLAIN YOGURT

Only plain yogurt is evaluated here. See page 26 for my take on flavored yogurt. Bottom line: It's a dessert.

BAD

These brands don't use hormones, but the animals are factory-farmed with genetically modified feed likely exposed to glyphosate and other pesticides. Antibiotics are likely used when "needed," and it's unknown whether these are antibiotics also used in humans, which is very problematic considering millions of people every year are infected with antibiotic-resistant bacteria in the United States.

Activia
Chobani
Fage
Mountain High
Yoplait Greek 100

BETTER

Human antibiotics not used, although other antibiotics likely are, and/or likely factory farmed. Not organic. Animal feed likely exposed to glyphosate and other pesticides. However, two of these brands are changing to non-GMO feed (marked with an asterisk) and one is grass-fed (double asterisk). One organic brand is from a factory farm via an investigation from The Cornucopia Institute.

Brown Cow
Dannon*
Dreaming Cow**
Oikos*
Trader Joe's Organic

BEST

All organic. No pesticides, antibiotics, hormones, GMOs. Two are 100 percent grass-fed and organic (marked with an asterisk for badassery).

365 Everyday Organic (Whole Foods)
Annie's Homegrown Organic Yogurt
Clover Sonoma Organic
Cultural Revolution
Green Valley Organic (goat yogurt)
Horizon Organic

Liberté
Maple Hill Creamery*
Nancy's Organic Greek Yogurt
Organic Valley Grassmilk*
Stonyfield Organic
Stonyfield 100% Grassfed Organic*
Straus Family Creamery Organic
Wallaby Organic Yogurt
White Mountain Organic

MILK AND CHEESE

BAD

These conventional brands are likely to contain hormones and antibiotics, and the cows are fed GMO feed and may be raised on factory farms.

Albertsons
Alta Dena (Dean Foods)
Anderson
BelGioioso
Borden Dairy (Dean Foods)
Cabot Farms
Cracker Barrel
Dairyland
Finlandia
Frigo
Hollandia
Kraft
Land O'Lakes
Laughing Cow
Lucerne

Publix
Precious
Sargento
TruMoo
Western Family

BETTER

These brands do not use added growth hormones or antibiotics for their dairy products, but the cows' diet may include genetically modified feed and grain. This list also includes organic dairy that is sourced from factory farms as investigated via The Cornucopia Institute.

Applegate Farms
Archer Farms (Target)
Back to Nature (Kraft)
Bravo Farms
Cadia
Challenge Dairy
Costco Organic
Darigold
Earth's Best
Friendly Farms (Aldi Organic)
Fresh & Easy
Great Value (Walmart Organic)
Horizon Organic
Kemps Dairy
Kerrygold
Kirkland Signature (Costco Organic)
Kroger

Natural Prairie

Nature's Place

O Organics (Safeway Organic)

Safeway

Shamrock Farms

Simply Balanced (Target Organic)

Simple Truth (Kroger Organic)

SimplyNature (Aldi Organic)

Spring Hill Jersey Cheese

Sprouts Organic

Swissland

Neighborhood Dairy

Tillamook Diary Co-op

Trader Joe's Organic

Wholesome Valley Farm

Wild Harvest (Albertsons Organic)

Winn-Dixie Organic

BEST

These organic brands are free of hormones and antibiotics, and the animals are grass-fed or given an organic diet. Those using raw milk are marked with an asterisk. Please be very careful when consuming raw milk. I would recommend getting it directly from the farm if you are going to purchase it and not from the supermarket shelves. I've gotten sick from it before when purchased from the supermarket, but never directly from the farm.

365 Everyday Value (Whole Foods Organic)

Amish Country Farms

Castle Rock Organic Farms

Cedar Grove Cheese

Chase Hill Farm*

Clover Sonoma

Crystal Ball Farms

Engelbert Farms

Evans Farmhouse Creamery

Fresh Breeze Organic Dairy

Glanbia Nutritionals

Green Field Farms

Harris Teeter

Hawthorne Valley Farm*

Helios Farms

Lifeway Kefir

Kimball Brook Farm

Maple Hill Creamery

MOM's Organic Market

Natural by Nature

New England Organic Creamery

Organic Creamery

Organic Pastures*

Organic Valley

Rumiano Cheese

Sassy Cow Creamery

Scenic Central Milk Producers

Sierra Nevada Cheese Company

Sky Top Farms

Strafford Organic Creamery

Stonyfield

Straus Family Creamery

Stremicks Heritage Foods

Sunnyside Farms
Thistle Hill Farm
Traders Point Creamery
Trimona Yogurt
Working Cows Dairy

CHICKEN & EGGS

BAD

These brands may use antibiotics; the birds are raised in confinement and their feed contains GMOs.

CHICKEN

Foster Farms
Sanderson Farms
Signature Farms (Safeway)
Tyson

EGGS

Eggland's Best
Land O'Lakes
Lucerne Farms

BETTER

These are antibiotic-free brands with a commitment to animal health and welfare. Also listed here are organic eggs that are confirmed or suspected to be factory farmed, according to the Cornucopia Institute.

CHICKEN

365 Everyday Value (Whole Foods)
Applegate Naturals

Bell & Evans
Coleman Natural
Eating Right (Safeway)
Foster Farms Simply Raised
GreenWise (Publix)
Nature's Place
NatureRaised Farms (Tyson Foods)
Nature's Rancher
Open Nature
Simple Truth (Kroger)
SmartChicken
Trader Joe's
Wellshire Farms

EGGS

4Grain
365 Everyday Value Organic
Archer Farms Organic (Target)
Cadia
Chino Valley Ranchers
Clover Sonoma Organic
Great Value Organic (Walmart)*
Herbruck's Poultry Ranch
Horizon Organic
Kirkland Signature Organic (Costco)
Meijer Organics
Natural Grocers Organic
NestFresh
O Organics (Safeway)
Open Nature
Publix Organic
Simply Balanced Organic (Target)
Simple Truth Organic (Kroger)
Trader Joe's Organic

Wegman's Organic
Wild Harvest
Winn-Dixie Organic

BEST

All of the chicken brands here are non-GMO, and are either organic or pastured. All eggs listed here are organic, non-GMO, and from hens that are either pastured or given ample access to a healthy outdoor environment. (Source: the Cornucopia Institute.)

CHICKEN

Applegate Organic
ButcherBox
Coleman Organic
Foster Farms Organic Chicken
Just BARE Organic Chicken
Kol Foods
Organic Prairie
Mary's Free Range Chickens
Mary's Organic Chicken
Roxy the Organic Chicken
Simple Truth Organic (Kroger)
White Oak Pastures

EGGS

Alexandre Kids
Happy Egg Co.
Red Hill Farms
Shenandoah Valley Family Farm
Vital Farms
White Oak Pastures

PROCESSED MEATS

I'm a big fan of bacon, but use it as a flavoring ingredient more often than serving it in strips, because—even if its uncured, organic pastured pork—bacon, sausage, prepared ham, prosciutto, and all that good stuff is, well, *not* health food. It has to be eaten in moderation. In fact, the World Health Organization has labeled processed meats, such as lunch meat, bacon, and sausage, as carcinogenic to humans.[138] On its own, that's enough to raise a big red flag. Bonus hazards: mucho sodium, harmful synthetic nitrate and nitrite preservatives, antibiotics fed to livestock that then contribute to the emergence of antibiotic-resistant superbugs (page 117), and an extensive array of other yucky additives, like hidden sugars and MSG. Here's a list to help you avoid the worst brands and zero in on the best choices.

BAD

These are the mystery meats to avoid; some brands have better options available in their product line.

Boar's Head

Buddig *and* Buddig Premium

Great Value (Walmart)

Hillshire Farms

Hormel

Land O'Frost *and* Land O'Frost Premium

Sara Lee Deli

BETTER

These brands fall midway on the scale. Remember that "natural" has no legal definition, so it's a meaningless label term. These brands are antibiotic- and hormone-free but not organic. They claim minimal processing, and they contain some not-so-good ingredients, such as added sugar or natural flavors, which are likely GMOs and MSG.

Applegate Naturals (kudos for removing GMOs from the animal feed!)

Boar's Head All Natural

Hillshire Farm Naturals

Hormel Natural Choice

Oscar Meyer *and* Oscar Meyer Natural

Open Nature (Safeway)

Publix GreenWise

BEST

These organic options are third-party–certified and carry the USDA Organic seal. They are free of GMOs, artificial ingredients, preservatives, antibiotics, and hormones. There are no added nitrites or nitrates.

Applegate Organic

Bilinski's Natural and Organic Sausage

Organic Prairie

Simple Truth Organic

White Oak Pastures

Whole Foods Organic

FIVE
GOOD EATS

IF YOU'VE READ ALL the way here, you have reckoned with some harsh realities and geared up to dial down the toxic tsunami in your family's food. So, enough already with foods that suck. Welcome to the part that's all about foods that rock. I'm talking deliciously good-for-you foods.

I mean genuinely delicious *real food*—whole, clean, healthy food, which, done right, is infinitely more enjoyable than feeding your face with processed junk.

It won't be effortless, of course, but it also won't be a ridiculously time-consuming pain in the ass. And it will be hella delicious. Pinkie promise.

TAKE IT SLOW

If there's anything I've learned over the course of cleaning up my own act, it's that positive transformation is gradual. You can be tortoise-slow here; the key is to keep your pace slow enough to stay in sync with the team—your family. That's why, for example, your processed-food cleanup

DR. TANYA'S PRESCRIPTION:

I see many kids complaining of headaches and tummy aches at school. By really limiting added sugar before noon and increasing protein at breakfast, these kids start to feel better. Instead of frozen name-brand waffles, have whole-grain toast with peanut butter or eggs. Make the oatmeal yourself and add a touch of cinnamon and honey instead of using the flavored instant packets that are loaded with sugar and other junk.]

concentrates on your most-used items rather the entire contents of your fridge, pantry, and freezer. Once you get rolling with whatever baseline shifts make sense for you and your family, you'll build momentum and reach further into your stock of food supplies. Having gone a few rounds bringing in healthier choices, you will have chalked up some wins, some compromises, and even a flat-out fail here and there, so you'll be well equipped when and how to make another push.

So my advice for morning and midday meals is to keep it casual—give the process of finding better cereals and sandwich breads and so forth plenty of time to find their way into the breakfast bowls and lunchboxes and get comfortably settled. That way, you are more likely to keep everyone on board while you forge into some new (or even just newish) territory at dinnertime.

DR. TANYA'S PRESCRIPTION:

Even small changes in healthy food choices can make a big change in your family's heath. Try serving new dishes with old favorites, or try to slowly incorporate one new meal a week or one new food item a day. Get your kids involved in choosing the new veggie or legume at the grocery store and helping prepare and cook in the kitchen too!

PLAY IT COOL

Now, if your family is accustomed to hunkering down over pasta several times a week, don't make an overly dramatic switch from that pattern. Reduce the frequency gradually, and *please* tread lightly. If you are going to try something rad—like introducing whole-grain or quinoa pasta—for the love of God, choose your moment wisely (and pair that grainier pasta with a good strong sauce so the more-pronounced flavor and texture of those noodles isn't super obvious). The harder a new food flops, the more closed the minds (and palates) you'll be dealing with on future attempts.

FOCUS ON DINNER

Dinnerwise, eating cleaner and keeping it delicious does mean doing some cooking. But not much. And not even every day, because you are going to *cook smart.* Here's how.

KEEP IT SIMPLE

This is not the time to try to be *anything* like Martha Stewart. It's back to basics, especially now, when you're just getting started. You know those chicks (and maybe you've tried being one of them) who spend their entire Sunday in the kitchen making lasagnas and stews? That is *not* what we're about here.

It took me a few years and more than a few twists and turns, but I figured out how to rustle up healthy dinners five-plus days a week—without driving myself or my loved ones bonkers. I've honed my fantastically foolproof family dinners down to a science. Healthy and delicious. Simple and streamlined.

SAY HELLO TO THE HOLY TRINITY

On a nightly basis, dinner has three central components—a nutrition-packed holy trinity:

Protein + Grain + Dark Green Leafy

DR. TANYA'S PRESCRIPTION:

Start introducing to your kids at a young age nutrient-rich foods such as green veggies, wild salmon, eggs, plain Greek yogurt, beans, and nut butter. Around 6 months of age, infants can eat almost *anything* in a form that they can handle—pureed, fork-mashed, tiny, soft pieces. (You only need to avoid raw honey and choking hazards.) It's true that it may take a dozen exposures for a child to accept a new food, so keep trying. If healthy choices are offered and your children see you eating it, they will eventually eat it too—I promise!

DR. TANYA'S PRESCRIPTION:

Complete proteins have all nine essential amino acids in appropriate amounts for our body to use (we can make other amino acids out of different building blocks, but we must consume those nine in food as our body cannot make them on our own).

Eggs, dairy, meat, chicken, fish, and soy are all examples of complete proteins. Plant-based proteins like beans and grains are lacking in one or more essential amino acid. But hooray for vegan and vegetarian meals. When we combine them in the right way, they become complete proteins together. Grains plus beans are one great example.

PETE DROPS SCIENCE:

Not farmed. Best when consumed with avocado and mango. OMG.

DR. TANYA'S PRESCRIPTION:

Wild salmon is great for young children's growing fatty brains! Introducing it early is really the easiest way to get kids used to the smell and taste of fish.

With this power trio rockin' the dinner plate, you've got the nutritional bases covered. Here's the trick to making it doable: Within each of these categories, you are going to concentrate on a select grab bag of go-tos, foods that offer maximum nutrition, deliciousness, and versatility with minimum time and effort. You'll use easy prep instructions for cooking these guys up, beginning on page 138, along with pointers on everything from making ahead and freezing (instant dinners, here we come!) to boosting flavor and improvising combos.

Here's the lineup.

PROTEIN

Chicken
Salmon (see page 149 for important info about choosing)
Eggs
Beans

GRAIN

Whole-wheat couscous
Quinoa
Farro
Rice (basmati; see page 156)

DARK GREEN LEAFIES

Baby spinach and other tender greens
Chard and other beefier greens

GET SAUCY

Using these simple standby dressings and such will keep plenty of bright, happy flavors in the mix. Most of these are quick and easy concoctions and many are bankable in the fridge or freezer so you can bust 'em out on a moment's notice. Tasty versatility is the name of the game—dips that double as soup starters, vinaigrettes that make great marinades, and sandwich spreads that play well with others.

There are three categories in the saucy section:

Purees, Dips, and Spreads
Dressings
Creamy Concoctions

VEG OUT

Just because dark green leafies are the only veggies that make the cut for the holy trinity does *not* mean there shouldn't be plenty of other vegetable action going down. I have been amazed to discover how very much more there is to love about vegetables when you treat them right—adding a nice little touch of flavor here and there or just venturing off the well-worn prep path for a change.

Asparagus
Broccoli
Brussels Sprouts
Carrots
Cauliflower
Onions
Potatoes/Yams
Tomatoes
Winter Squash
Zucchini/Summer Squash

Plus, I've got a few solid ways for salvaging the sad vegetable situation that

PETE DROPS SCIENCE:

Stepping out of my role as a scientist: I used to avoid Brussels sprouts like the plague because I'd only ever had them boiled. Yech! Now I devour them sautéed and even order them in restaurants. What a difference!

DR. TANYA'S PRESCRIPTION:

Including a protein, grain, and green veggie makes it super simple to plan. The protein doesn't have to be animal-based; you can also use beans and lentils. All three of these are also part of my 11 Foundation Foods for young kids and families—chicken, beans/lentils, whole grains, and green leafies.

frequently occurs in the produce bin of just about everybody's fridge, a.k.a. **the Drawer of Good Intentions**. Up until recently, I would more often than not ignore the wilting items for way too long, then be all pissed off with myself when I found things so far gone, it was compost or chicken feed. But now I've embraced that this is sometimes inevitable, and I've come up with a few clever recipes that help me use up at least some of that past-its-prime produce before it turns to slime.

DRAWER OF GOOD INTENTIONS (DOGI) RECIPES: LETTUCE SPREAD/ PESTO (SOUNDS GROSS, BUT IT'S DELICIOUS, I SWEAR)

DoGI Slaw (page 180)
Roasted Tomato Soup (page 199)
Quick Minestrone (page 141)
Build-a-Frittata Dinner (page 205)
Build-a-Casserole Dinner (page 204)

DO WHAT YOU CAN

Part I: Keep it real. As in real in *your* world. Even if you bought *nothing* organic—produce, chicken, eggs, dairy—it would still be beneficial to everyone in your family for you to cherry-pick whatever go-to basics or other recipes you can manage, rather than continuing to rely on processed foods. Can't get fresh? Go with frozen. I'd love for you to give cooking your own beans a go, but if you're just not up for that, by all means, use Tetra Pak or jarred (becoming more widely available), and *feel good about it*. Unfortunately, canned is just not a good idea (see pages 70–71).

Part II: You may encounter some new-to-you foods. Don't let that scare you off; embrace the new experience. There's a lot of healthy cooking out there that is just plain boring, but this isn't that. The go-to recipes show you how to treat ingredients right, so take 'em for a spin. If it turns out you really just don't like kale, that's okay! But give chard a chance.

NOW COOK SMART!

Once these basic building blocks become part of your weekly dinner routine, there's no going back. They're easy to put together on the spot, they make you feel like an über-domestic goddess, and I never get tired of salmon with garlicky Swiss chard.

You've heard people say, "Don't work hard, work smart"? Well this is how you cook smart—you're not multitasking because the food you cook is doing that for you. Make 3 pounds of salmon rather than 1½ so you can throw together a slammin' Niçoise salad (page 194) a couple days later in zero time. Pile of leftover sautéed veggies and barely any time to cook dinner for the whole fam? Hello, frittata—the one-pan dinner of champions (page 205). Whip up a big batch of hummus (page 169) for snack and lunches throughout the week—and to use for soup base. (Full disclosure: In my house, I can rarely keep homemade hummus around long enough to use for soup because it gets snarfed up so quickly.)

Because you're banking up those cooked beans and grains and greens and chicken breasts, there's a ton of great food about to happen at any given moment in your kitchen, and you're always able to spin the remains of one meal into a different dish later on (#leftoversRULE).

BUILDING BLOCKS

GO-TO PROTEINS

Basic Beans (black, cannellini, garbanzo)

Make It a Meal:

- Huevos Rancheros 1
- Warm Cannellini Quinoa Potato Salad
- Quick Minestrone (DoGI)

French Green Lentils

Make It a Meal:

- Savory Lentil Soup with Potatoes and Greens

Basic Roasted Salmon

- var: Honey Mustard–Dill
- var: Soy Ginger Sesame

Basic Baked Chicken Breast
- var: Lemony
- var: Aromatic
- var: Herb-Infused
- var: Peppery-Garlicky

Make It a Meal:
- Quick Chicken with Roasted Tomato Vegetable Sauce
- Leah's Upside-Down Roast Chicken
- var: Garlicky Bird
- var: Lemony Bird

GO-TO GRAINS

Quinoa

Make It a Meal:
- Quinoa Frittata (DoGI)

Farro

Make It a Meal:
- White Bean & Farro Salad

Whole Wheat Couscous

Make It a Meal:
- Whole Wheat Couscous & French Lentil Salad

Long-grain/Basmati White Rice; Long-Grain/Basmati Brown Rice

Make It a Meal:
- Warm Rice Salad with Roasted Asparagus and Shiitake Caper Butter and Sliced Basic Chicken or Salmon

GO-TO DARK GREEN LEAFIES

Spinach
- Basic salad
- Basic sauté

Chard & Kale
- Basic salad (lemon, olive oil, shaved Parmesan cheese)
- Basic sauté

GET SAUCY

Basic Vinaigrette
- var: Citrus
- var: Soy Ginger Sesame
- var: Pesto

Slow-Roasted Tomatoes
- var: Bruschetta Spread
- var: Rich Tomato Sauce

Basil Pesto
- var: Pistachio-Mint Pesto
- var: Lettuce-Parsley Spread (DoGI)

Hummus
- Savory White Bean Dip
- Chipotle Black Bean Dip
- Roasted Shiitake Shallot Caper Butter
- Creamy Yogurt Sauce
- var: Creamy Dill Sauce
- var: Tzatziki
- var: Feta Dip

VEG OUT

Asparagus
- Blanched
- Roasted

Broccoli
- Cheesy Baked
- Roasted

Cauliflower
- Caramelized
- "Rice"
- Slaw with Apples (DoGI)

Onions
- Caramelized Yellow
- Pink Quick-Pickled

Potatoes
- Vinaigrette
- var: Shiitake-Caper
- var: Green
- Herb Roasted
- var: Oven Fries

Squash
- Lemon Roasted Butternut
- Sautéed Zucchini with Pesto
- var: Pesto Tomato Zucchini Salad
- Dry-Roasted Zucchini

MORE GOOD EATS
- Kale Salad with Lentils & Butternut Squash
- Creamy Chicken Salad
- Grain Salad with Dried Fruit
- var: Coconut Ginger Grain Salad with Dates
- var: Fruity Minty Grain Salad
- Garbanzo Farro Salad
- Black Bean & Corn Salad with Avocado
- Warm Grain Salad with Roasted Asparagus and Chard
- Salmon Salad Niçoise
- Chicken with Pistachio-Mint Couscous
- var: Caprese-ish
- var: à la Salmon-Avocado Roll
- Hearty Chili
- var: Con Carne
- White Bean Soup
- Roasted Tomato Soup (DoGI)
- Chicken Soup with (Cauliflower) "Rice"
- Eggs Poached in Tomato Sauce
- var: Puttanesca-esque
- var: (All-day) Breakfast of Champions
- var: Huevos Rancheros 2
- Build-a-Casserole Dinner (DoGI)
- var: Less Mex, More Med: White Bean, etc
- Build-a-Frittata Dinner (DoGI)

GO-TO PROTEINS: BEANS

It's time to change the way you think about cooking up dried beans. Compared to canned, you do cut costs, and you do avoid bisphenol A (BPA) and other problematic can linings.

There are many, many kinds of beans out there. I'm going to set you up with just a starter sampler featuring a few of the most basic, easy-to-find, and versatile ones: black beans, cannellini beans, and garbanzo beans.

And here's how easy it is: Chop up some onion, carrots, and celery, give them a little sauté in a big soup pot, and add beans and lots of water (if you happened to have any Parmesan cheese rinds or a ham bone or some such lying around, I would not discourage you from chuckin' that in there as well). Then fire up the stove, bring on a good hard boil, and keep it going for 15 minutes before dialing it back to a simmer, and cook gently for about an hour, depending on type of bean (see page 140).

TIPS

- Don't abide by the no-salt-till-they're-fully-cooked rule, because it's been conclusively proven that it doesn't make them tough, and it makes them ever so tasty if you time the salting step right: late enough that it doesn't prolong the cooking time by much *but* soon enough that the salt penetrates the beans rather than just creating salty broth.

- Use a deep soup pot because you can cover the beans with plenty of water and not worry about having to check that too much of it has cooked off. (A shallower pot makes it harder to keep the simmer level low and steady *and* requires close attention to the water level; if the top layer of beans ends up exposed, they won't cook at the same rate as the underwater ones, and may even come out dry and tough.)

COOK

BASIC BEANS

Makes about 5 cups cooked beans

This recipe yields a substantial amount of cooked beans and soup-ready broth, setting you up to make an assortment of tasty meals. I like to use some of the beans right away, stash another recipe's worth (plus plenty of liquid to cover) in the fridge to make something else later in the week, and bank the rest of the beans and liquid in the freezer. See page 140 for the estimated cooking times for the types of beans used in this book.

> 2 tablespoons unsalted butter, ghee, or avocado oil
> I onion, diced small
> I to 2 celery stalks, diced small
> 2 to 3 carrots, diced small
> I pound (about 2 cups) dried black beans, cannellini beans, or
>   garbanzo beans
> I bay leaf
> I or more garlic cloves, crushed and peeled
> Sprigs of fresh herbs, or pinches of dried herbs, such as thyme,
>   sage, or rosemary (optional)
> I teaspoon kosher or sea salt, plus more as needed

1. Set a soup pot or other large, deep, heavy-bottomed pot over medium-low heat; add the butter, stir in the chopped vegetables, season generously with salt and pepper, and cook, stirring occasionally, until the onions are soft and translucent, about 10 minutes.

2. Meanwhile, put the beans in a strainer or colander large enough that you can spread them out, so that while you're rinsing them under cold running water you can paw through and pick out any teeny rocks or funky-looking beans.

3. Dump the clean beans into the pot along with the bay leaf, garlic, and herbs, and add lukewarm water to a depth of several inches above the beans. Bring to a boil over medium-high heat and continue to boil for 15 minutes, then lower the heat to a simmer.

4. Continue cooking the beans at a gentle but steady simmer, occasionally skimming off and discarding any foam that forms on the surface, for 30 to 40 minutes, just until the beans begin to go from hard to a bit tender (for garbanzos and other beans on the larger and/or older side, this can take an hour or so). Add the salt.

5. Continue cooking until the beans are tender but not soft; see below for estimated cooking times for the beans used in the recipes in this book. Taste and adjust seasoning with additional salt if needed.

COOKING TIMES

The estimated cooking times listed below should work for varieties of beans that are similar sizes and shapes. But always remember that times can range very widely, so start checking sooner than you think you need to and use a timer throughout the whole process so you don't space out and end up with mushy beans instead of gorgeously tender ones.

Black beans: 45 to 60 minutes
Cannellini beans: 1 to $1\frac{1}{2}$ hours
Garbanzo beans (chickpeas): $1\frac{1}{4}$ to 2 hours

BANK

FRIDGE: Store the beans in an airtight container (along with enough cooking liquid to cover or they'll dry out), for up to a week; additional broth can also be kept in jars in the fridge for up to five days, or frozen (see below).

FREEZER: Separate the beans from the cooking liquid (don't pour it down the drain!); store in airtight 1- or 2-cup containers or freezer bags (press all air out before sealing) and freeze for up to three months. Fish out and discard the bay leaf, garlic cloves, and herb stems, transfer the broth to tempered glass containers, and freeze for up to three months.

MAKE IT A MEAL

🌿 **HUEVOS RANCHEROS NO. I:** Divide 2 cups hot, cooked and drained black beans among 4 plates, top each with a freshly fried, poached, or scrambled egg. Serve with diced avocado, salsa and/or hot sauce, chopped scallions, and whatever other toppings you like. More options: Pile the beans on top of leftover rice or other grains and/or fresh or cooked spinach or other greens; stir $\frac{1}{4}$ to $\frac{1}{2}$ cup leftover Chipotle Black Bean Dip (page 171) into the beans.

🌿 **WARM CANNELLINI QUINOA POTATO SALAD:** In a largish bowl, stir $\frac{1}{4}$ cup Basic Vinaigrette (page 164) into 2 cups steaming-hot cooked quinoa (page 151), then add $\frac{1}{2}$ the recipe (about 2 cups) leftover Warm Potato Salad (page 183; room temp or rewarmed) and mix gently to combine. Add 2 cups cooked and drained cannellini beans and $\frac{1}{2}$ cup Slow-Roasted Tomatoes (page 165) or $\frac{1}{2}$ pint cherry or grape tomatoes, quartered or halved, and 1 cup coarsely chopped artichoke hearts (drained jarred or thawed frozen). Serve on a lightly dressed bed of simple baby greens or shredded chard.

🌿 **QUICK MINESTRONE:** Combine 3 cups cooked garbanzos and 4 cups of their cooking liquid with 1 cup Slow-Roasted Tomatoes (page 165), $\frac{1}{2}$ cup Hummus (page 169), 1 cup chopped cooked greens (page 162), and 1 cup cooked farro (page 153). Bring to a simmer and cook gently for 10 to 15 minutes. Season to taste with kosher or sea salt and freshly ground black pepper. More options: Top with freshly grated Parmesan cheese before serving; swap in good-quality store-bought subs such as jarred roasted tomatoes, packaged hummus, frozen chopped spinach, or small whole-grain pasta shapes.

GO-TO PROTEINS: LENTILS

Unlike the more familiar brown and orange lentils, French greenies keep their shape and don't taste like wet dirt. In fact, their innately rich and multidimensional flavor makes for dishes that taste deceivingly complex. Also, in my experience, French lentils go over surprisingly well with kids, who tend to hesitate at first because a lentil dish might not look like something they'd ordinarily enjoy, but if they can be persuaded to taste it, many discover it's delish. All of which is to say, if you've never liked lentils in the past, pretty please give these a try anyway. (A very nice but often pricey substitute you might come across is black Beluga lentils, which also retain their shape and firmness.)

The following basic method gets you a large supply of mighty tasty lentils and a richly flavorful broth within about a half hour, a portion of which you can opt to transform into a lovely soup within another 15 minutes (page 144). Uses of French green lentils go way beyond soup, so it's good to have plenty precooked and banked; you can divide up the remaining supply between fridge and freezer.

COOK

BASIC FRENCH GREEN LENTILS

Makes about 10 cups cooked lentils

I pound (about 2¼ cups) dried lentils

6 cups homemade or low-sodium store-bought chicken stock or
    vegetable stock or water (or enough to cover the lentils by I
    inch), plus more if needed

I small onion, quartered

3 carrots, peeled and cut into several chunks

2 celery stalks, stringy fibers stripped off and discarded, stalks
    cut into several chunks

I bay leaf (optional)

A few sprigs fresh or I pinch dried thyme (optional)

$1/2$ to I teaspoon kosher or sea salt

Freshly ground black pepper

1. Deposit the lentils in a strainer large enough to allow you to thoroughly pick through them, as you rinse well under cold running water, and remove any tiny stones or dirt.

2. Transfer the lentils to a saucepan large enough to hold enough water to cover the lentils by at least 2 inches. Add the veggies, bay leaf, and herbs to the pan, bring to a boil, then immediately reduce the heat to low and simmer gently, partially covered, until tender but not soft. Begin checking for doneness after about 15 minutes; the lentils should be perfectly tender within about 25 minutes, but, as with dried beans, time will vary depending on freshness. Skim off and discard foam that forms on the surface.

3. Fish out and discard the bay leaf. Strip off any leaves remaining on the herb stems, stirring the leaves back into the lentils and discarding the stems. Pluck out the vegetables, chop finely, and stir back into the lentils. Season to taste with salt and pepper.

BANK

TO STORE IN THE FRIDGE: Cool the lentils and store in their broth in an airtight container for up to one week. (Note: If you will be using some of the lentils within a few days for salad (page 156), you can drain that portion, gently toss with a couple of tablespoons of vinaigrette while still warm, and then store them in an airtight container.)

TO FREEZE: Cool and strain the lentils, reserving the broth. Transfer the lentils to airtight containers or freezer bags (press out air before sealing), and keep for up to three months. Thaw in the refrigerator before using or, if adding to soup or another cooked dish, you can stir them in still frozen and warm to heat through.

MAKE IT A MEAL

✎ SAVORY LENTIL SOUP WITH POTATOES AND GREENS: When you cook up the lentils, use a slotted spoon to scoop out about 6 cups of lentils and set them aside to bank however you like. In the saucepan, you'll have about 4 cups lentils left and all of the cooking broth; transfer everything to a bowl and give the saucepan a good rinse to clean off the residue that will have built up around the upper edge. Use a food processor to puree about 2 cups (half) of the reserved lentils (along with any incidental veggies) until smooth. Pour the puree back into the clean pan along with the intact lentil-veggie-broth mixture and 3 cups low-sodium vegetable or chicken broth (more if you didn't have much lentil broth to start with), 4 diced Yukon gold potatoes, 1 to 2 cups sautéed chard or kale (which can be frozen and unthawed, page 160), and 1 fat pinch nutmeg (preferably freshly grated). Season with kosher or sea salt and freshly ground black pepper and bring to a simmer over medium heat. Turn the heat to low and simmer the soup for about 15 minutes, or until the potatoes are tender, stirring occasionally to prevent scorching and skimming off foam that forms on the surface. If the soup seems too thick, add more broth. Check seasoning and adjust with additional salt to taste. Serve immediately, or cool and hold in the refrigerator for up to seven days, or freeze.

GO-TO PROTEINS: CHICKEN

When I say "simple and streamlined," this right here is what I mean. It's also what I mean when I say *delicious:* perfectly cooked chicken breast every time. The base recipe is überminimalist and delivers tender chicken breast that's far more tender than if you'd simply baked it in the oven and much more flavorful than if you'd poached it on the stovetop—tasty enough to enjoy as is and also an ideal blank slate for incorporating into other dishes. Add the simplest of seasonings—a sprinkling of smoked paprika or a sprig of fresh rosemary, for example, for a big flavor payoff. (See pages 146–147 for a sampling of suggestions.) Quantitywise, you can make as much or as little as you need (it works as well for a single breast in a Pyrex pie pan as it does for several pounds of chicken in an oven full of ceramic baking dishes, though the cook times will vary). And they freeze very nicely, so you can keep them on hand at all times.

TIPS

- Don't skimp on the ghee or whatever fat you're using because a light but thorough coating is essential to getting a good, tight seal between the parchment and the chicken—crucial to moisture retention—and also prevents the meat from sticking to the pan.
- Also, use both a timer and an instant-read thermometer—it only takes a few minutes/degrees to go from just right (juicy) to over-cooked (dry).

COOK

BASIC CHICKEN BREAST

Makes 1 or more chicken breasts

Unsalted butter, ghee, or avocado oil
I or more boneless, skinless chicken breasts
   Sea or kosher salt
Freshly ground black pepper

1. Preheat the oven to 400°F with a rack in the middle position. Butter the bottom of a shallow baking dish large enough to fit the chicken breasts without touching each other. Cut a piece of unbleached parchment paper large enough to fit over the pan, and butter one side of the paper.
2. Pat the chicken dry with paper towels and rub all over with a little butter. Set the chicken breasts in the baking dish, spacing slightly

apart. Season generously with salt and pepper.

3. Lay the parchment, greased-side down, over the chicken. Tuck the edges of the parchment into the pan and press down to snug the paper right up against the meat and the bottom and sides of the pan. You want the chicken completely covered, with no air pockets or gaps that would allow dry heat in (and moisture out). If need be, you can tuck the edges of the paper underneath the chicken to be sure it's securely covered.

4. Bake 20 minutes, then start checking for doneness by inserting an instant-read thermometer into the thickest part of chicken breast; you want to pull the chicken out of the oven the moment it hits 165°F (I usually take it out when it starts to creep above 160°F and let it sit for 5 minutes to cook the rest of the way from retained heat; and I always check that it's opaque all the way to the center). This can take up to 30 minutes, but varies depending on how much you have in the oven, size of pan, etc.

5. Serve immediately or cool to room temperature.

RIFF

LEMONY: In Step 2, zest a lemon (or lemons, depending on how much chicken you're making). Reserve the zest. Thinly slice the lemon(s) and lay the rounds in the buttered pan. Butter the chicken, set it on top of the lemon slices in the pan, season with salt and pepper, and sprinkle with the lemon zest. If you want to add another delicious dimension, top the chicken with leaves or whole sprigs of thyme before you layer on the lemon slices. Proceed with Step 3.

AROMATIC: In Step 1, line the buttered pan with thin slices of lemon. In Step 2, lightly dust the buttered and seasoned chicken with sweet smoked Spanish paprika (for smoky flavor), cumin (for pungent flavor), or Italian seasoning (for a somewhat Mediterranean flavor). Proceed with Step 3.

HERB-INFUSED: In Step 1, lay sprigs of tarragon, rosemary, or sage in the buttered pan; in Step 2, top the buttered and seasoned chicken with additional herb sprigs. Proceed with Step 3.

PEPPERY-GARLICKY: In Step 2, be especially generous with the black pepper and top each buttered and seasoned chicken breast with a few slices of garlic. Proceed with Step 3.

MAKE IT A MEAL

QUICK CHICKEN WITH ROASTED TOMATO VEGETABLE SAUCE: Use the basic recipe or any of the variations to prepare 4 chicken breasts. While the chicken cooks in the oven, set a saucepan on the stove and throw in $1/2$ recipe (about $1^1/_2$ cups) Slow-Roasted Tomatoes (page 165) and 1 cup Roasted Broccoli (page 177, or Dry-Roasted Zucchini, page 187, or whatever tender but sturdy cooked vegetable you have on hand that seems well suited to tomatoes) and bring to a simmer. Stir in 1 cup Sautéed Baby Spinach (page 158) or 2 cups raw baby spinach or baby dark greens and cook to warm through. Season to taste with kosher or sea salt and freshly ground black pepper. Rewarm some cooked grains or pasta and, when the chicken is done and out of the oven, mound a portion of grains or pasta into 4 wide shallow bowls, layer on a chicken breast, and top that with a large spoonful of the tomato-vegetable sauce (make sure you get plenty of juices). Sprinkle on some Parmesan cheese and/or chopped Italian parsley leaves if you have them/feel like it.

BANK

Double-wrap cooked and cooled chicken breasts in a tight layer of wax paper or foil followed by a tight layer of plastic wrap, put these in an airtight tempered-glass container or freezer bag (squeeze out all air before sealing), and store in the freezer for up to 3 months. Remember to label! Defrost in the fridge. Rewarm very gently.

SWAP

LEAH'S UPSIDE-DOWN ROAST CHICKEN: Instead of boneless skinless chicken breast, go with a whole bird (about 3 pounds). Remove excess fat from the cavity, pat dry, and set breast-side down in an oven-proof casserole dish. Rub all over with unsalted butter, ghee, or coconut oil, and sprinkle all over with coarse salt (I love to use pink Himalayan) and cracked black pepper. Roast at 400°F until the juices run clear when the skin is pierced or an instant-read thermometer inserted in the thickest part of one of the thighs registers 165°F.

RIFF

GARLICKY BIRD: Before salt-and-peppering, coarsely chop 4 garlic cloves, poke little holes in the skin and stick in the garlic pieces, then sprinkle all over with garlic salt and cracked black pepper. (Sometimes I also squeeze an orange over the bird to cover with juice.)

• HERBY BIRD: Before salt-and-peppering, stick half a lemon, a sprig of rosemary, and a few garlic cloves in the cavity, then cover the outside with garlic salt and cracked pepper.

Note: Roasting breast-side down keeps the meat juicy. It's not the prettiest roast chicken you'll ever see, and only the skin on the back gets crispy, but it's a terrific family supper with plenty of leftovers to incorporate into other meals.

GO-TO PROTEINS: SALMON

A good fresh piece of salmon needs very little done to it to become a delicious dinner. In fact, salmon is so innately lush in texture and flavor that cooking it well is mainly a matter of what *not* to do: 1) don't overcook; 2) don't overcomplicate. So that's what the following recipe is all about. It serves up enough perfectly cooked salmon to feed four at least twice, and the fish is every bit as delicious deeply chilled as it is freshly cooked.

TIPS

I always go by touch to tell when salmon is done—that moment when the thickest part of the fillet goes from having a very slight squish to it (which means it's getting there, but needs a few more minutes of good, steady oven heat) to being just a tad shy of firm (which means it's close enough to done that it's time to get it out of the oven). You can use an instant-read thermometer rather than your fingertips to determine when this moment has

PETE DROPS SCIENCE:

If you have a choice, avoid farmed salmon. Scientific studies show that wild-caught salmon, especially from Alaska, are lower in persistent organic pollutants, such as PCBs and dioxin, than farmed salmon.

arrived: Insert the thermometer into the thickest part of the fillet; once the temp has hit at least 130°F, I pull it out and let retained heat finish the job of bringing the internal temp closer to the FDA's 145°F threshold.

- Use a timer. Just do it. Overcooked salmon is a total bummer.
- Note: If you use cut portions rather than whole fillet, the fish will cook a little more quickly.

COOK

BASIC SALMON

Makes 8-plus servings

I large (about 2 pounds) fresh, skin-on salmon fillet, pinbones
    removed
Avocado oil
Kosher or sea salt
Freshly ground black pepper
$1/2$ lemon, plus more as needed
Lemon wedges, for serving (optional)

1. Preheat the oven to 375°F with a rack in the center. Line a baking sheet with parchment or foil.
2. Lay the salmon on the prepared baking sheet, lightly drizzle it with oil, and season generously with salt and pepper. Slide the pan into

the oven and roast the salmon 15 minutes.

3. Pull the pan out of the oven and check for doneness by gently pressing the center of the fillet with your fingertips; it should feel nearly firm, which means it is nearly done. (If not, put it back in the oven, cook it for a few more minutes, and check again.)

4. Switch the oven to broil. Squeeze the lemon over the fish (see Tips and repeat with another lemon half if the first isn't juicy enough to coat the whole fillet). Return the pan to the oven and broil just until it is barely firm to the touch and the top surface is golden, 2 to 5 minutes. You can carefully cut partway into the center of the fillet to take a peek to be sure it is opaque all the way through. Or you can use an instant-read thermometer (see Tip).

5. Serve hot, at room temperature. The salmon keeps well in the fridge, tightly covered, for several days.

TIP

A spritz of lemon has magical brightening powers, bringing tart acidity that can make flavors really sing. So it's a good idea to stock at least one lemon in the fridge at all times. Soften up the tough fibers in the peel and pith of the lemon by firmly rolling the whole lemon around on the countertop several times before you cut it in half; this makes it easy to squeeze juice out with one hand while holding your other hand over the cut side of the lemon to catch the seeds.

MAKE IT A MEAL

Serve each fillet on bed of fresh or cooked greens tossed or topped with cooked grains; if serving warm, drizzle on Lemon Yogurt Sauce (page 173); if serving chilled or at room temperature, add $1/2$ pint cherry or grape tomatoes, halved, and drizzle everything with Pesto Vinaigrette.

RIFF

HONEY MUSTARD-DILL SALMON: In step 2, skip the oil; instead, slather the fillet with honey mustard (or Dijon followed by a drizzle of honey, smoothed together with a butter knife), sprinkle on lots of fresh dill and season with kosher or sea salt and freshly ground black pepper. Bake at 375°F, skipping the lemon squeeze and the broil step.

MAKE IT A MEAL

Serve basic salmon on a bed of cooked rice that you've tossed with the salmon pan juices and a few tablespoons of Soy Ginger Vinaigrette. Top with sliced avocado spritzed with lemon juice and seasoned with salt and pepper, and serve with sautéed greens or a simple salad of baby greens alongside.

BANK

Cooked salmon keeps well in an airtight container in the fridge for about 5 days.

GO-TO GRAINS

Here is a starter-kit bouquet of distinct, versatile, and deliciously nutritious grains. All four of these go-tos freeze beautifully. Cooking each one in bulk and banking up a supply of clearly labeled, portioned-out packets is a smart move toward a wide range of shortcut meals. (Even for fairly quick-cooking grains, ready-made on tap in the freezer means perfect grains in minutes, no pots and pans to wash. You can't beat that on a weeknight.)

GO-TO GRAINS: QUINOA

Yield: 1 cup dry quinoa makes about 2 cups cooked
Cook time: about 25 to 30 minutes total
(5 to 10 minutes to toast, 15 to 20 to cook)

This grainlike seed comes in lots of colors—most commonly blonde, red, and black—each of which has its own subtly unique flavor, and a rainbow combo can be a fun way to go. Whatever the shade, all quinoa is packed with protein—a legit superfood—but please take my word for it when I tell you quinoa is a lot tastier (no bitterness, lots of nuttiness) if you bother to rinse it first and then toast it.

PREP

Even if the package indicates the quinoa is ready to cook, get those grains into a (very) fine-mesh strainer and rinse thoroughly under running water, shaking the strainer to make sure they all get a good washing (each teeny little seed has a natural, bitter-tasting coating that clings tenaciously).

Then toast: If you're making 1 cup or less, transfer the rinsed quinoa to a dry, medium-size, heavy-bottomed saucepan and toast gently, stirring often, over low heat, 5 to 10 minutes or until it has dried, darkened slightly (if it started out light-colored), and gives off a nutty aroma. If you're cooking more than 1 cup, spread the washed quinoa on a parchment-lined, rimmed baking sheet and bake at 350°F for 5 or 10 minutes, stirring a few times. Either way, keep a close eye on your quinoa so it doesn't overbrown and go bitter.

COOK

If you're starting with 1 cup or less, then leave the quinoa in the pan you just toasted it in and add water or broth to the saucepan at a straight 2:1 ratio of liquid to quinoa. Broth will get you more flavor, but water's also fine (just be sure to add a generous pinch or two of salt). Bring to a boil over high heat, then immediately lower the heat to a simmer, cover, and cook until the liquid is absorbed and the squiggly little tails have sprung loose, 15 to 20 minutes. Fluff with a fork.

For larger amounts, cook just as you would pasta: Bring a big pot of generously salted water to boil (optional, but nice: add flavor by tossing in a bay leaf and or branches of a sturdy fresh herb like thyme or rosemary, and or onion/shallot/leek, carrot/celery). Use the parchment lining the pan to funnel the toasted quinoa into the pot for cooking. (Put the parchment back on the baking sheet; you'll be using it again.) Start checking for doneness (little tails sprung loose) after 10 to 12 minutes—quinoa cooks even faster this way than it does the lid-on way. Drain well using a fine-mesh strainer, removing and discarding any veggies or herbs. Transfer back to the baking sheet, spreading out evenly, then put the pan in the fridge and let the quinoa dry and chill, uncovered, before using or storing (this step prevents the grainlike seeds from going gummy).

BANK

Cooked quinoa keeps well in an airtight container in the fridge for several days. To freeze, portion out fluffed, cooled quinoa into clearly labeled 1- or 2-cup containers or freezer bags.

MAKE IT A MEAL

Build-a-Frittata Dinner (page 205), substituting 1 cup quinoa for about $\frac{1}{2}$ cup of the vegetables. (Skeptical? I didn't think this sounded all that good either—but it's delicious; the quinoa blends in, adding nice flavor and texture without being at all noticeable.)

GO-TO GRAINS: FARRO

Yield: 1 cup dry farro makes about 1½ cups cooked
Cook time: about 30 minutes total
(5 to 10 minutes to toast, 20 to 25 to cook)

Farro is a plump, juicy, whole-grain Italian wheat that's not new but newly rediscovered, and gaining popularity for its nutty flavor and luxurious texture, as well as its excellent nutritional profile. I use pearled farro, which has been polished to remove the hard husk so the grains are tender and cook quickly (and don't need overnight soaking), but still retains good amounts of fiber, protein, and iron. Toasting brings out a lovely nutty flavor, totally worth the extra few minutes it takes.

PREP

Rinse the grains under cool running water. If you're cooking 1 cup or less, transfer the rinsed farro to a dry soup pot and toast gently, stirring often, over low heat, 5 to 10 minutes or until the grains are dry, darkening just a bit and giving off a nutty aroma. If you're cooking more than 1 cup, spread the grains on a parchment-lined, rimmed baking sheet and toast at 350°F for 5 or 10 minutes, stirring a few times. Either way, keep close watch so the farro doesn't overbrown and go bitter.

COOK

Cook the farro as you would pasta (if you used the pot to toast the farro, you'll need to transfer it to a bowl to free up the pot), in several quarts of generously salted boiling water. Start checking for doneness after the farro's been boiling for 20 minutes, cooking to however al dente or tender you like, and taking care not to overcook.

TIP

Infusing your farro with flavor is as easy as tossing some or all of the following into the cooking water: a bay leaf, a branch or two of a sturdy fresh herb like thyme or rosemary, a few chunks of onion (or shallot or leek), carrot, celery. Fish them back out before serving/storing the cooked farro.

MAKE IT A MEAL

✐ WHITE BEAN & FARRO SALAD: In a largish bowl, combine 1 cup each cooked and cooled farro, cooked and drained cannellini beans (page 139), and chopped sweet bell pepper; ½ cup each feta cheese and sliced kalamata olives; 1 to 2 cups baby spinach; and ¼ cup Pesto Vinaigrette (page 165). Toss to mix, seasoning with salt and pepper and/or adding a little more vinaigrette, if needed.

GO-TO GRAINS: WHOLE WHEAT COUSCOUS

Yield: 1 cup dry whole wheat couscous makes about 3 cups cooked
Cook time: About 20 minutes total (5 to 10 minutes to toast, 10 to cook)

First off, let's get two things straight. One: There are a few different kinds of couscous, but what we are working with here is whole wheat couscous—neither the product simply labeled "couscous" nor the one labeled "Israeli" or "pearl" couscous. (Whole wheat couscous is made with high-protein, whole-grain durum wheat, which means it's rich in fiber, although tastes virtually identical to the low-fiber version, plus it cooks just as quickly; a bargain all the way round.) And two: All couscous is actually pasta—so truth be told, whole wheat couscous isn't a grain in and of itself. (I won't tell if you don't.)

COOK

Use a heavy-bottom skillet that you have a tight-fitting lid for (the more couscous you're making, the larger the skillet needs to be). Pan-toast the couscous in the dry skillet over medium heat, stirring almost constantly, until the couscous takes on a little color and gives off a nutty aroma. For every 1 cup couscous, add $1\frac{1}{2}$ cups water (or broth), plus a fat pinch of salt (and, if you're feelin' it, a pat of unsalted butter). As soon as the water comes to a boil, which will happen almost immediately, slap on the lid and remove the pan from the heat. Let sit, covered, for about 10 minutes, at which point the couscous will have absorbed all of the liquid. Fluff with a fork.

BANK

Cooked, cooled whole wheat couscous keeps well in an airtight container in the refrigerator and also freezes beautifully. If you're making a large amount, I recommend spreading the hot, cooked and fluffed couscous out on a sheet pan to cool thoroughly and evaporate any extra moisture.

MAKE IT A MEAL

◾ **WHOLE WHEAT COUSCOUS AND FRENCH LENTIL SALAD:** In a medium-size serving bowl, combine 2 cups cooked whole wheat couscous (page 155), 1½ cups cooked and drained French green lentils (page 142), 1 cup mixed diced crisp vegetables (such as bell pepper, celery, carrots), and 1 minced small shallot. Add ¼ cup Basic Vinaigrette (page 164), juice of one lemon, ½ cup chopped Italian parsley leaves, and ½ teaspoon chopped fresh thyme (optional). Season the salad with a pinch of kosher or sea salt and a few grinds of black pepper. Toss lightly to mix; taste and adjust with a little more salt and pepper if needed. Serve chilled or at room temperature, atop lightly dressed salad greens.

GO-TO GRAINS: BASAMATI RICE

Okay, so here's my take on rice. It's not the only grain—or food plant for that matter—that can have trace amounts of arsenic, but the rice plant is especially adept at pulling this particular toxic pollutant out of the ground. After years of concerning reports, even the slow-on-the-uptake FDA is recommending some degree of caution about heavy rice consumption. I have not sworn off rice entirely, but to be safe, I do serve it less often, especially brown rice because it tests higher than white. That means white basmati rice is in the mix of my family's meals, just as there is often some non–whole grain sourdough bread happening. Remember: When

DR. TANYA'S PRESCRIPTION:

I rarely recommend white rice for any age. It has no fiber, little nutrition, and simply primes young palates for a lifetime of eating white carbs. That, combined with arsenic concerns, is why I prefer feeding infants and children oatmeal, quinoa, and other whole grains. When I do feed my family rice, I choose brown rice over white for the fiber.

y'all are loading up on fiber, vitamins, and minerals from a steady intake of fresh produce, there's room in the dietary budget for some fairly empty carbs.

Brown basmati is also a favorite; my choice brand is Lundberg Family Farms because they regularly test their rice and publish the results, and those results show the lowest trace levels for brown basmati (my family threw down over rice, so we still have it in our diet—which is an example of not making others crazy. We do tons of basmati rice from California as a safe option).

Rinsing heavily and cooking in large amounts of water, while it can reduce nutrient content, has also been shown to minimize the already very low detections of arsenic in basmati rice. P.S.: This fuss-free, stress-free method gets you perfectly plump, fluffy rice every time.

Both brown and white basmati have a long, delicate grain and a fragrant aroma.

PREP

Wash rice thoroughly, for a least a few minutes, under cool running water.

PETE DROPS SCIENCE

Unfortunately, arsenic is much more pervasive in the environment and some of our foods and drinking water than you might imagine. [http://bit.ly/29sCDOf] Rice is particularly problematic, as is drinking water in some areas of the United States. Arsenic is a well-known poison, but at what might seem to be low levels of exposure, it also interferes with hormones: It is an endocrine-disrupting chemical that messes with our ability to defeat tumors. Arsenic is a naturally occuring element in the environment. Some drinking-water systems have more than others, some a lot more. But we have also used it as a pesticide in agriculture and to protect wood from pests, so it lurks in unexpected places. Arsenic-based pesticides used to commonly be in apple orchards. Whoops! Do you know of any developments in your community that are built on old orchards? Their soil is likely to have elevated arsenic levels. Fortunately, the use of arsenic-based preservatives has been stopped in treated wood, but there are old structures still around that used that treatment.

COOK

Bring a pot of generously salted water to a boil. Add the rice and lower the heat to keep the water at a gentle boil. Begin checking for doneness after about 15 minutes for white basmati, about 25 minutes for brown basmati. As soon as it's done to your liking, dump the rice into a colander set in the sink and drain thoroughly.

BANK

Brown and white basmati both freeze beautifully. Cool first—ideally spread out on a rimmed baking sheet, which will allow moisture on the individual grains to evaporate. Portion out into 1- or 2-cup containers or freezer bags (squeeze out air before sealing).

MAKE IT A MEAL

Warm Rice Salad with Roasted Asparagus and Shiitake Capers (page 172) + sliced chicken (page 144) or salmon (page 148) or poached egg (page 202)

GO-TO DARK GREEN LEAFIES: BABY SPINACH

Sweet with a tender yet substantial leaf, baby spinach requires zero prep and is endlessly versatile. It could easily be your one-and-only go-to dark green leafy—seriously, you could keep your fridge stocked with a 1-pound tub of prewashed baby spinach and you'd be set, able to make pretty much any of the recipes in this book and improv a whole lot more.

TIP

One seriously annoying drawback to buying prewashed greens is the inevitable wilt and waste from trapped moisture inside that bag, clamshell, or tub. If you can buy your greens loose, then by all means go for it. Closely scrutinize packaged greens before buying and pass over any with signs of wilt having already started—it quickly gets worse once you schlep those greens home. If you won't be using the whole container very soon after bringing it home, you can prevent your carefully selected, pristine greens from meeting a sad and slimy fate if you can spare a few minutes of minor fussing and several clean, dry lightweight dishtowels (or paper towels). Use a couple of towels to line an expanse of your kitchen counter; turn the greens out onto the towels, spreading the greens out so that they're not piled deeply; cover with a couple more towels and gently roll up the bottom pair of towels with the greens and the top towels inside. Set aside. Wipe the inside of the container dry and spread one last dry towel across the bottom so that the ends overlap the sides of the container. Unroll the towels holding the greens, transfer the greens to the towel-lined container, close it back up, and stow it in the fridge for 5 days. Depending on how fresh it was to start with and the humidity level in your fridge, wrapped spinach can keep well for 10 days or more.

PREP

Unless there are some thicker stems you want to pick off, baby spinach is ready to use straight out of the tub (although see Tip about wrapping to prevent wilt).

SWAP

Non–baby spinach is just as sweet and tasty, just a good bit thicker in the leaf (especially if it's a ruffled variety); thorough washing in multiple changes of water is necessary, as is the somewhat tedious task of removing the fibrous stems. Feel free to substitute in any recipe. I grow a few varieties in my garden and use it (and/or the neighboring chards) just about every day, year-round (thank you, SoCal climate).

GO RAW

Lightly seasoned with kosher or sea salt and delicately dressed (with vinaigrettes on page 164, or just lemon and extra-virgin olive oil), baby spinach is a great go-to salad all by its lonesome, and it also makes a lovely bed for substantial bean and grain salads, as well as a serving of

chicken or salmon. Other uses include making a fresh-tasting and fortifying addition to soups; you can stir it into the pot just before serving or
put a handful in each bowl and spoon soup on top.

COOK

Be warned, a whole pound of spinach cooks down to about 1 cup, so it's
not the most economical use in terms of actual dollars, nor delicate flavor and texture. Which is not to say that a quick garlic sauté of baby (or
adult) spinach isn't a mighty tasty treat every now and again. Plus it's
wicked easy: Mince a couple garlic cloves and heat a tablespoon or two—
depending on how big a batch of spinach you're making—of extra-virgin
olive oil in a large-enough skillet over medium-low heat. Add the spinach
and the garlic and cook, stirring, until the spinach is wilted and the garlic is fragrant but not browned, 2 to 3 minutes. Tongs work best for getting the spinach out of the pan without bringing a lot of watery liquid
along, and you can use the tongs to give each little bunch a squeeze to
wring out more of the water over the pan.

BANK

Well-drained, chopped, cooked or uncooked spinach freezes quite well,
but baby spinach is sweetest and tastiest raw or freshly cooked. So I do put
a bit of effort into keeping fresh spinach fresh (see Tip), and I keep a package of high-quality store-bought frozen spinach in the freezer for the occasional improv addition to soups, frittatas, and such—but I most often use
other dark green leafies I've banked (chard and kale, page 160).

GO-TO DARK GREEN LEAFIES:
CHARD & KALE

Compared to spinach, the various chards have great big, gorgeously
shiny, and sometimes wildly colorful leaves that are in the same range of

tenderness as spinach, but each chard leaf has a thick and juicy stalk forming a rib up its full length, branching out into veins and varying in color from white to red to a range of nearly neon yellow, orange, and pink.

Kale leaves are quite a bit beefier, and the stems are dense and often very fibrous. Some kale varieties sport curly-edged green leaves, while others feature pretty purple stems; texture can be on the coarse and chewy side, but it's easily coaxed into submission. The variety I find easiest to prepare, most versatile, and generally most palatable is the dark-leafed beauty known as dinosaur, lacinato, or Tuscan kale. I especially recommend this variety for using raw in salads. And if you haven't liked kale in the past or you're new to kale altogether, dino's the place to start.

SWAP

Baby dark greens—prewashed and a good bit more tender and mild—are a fully legit substitute for chard and kale, both raw in salads and cooked in other dishes, so feel free to swap in any packaged baby blend anytime—or even all the time, if that's what gets the good green stuff on the table and into the bellies.

PREP

Fill a large bowl or your kitchen sink with cool water and immerse the greens, swishing the leaves around to rinse off any grit and lifting the leaves out of the water so that said grit gets left behind. Rinse under running water, and shake to get the leaves somewhat dry.

Remove the center stem/rib either by holding the base of the stem in one hand and sliding the other hand up the length, or by folding the leaf in half along the stem, laying it flat on a cutting board, and slicing out the rib with a sharp knife.

Trim off and discard the thickest and most fibrous portion of the stems. For both chard and kale, if you'll be sautéing the leaves, set the chopped stems aside (they'll go into the pan first, a few minutes before the leaves).

For chard that you're going to serve as a raw salad, you can chop the stems—which are crisp and tasty—and include them in the salad if you like; your call. If not, you can do the same as for kale that's destined for salads: pack the chopped stems away for future use (they're good in the base sauté for cooking dried beans, and they also blend well into sautés and stir-fries of crisp, substantial veggies; I also keep a designated container in the freezer for these sorts of bits to brew up into the occasional vat of soup stock). Coarsely chop the leaves and set aside.

GO RAW

For chard, simply slice the leaves into thin strips and dress with a simple vinaigrette. Or try my fave simple salad: Squeeze on the juice of a lemon (or two) drizzle in some extra-virgin olive oil, season with salt and pepper, and toss to coat, and—essential, as far as I'm concerned, but technically optional—top with copious amounts of shaved Parmesan (Parmigiano-Reggiano, if at all possible).

Kale can be dressed much the same way as chard, but because it's so fibrous you either need to slice it *very* thinly or massage it with olive oil, lemon juice, and salt (or any vinaigrette) for several minutes, until the fibers soften and the leaves become glossy and silky. To cut back on massaging time, you can also dress the leaves, tossing to coat thoroughly, and park them in the fridge for a couple hours or even overnight, after which they will have softened considerably so you'll have much less, if any, massaging to do. Tenderized kale keeps well in the fridge for about a week.

COOK

BASIC CHARD OR KALE

Makes 2 to 4 cups cooked greens

Avocado oil or extra-virgin olive oil
2 to 4 garlic cloves, minced

Crushed red pepper (optional)

I to 2 bunches chard or kale, trimmed and prepped (page 161)

Kosher or sea salt

Freshly ground black pepper

1. Set a large pan over low heat and add enough oil to generously coat the bottom of the pan. Add 1 to 2 cloves minced garlic and a pinch of crushed red pepper (optional, but it adds a nice whiff) and cook just until the garlic is gently sizzling and fragrant, about 2 minutes. Then stir in the chopped stems and cook, stirring often to prevent the garlic from browning, until the stems are slightly tender—about 5 minutes for chard, 8 minutes for kale.

2. Add the chopped leaves to the pan, a few handfuls at a time, and a healthy pinch of salt, mixing gently to evenly distribute the garlicky oil and the salt.

3. For chard, it will only take about 5 attentive minutes longer for everything to be done; you're aiming for tender, bright green, glossy, and still a bit perky—not brown—so stir frequently, and keep tasting little pieces, adding a teeny bit more salt and tasting again, until the slight edge of bitterness gives way. If the pan seems dry at any point, toss in about a tablespoon of water. The process is the same for kale, but takes longer—more like 10 to 15 more minutes (and the salting and tasting is especially crucial).

BANK

Portion cooled greens into 1- or 2-cup containers or freezer bags (squeeze out air before sealing) and keep in the fridge for about a week or freeze (remember to label!). It's great to have a stack of bagged precooked greens on tap in the freezer as a time- and labor-saving step to a steady stream of hearty soups and stews (you can even stir the greens in without thawing), frittatas, and casseroles.

GET SAUCY

Eight sauces/dips/dressings, plus eight variations—all flavor-packed, all
bankable, all endlessly versatile.

BASIC VINAIGRETTE

Makes 2 cups

*A good dressing accentuates, rather than overshadows, whatever you put
it on. Example: A forkful of the simplest all-lettuce salad should land in
your mouth as a clean, crisp bite of ever-so-slightly sweet leafiness—not
a puckering blast of vinegar. In proper balance, vinegar (or other acid,
such as lemon) brings a hint of piquancy, just enough to keep things perky.
Combine that with skillful seasoning (always season lightly with salt and
pepper before dressing, and always taste, adjust, and taste again) and you
are good to go. The low vinegar-to-oil ratio makes the following go-to
basic vinaigrette a mild dressing very well suited to all sorts of salads,
simple side veggies, and sandwiches. You can always bump up the acidity
with an additional splash of vinegar or squeeze of lemon, but hold off until
the dish is complete and nicely seasoned, then taste again to see if a touch
more acid still seems needed. Alternatively, you can just go with one of the
zippier variations on this recipe.*

   1 $^3/_4$ cups avocado or extra-virgin olive oil
   $^1/_4$ cup red wine vinegar
   1 small garlic clove or shallot, finely minced
   1 fat pinch dry mustard
   1 fat pinch kosher or sea salt
   A few grinds black pepper

Whisk all of the ingredients together in a small bowl, or combine in
a jar and shake well. Store in an airtight glass jar or bottle in the
refrigerator.

RIFF

CITRUS VINAIGRETTE: Combine 1 cup basic vinaigrette with ¼ teaspoon each freshly grated lemon zest and orange zest, and 1 tablespoon each freshly squeezed lemon juice and orange juice (or ½ teaspoon lemon zest and 2 tablespoons lemon juice).

SOY GINGER: Use avocado oil; use rice vinegar instead of red wine vinegar; add 2 tablespoons low-sodium soy sauce and ½ teaspoon toasted sesame oil; add 1 to 2 teaspoons minced fresh ginger (or 1 teaspoon minced pickled ginger) along with the garlic.

PESTO VINAIGRETTE: Combine ½ cup Basic Vinaigrette with ¼ cup Basil Pesto (page 167).

SLOW-ROASTED TOMATOES

Makes 3 cups

If I had to pick just one make-ahead to always have on hand, it might very well be these flavor-packed, melt-in-the-mouth, crazy versatile goodies. Serve as is for a tasty side, use as topping for plain chicken breast (page 145) or salmon fillet (page 149)—with or without a little pesto mixed in—or as a saucy stir-in for pasta, grains, or vegetables. Fold into salads and soups galore. And so on and so forth! Make with meaty plum tomatoes or a mix of different varieties.

4 pounds ripe tomatoes, cored and roughly diced

4 or more whole cloves garlic, smashed and peeled

Extra-virgin olive oil, as needed

2 sprigs fresh basil (optional)

3 to 4 sprigs fresh thyme (optional)

Sea salt

1. Preheat the oven to 275°F, with convection on if possible. Line two rimmed baking sheets with unbleached parchment paper.
2. Divide the tomatoes and garlic between the two baking sheets. Drizzle with oil and toss with your hands, then spread out in an even

layer. Tuck the herbs underneath the tomatoes and salt both pans generously.

3. Bake for 2 hours, checking after an hour and a half to be sure they're not drying out too quickly. The tomatoes are done when they are shriveled, very dry, and taste like candy. If you prefer them a little juicier, check on them after 1 hour of cooking.

4. Pick out and discard the herb stems, first stripping off the leaves and adding them back into the tomatoes. Pick up the parchment by the corners and tip the warm tomatoes and garlic into a serving dish or storage container.

TIP

In summertime, use bulk quantities of fruity ripe tomatoes to make loads of roasted tomatoes and/or the sauce (below); bank up as much as you can in the freezer to use throughout the next nine months.

> Note: Roasted tomatoes keep well in the fridge for a week or so, and they freeze like a dream: Pack flat in a plastic freezer bag and press all the air out before freezing for up to 6 months.

RIFF

ROASTED TOMATO BRUSCHETTA SPREAD: Once cooled to room temperature, transfer 1 tray of the tomatoes along with one or more of the roasted garlic cloves (your call) to a food processor and pulse to a coarse puree, adding extra-virgin olive oil as needed to moisten. Spread on toasted sourdough baguette and serve as bruschetta. Keeps for weeks in a jar in the fridge.

ROASTED TOMATO SAUCE: Once cooled to room temperature, transfer 1 tray of tomatoes and garlic cloves to a food processor, add one (18.3-ounce) jar tomatoes along with their juice (about 2 cups), and pulse to a coarse puree. Transfer the tomatoes to a skillet and add $1/_2$ stick unsalted butter. Bring to a simmer over low heat and continue cook at a gentle simmer, stirring often, until consistency is thick and the flavor is rich and mellow (if it's still acidic, add another tablespoon or two of butter and simmer a few more minutes). The roasted tomatoes are so well seasoned that the sauce will probably not need any additional salt or pepper.

BASIC BASIL PESTO

Makes about 1 cup

The price of pine nuts shot through the roof a few years back and has yet to come back down, but it turns out blanched slivered almonds work just as well. Bank up a supply in the freezer (in cubes, see Tip), so you can bust it out any time to perk up just about anything: sandwiches, dressings, salads, vegetable sides, simple servings of chicken and salmon, and rice and other grains (drop a frozen cube into a bowl or pot of steaming hot grains, stir to cover with the grains, and leave it for a few minutes; it will be melted and mixable when you come back—and oh so delish).

I small garlic clove, smashed and peeled

2 cups fresh basil leaves, tightly packed (about 8 ounces before removing stems)

$1/2$ cup blanched slivered almonds or pine nuts

$1/2$ to $3/4$ cup fruity extra-virgin olive oil

$1/2$ teaspoon sea salt, plus more as needed

Freshly ground black pepper

About $1/2$ cup Parmesan cheese (omit if freezing)

1. Whiz the garlic clove in a food processor to pulverize. Add the basil and almonds. With the machine running, drizzle in $1/2$ cup of the olive oil. Process to a pourable consistency (add more olive oil if necessary).

2. Stop the machine, scrape down the bowl, and add a good-sized pinch of salt and a few grinds of pepper. Process to blend, taste, and adjust seasoning as needed.

3. If you are using all of the pesto right away for pasta or another dish that calls for pesto with Parmesan included, add the Parmesan and process to blend. Store in an airtight (preferably glass) container in

the fridge for up to 1 week (you can add a thin skim of olive oil to the top to help preserve the big flavor and bright green color). Or freeze Parm-less.

RIFFS

PISTACHIO MINT PESTO: Keep the garlic (make sure it's a very small clove), but instead of the basil use $1/4$ cup fresh mint leaves plus $1/4$ cup fresh Italian parsley leaves; replace the almonds with toasted unsalted pistachios; reduce the amount of olive oil to $1/2$ cup; add the zest and juice of 1 lemon and the juice of $1/2$ orange (or whole clementine). Omit the Parmesan. Makes about $3/4$ cup.

DRAWER OF GOOD INTENTIONS LETTUCE PESTO: Omit the nuts, use a medium-size clove of garlic, and replace the basil, with $1/2$ cup loosely packed fresh Italian parsley leaves and 4 cups loosely packed chopped romaine or other lettuce (tender-crisp varieties, such as butter crunch or Boston, are best). Puree all of that in the food processor, then scrape down the bowl, add $1/2$ cup grated Parmesan cheese, and season with about $1/4$ teaspoon salt and several grinds of pepper. Process to mix, then check seasoning, adjusting with more salt as needed. Use immediately—as a sandwich spread, dip for crackers or vegetables, or sauce for simple chicken breast, salmon fillet, or rice or other grain—or keep in an airtight container in the fridge; it will retain its flavor and color for several days. It's also freezable, but not as flavorful thereafter as basil or pistachio-mint pesto.

BREAK AWAY FROM BOTTLED DRESSING

Bottled dressings—and conventional condiments, in general—tend to be loaded with ridiculous amounts of sodium and sugar, and many are also packed with preservatives and other unhealthy—and totally unnecessary—ingredients (see "Naming Names," page 51). It is seriously *so* easy and *so* worth it to shake up a jar of homemade dressing. The stuff keeps for weeks in the fridge, makes everything you put it on taste better than any bottled crap ever could, and contains only healthy ingredients. If you use good-quality extra-virgin olive oil or avocado oil, the dressing will solidify in the fridge (that is the natural behavior of healthy monounsaturated fats), so just leave it out at room temp for a spell to reliquefy; if you forget this step, no worries—stand the jar in a bowl of warm (not hot) water to hasten the process along.

HUMMUS

Makes about 4 cups

My family can take down a lot of hummus, so I whip it up in large quan-
tities. You can certainly scale back this recipe by half, or just portion out
any leftovers into ½-cup containers for future use—it freezes surpris-
ingly well for use as dip, and is a must-have in the bank for Quick Mine-
strone (page 141).

2 to 3 garlic cloves, smashed and peeled, divided
4 cups cooked and drained garbanzo beans (page 140)
½ to 1 cup bean cooking broth
1 teaspoon toasted sesame oil
¼ cup extra-virgin olive oil
½ teaspoon kosher or sea salt, plus more as needed
Juice of 2 lemons, plus more as needed
Freshly ground black pepper

1. Whiz 2 cloves of the garlic in a food processor to pulverize.
2. Add the beans, ½ cup of the broth, oils, salt, lemon juice, and a few grinds of pepper, and process until smooth. Add more broth as needed to get to a nice creamy texture.
3. Taste and adjust seasoning with additional salt and/or additional lemon juice, and/or additional garlic, if needed.
4. Serve immediately or keep in an airtight container in the fridge for up to 1 week, or freeze for about 3 months.

SMOKY WHITE BEAN DIP

Makes about 2½ cups

Using sautéed rather than raw vegetables bolsters the mellow
flavor and rich texture of this crowd-pleasing dip, which doubles as
a delicious sandwich spread and makes a genius shortcut soup
component.

3 tablespoons extra-virgin olive oil, divided

I small shallot, minced

2 garlic cloves, minced

I carrot, finely chopped or grated

I celery stalk, finely chopped or grated

$\frac{1}{4}$ to $\frac{1}{2}$ teaspoon smoked paprika

Pinch cayenne pepper (optional)

Kosher or sea salt

Freshly ground black pepper

2 cups cooked cannellini or other white beans (page 139)

Juice of I lemon

$\frac{1}{2}$ cup reserved bean liquid, low-sodium vegetable or chicken
    broth, or water

Chopped parsley (optional)

1. Heat 1 tablespoon of the oil in a small sauté pan over low heat. Add the shallot and cook 1 minute, then add garlic and cook 1 more minute, stirring almost constantly, or until the mixture sizzles and is fragrant, but not brown. Add the garlic, carrots, celery, smoked paprika, and cayenne, and season with a pinch of salt and few grinds of pepper. Cook, stirring, until the vegetables are very tender, about 6 minutes. Take the pan off the heat and let the vegetables cool to room temperature.

2. Combine the beans, cooled sautéed veggies, remaining 2 tablespoons olive oil, the lemon juice, and $\frac{1}{4}$ cup of the bean liquid in the bowl of a food processor. Process for 1 to 2 minutes, stopping a couple of times to scrape down the bowl and add more liquid to adjust thin the puree, if needed.

3. Taste and adjust seasoning. Top with chopped parsley and serve.

CHIPOTLE BLACK BEAN DIP

Makes about 2 cups

Remember to add salt gradually, a teeny pinch at a time, blending thor-oughly and tasting, until the dip is flavorful—you're using the salt to heighten overall taste, not make the dip taste salty. Leftovers? Dollop atop the melted cheese on a quesadilla, add sliced avocado, salsa and/or hot sauce, and chow down. Also a great shortcut to delicious black bean soup.

I jalapeño pepper, seeded and coarsely chopped

$\frac{1}{2}$ cup chopped red onion

2 cloves garlic

$\frac{1}{2}$ cup loosely packed fresh cilantro, thicker stems removed

I$\frac{1}{2}$ cups cooked and drained black beans

I tablespoon avocado oil or extra-virgin olive oil

$\frac{1}{2}$ teaspoon kosher or sea salt, plus more as needed

Freshly ground black pepper

$\frac{1}{2}$ lime, plus more as needed

$\frac{1}{4}$ teaspoon chipotle chili powder, plus more as needed (optional)

Tortilla chips and/or cut up veggies, for serving

1. Combine the jalapeño, onion, and garlic, and cilantro in the bowl of a food processor and whiz them to finely mince. Add the beans and the oil, the salt and a few grinds of pepper, and squeeze in the lime juice. Process to a puree, pausing to scrape down the sides of the bowl and to taste and adjust seasoning with a pinch or two more salt and/or additional lime juice. Process to blend, then taste and adjust seasoning again, as needed.

2. If there's time, stick this in the fridge for an hour, or longer, to let the flavors meld. Keeps well in an airtight container for about 1 week. Leftovers can be frozen for use in Black Bean Soup.

ROASTED SHIITAKE SHALLOT CAPER BUTTER

Makes about ³/₄ cup

This is a secret-ingredient concoction you can deploy in all sorts of situations: Toss with roasted veggies (it's a match made in heaven with roasted asparagus) or warm potato salad, stir into grains, swirl into soups and frittatas, or schmear on a toasted baguette like a paté. It keeps in an airtight jar in the fridge for ages.

2 dozen fresh whole shiitake mushrooms (about 8 ounces)

2 or 3 large shallots, thinly sliced

¹/₄ cup white wine

2 to 4 tablespoons avocado oil

2 sprigs each fresh thyme and rosemary

Kosher or sea salt

Freshly ground black pepper

¹/₃ cup ghee or butter

2¹/₂ teaspoons capers

2¹/₂ teaspoons caper brine (from the jar)

1. Preheat the oven to 350°F. Line two large baking sheets with unbleached parchment paper.
2. Use scissors to snip the stems off of the mushrooms. Rinse off the stems, pat them dry, and reserve in an airtight container in the freezer to use for soup stock.
3. Quickly rinse the mushroom caps in a colander, then pat dry with paper towels.
4. Transfer the mushrooms to the prepared baking sheets, arranging in a single layer with a little space around each one. Scatter on the shallots. Drizzle half of the wine, then half of the oil over each sheet of mushrooms. Scatter on the herbs (if using dried herbs, sprinkle on evenly). Lightly season with salt and pepper. Turn each of the mush-

rooms a couple of times to lightly coat with the wine mixture and season again a bit more salt and pepper.

5. Slide the baking sheets into the oven and roast the mushrooms 30 minutes. Turn and roast 10 more minutes, or until nicely browned and tender to the center (the tip of a small sharp knife should meet with no resistance).

6. Cool the mixture, pick out the herb stems, transfer the mushrooms and shallots to the bowl of a food processor, and process to a coarse puree. Scrape down the sides of the bowl, add the butter, capers, and caper brine, and puree until smooth. Taste and adjust seasoning with additional salt and pepper, if needed.

CREAMY YOGURT SAUCE

Makes about 1 cup

This complements pretty much everything: all manner of cooked veggies; simply prepared (or leftover chilled) salmon or chicken; you name it. Is it nice to have this on hand in the fridge? Sure. However, because it couldn't be easier prepwise (1 minute flat) and life is, well, life, I usually throw it together either when I find myself in need of a dip for raw veggies or when I've already got the rest of dinner done and ready to put on the table and I realize I want a little something in the way of drizzle. Now that's what I call a go-to. Feel free to throw in a pinch of cumin or smoked paprika, or some chopped herbs.

I cup whole milk yogurt
Juice of $\frac{1}{2}$ lemon
Sea salt or kosher salt
Freshly ground black pepper

1. Put the yogurt in a small bowl, squeeze in the lemon juice (use two hands, one to squeeze, the other to sieve out the seeds; or a little strainer), add a generous pinch of salt, a couple grinds of pepper, and

whisk the mixture together until thoroughly combined.

2. Use indiscriminately.

RIFFS

CREAMY DILL SAUCE: Double the lemon juice, grate in a little bit of red onion (if you have it), and snip in a couple tablespoons worth of dill (feathery leaves only). Serve over salmon or slabs of summer tomato, and swoon.

TZATZIKI: Use Greek yogurt; add 1 cucumber, peeled, seeded, and coarsely grated or finely chopped; 1 to 2 tablespoons finely chopped fresh mint; and, if you want your dip rather zippy, one very small, very finely minced clove of garlic. Enjoy as dip for grilled pita or raw veggies; as a sandwich condiment; as a sauce for cold chicken or salmon.

FETA DIP: Cut back the amount of yogurt to ¼ cup and put it in the bowl of a food processor along with the lemon juice, ½ cup crumbled feta cheese (packed); 2 tablespoons extra-virgin olive oil; 1 very small smashed and peeled clove of garlic, and 1 teaspoon smoked sweet Spanish paprika. Grind in enough black pepper to lightly cover the surface of the yogurt. Process the mixture until thick and smooth. Cover and chill (in a bowl or jar) for 1 hour before serving, if possible. Keep in an airtight container in the fridge for up to 2 weeks.

> ## DR. TANYA'S PRESCRIPTION:
>
> Yogurt is a natural, healthy, non-pill way to feed beneficial bacteria to our gut.

VEG OUT

Tasty, easy ways to prep a select few fortifying and flavorful veggies that make terrific straight-to-the-plate sides and, as leftovers, repurpose into shortcut components for outstandingly easy, deliciously substantial salads, soups, and mains. Here and there, "Dress Up" recommendations offer prime pairings with saucy stuff.

BLANCHED ASPARAGUS

Makes 6 to 8 servings

A very brief and briny boil followed by an ice-cold dunk is the surest way to get delectably tender-crisp, brilliantly bright-green asparagus. This method is best suited to very fresh asparagus harvested at the height of the season, when the spears are at their crispy sweetest.

2 large bunches medium-thick asparagus, trimmed and washed (see Tip)
Kosher or sea salt

1. Set a large soup pot of heavily salted water on to boil over high heat.
2. While the water is heating, set up an ice bath: a large bowl of cool water with plenty of ice so that the water temperature is very cold. Set a colander in the sink.
3. When the pot of water comes to a boil, add the asparagus and cook for about 3 minutes, just until barely tender-crisp, then immediately drain in the colander and transfer to the ice bath to cool for 2 to 3 minutes.
4. Drain and serve cold, rewarm with a very quick sauté in melted butter, and serve immediately, or refrigerate in an airtight container for up to 3 days.

DRESS UP

Splash chilled asparagus spears with any vinaigrette (pages 164 and 165), give them the olive oil + lemon juice + Parm treatment. A drizzle of Lemon Yogurt Sauce is very nice for hot or cold asparagus. And one of the most delicious things evah is a pile of perfectly cooked, peak-of-season asparagus topped with a poached egg.

ROASTED ASPARAGUS

Makes 6 to 8 servings

Whereas blanching asparagus highlights its bright fresh flavors, roasting calls forth the vegetable's earthier nature. This is a delicious way to enjoy asparagus anytime, and the best route to go when the primest peak of the season is past, taking the sweetest of the asparagus with it—or when you're working with imported asparagus, which travels too far (often all the way from Peru) to be field-fresh.

2 large bunches asparagus with medium-thick stalks

I to 2 tablespoons avocado oil

Kosher or sea salt

Freshly ground black pepper

1. Preheat the oven to 400°F, with convection on, if possible, and line two large rimmed baking sheets with parchment paper.
2. Spread the asparagus in a single layer on the prepared baking sheets. Drizzle on the oil, turning the stalks to lightly coat, and season them all over with salt and pepper. Slide the sheets into the oven and roast 20 to 30 minutes, or just until tender and slightly browned, shaking the pans or using tongs to turn the spears once or twice during the cooking time.

DRESS UP

Roasted asparagus with Shiitake Shallot Caper Butter (page 172) = *heaven.*

CHEESY BAKED BROCCOLI

Serves 4 generously

Two words: Crowd-pleaser.

> Butter or ghee
> I large bunch broccoli
> I cup low-sodium chicken or vegetable broth
> 6 ounces grated cheese (such as Cheddar, or 4 ounces Cheddar
>   and 2 ounces Parmesan)

1. Preheat the oven to 400°F. Butter a casserole dish (a 9″ x 13″ Pyrex one works well).
2. Cut the broccoli, including stems (see Tip) into 2-inch pieces.
3. Spread the broccoli in the buttered dish and pour the broth over top. Cover tightly with foil and bake 15 minutes at 400°F.
4. Slide the pan out of the oven, take off the foil, and sprinkle on all but 3 tablespoons of the cheese. Put the foil back on and bake 5 to 10 more minutes (depending on how soft your family likes their broccoli).
5. Slide the pan out of the oven and switch to broil.
6. Sprinkle the remaining cheese all over the top of the broccoli, and broil, uncovered, for 2 minutes or until golden brown. Serve immediately.

ROASTED BROCCOLI

Serves 4 to 6

I can't imagine why roasted broccoli isn't a lot more popular. The crispy edges and deeply savory flavor are delicious new twists for any broccoli fan more accustomed to steamed or sautéed. For nonfans, this is more likely to bring about a broccoli breakthrough than any stovetop prep I know of.

> 2 bunches broccoli, separated into small florets, and stem
>   trimmed and chopped into bite-size pieces

Avocado oil or ghee, as needed

Sea salt

Freshly ground black pepper

1. Preheat the oven to 400°F, with convection on, if possible.
2. Drizzle 2 large rimmed baking sheets with oil to coat. Spread the broccoli out in an even layer on the pan. Add another drizzle of oil over the broccoli, mixing with your hands to coat, then salt and pepper generously.
3. Roast for 10 to 15 minutes, until the broccoli is browned and crisp at the edges. Serve hot.

DRESS UP

Leftover roasted broccoli is very nice lightly bathed in Citrus Vinaigrette (page 165)—or just spritzed with lemon juice—and tossed with crumbled feta cheese.

CARAMELIZED CAULIFLOWER

Makes about 6 cups

The way roasting renders cauliflower into a sort of savory candy is nothing short of a vegetable miracle.

2 heads cauliflower, cut into florets

Avocado oil

Kosher or sea salt

Freshly ground black pepper

1. Preheat the oven to 450°F, with convection on if possible.
2. Spread the florets on two large rimmed baking sheets, drizzle with oil, and mix with your hands to coat thoroughly, adding more oil as needed. Sprinkle each tray with a large pinch of salt and a few grinds of pepper.
3. Slide the trays into the oven, close the door, and turn the temperature down to 375°F.

4. Roast for 15 to 20 minutes, until the florets are nicely browned on their undersides, then turn them, put the trays back in the oven and cook the cauliflower another 10 to 15 minutes, or until nicely browned on both sides. Serve immediately.

DRESS UP

It isn't really possible for roasted cauliflower to get any better, but tossing it with Pistachio Mint Pesto (page 168) might come close. In the unlikely event you have leftovers, you could shake up a mix of that pesto and some Citrus Vinaigrette (page 165), drizzle, and dig in.

ROAST 'EM

Most of these veggie recipes involve roasting because that's what does the most magic with the least time and effort. Important: high heat, good air circulation (that's why baking sheets work so well, rather than pans with higher sides, which trap moisture and contribute to more steaming and less browning); oil that's good for roasting; parchment paper for easier cleanup.

CAULIFLOWER "RICE"

Makes 4 to 5 cups

So I am fully on board with the cauliflower rice thing because it is just plain yummy. In this recipe, the cauliflower rice is roasted and dressed with butter and Parm, and the resulting texture and flavor is a lot like orzo, the rice-shaped pasta. This recipe uses the whole head of cauliflower and makes a large quantity, but leftovers are freezable and excellent in Chicken and (Cauliflower) Rice Soup (page 201). You could also scale the recipe down by half and use the other half of the cauliflower for a tasty slaw (page 180).

I head cauliflower (about 1½ pounds)
About 2 tablespoons avocado oil
½ teaspoon kosher or coarse sea salt
Freshly ground black pepper
2 tablespoons unsalted butter (optional)
¼ cup grated Parmesan cheese, plus more as needed
Fresh basil leaves and chopped tomatoes, for serving (optional)

DRAWER OF GOOD INTENTIONS SLAW

Slaw is an excellent go-to solution to the problem of various veggies on the verge, especially fibrous ones like cauliflower, broccoli, carrots, and celery. (Softer, juicier ones—cucumbers, bell peppers, and even zucchini unless it's quite firm—make for soggy slaw.)

To whip up a quick and tasty slaw, trim any sketchy patches off the veggies (including stems for cauliflower and broccoli) and shred them up using a box grater (side with largest holes) or a food processor fitted with the coarse grating blade. For every 5 or 6 cups of grated veggies, mix in about $1/2$ cup vinaigrette of your choice (page 164). Mix the whole thing up in a bowl, cover, and set it in the fridge to marinate for an hour or two, stirring every now and then, if you get a chance. Grated apple makes a nice addition, if you've got one rolling around in the fridge that needs using; use the Citrus Vinaigrette to help keep the apple from turning brown. Serve the slaw as a side or salad; leftovers will soften with each passing day, but can be stirred into big leafy green salads and can also make a good addition to sandwiches, burgers, and tacos.

1. Preheat the oven to 400°F. Line a large rimmed baking sheet with unbleached parchment paper.

2. Break the cauliflower into manageable pieces (florets and trimmed, tender stems) and grate with a box grater, using the side with largest holes, or a food processor fitted with a coarse grating blade. You should end up with several cups of rice-shaped cauliflower bits.

3. Transfer the grated cauliflower to a mixing bowl, add the oil, salt, and several grinds of black pepper, and toss well to blend.

4. Spread the cauliflower on the baking sheet. Roast for 10 to 15 minutes, until it is no longer crunchy but still firm to the bite.

5. Transfer the roasted cauliflower to a serving bowl and mix in the butter and cheese. Check seasoning and adjust to taste with additional salt and pepper; add more cheese, as needed. Serve immediately, topped with some snipped basil and chopped tomato, or store in an airtight container in the fridge for several days. Rewarm gently to keep the cauliflower nice and firm.

DRESS UP

Go all the way with the orzo pasta facsimile and toss the hot cauliflower with Basil Pesto (page 167; this is a perfect use for a banked away frozen cube or two). You could parlay cold leftovers into a faux orzo salad, combining with chopped fresh veggies (like tomatoes, sweet bell pepper, cucumber) or leftover cooked ones (like zucchini); garbanzo beans would be good in there, too; bring it all together by tossing with plenty of Pesto Vinaigrette (page 165).

CARAMELIZED ONIONS

Makes about 2 cups

Cooking plain old yellow onions low and slow makes them delectably sweet and tender. They serve as a lovely side on their own and play extremely well with others—from veggie side to meaty or egg-based main—and form a phenomenal foundation for soups (page 201). Even the smallest amount of leftovers is worth saving, to work some condiment magic on a sandwich or burger. If you have a food processor, slicing up a large quantity of onions takes barely any time, effort, or tears, so it makes sense to double or triple this recipe so you end up with enough caramelized onions to sock away in the freezer. Just be sure to use as wide a pan as possible so you don't have epic cook time.

I tablespoon unsalted butter or ghee
I tablespoon extra-virgin olive oil
2 large yellow onions, sliced into rounds or half moons
I to 2 teaspoons fresh thyme leaves (optional)
Kosher or sea salt
Freshly ground black pepper

1. Melt the butter and oil together in a large, stainless steel skillet over medium-low heat. Add the onions and thyme, season generously with salt and pepper, and leave to cook undisturbed for about 10 minutes (keep an eye on them and lower the heat under the pan if the onions are cooking quickly or crisping at the edges), or until the onions have softened considerably and are golden brown on the bottom (peek to check before doing any stirring).

2. Stir the onions and continue cooking, moving them around the pan occasionally and keeping the heat low enough to prevent crisping,

until very tender (taste one: there should be no crunch whatsoever) and a deep golden brown. The whole process can take 45 minutes to 1 hour.

DRESS UP

When the onions are done cooking, transfer them to a dish and don't wash the pan—it's full of yumminess. Add some wine, broth, or just plain water to the pan—$1/4$ to $1/2$ cup, or however much it takes to cover the bottom of the pan. Crank the heat under the pan up to high and stir nonstop to scrape up all the tasty brown bits while the mixture bubbles furiously. Within a minute or two the liquid will reduce to a syrupy consistency, which means you've got a lovely pan sauce and you need to get the pan off the heat, pronto. Pour it over the onions.

PINK QUICK-PICKLED ONIONS

Makes about $1^1/_2$ cups

The optics alone—pretty and pink!—make these babies worth the very few minutes of prep time, but you also get yourself a versatile condiment. This is the jar to reach for next time you serve tacos or burgers—or a salad, sandwich, or veggie side that's in need of a little somethin'-somethin'. You can switch up the citrus juices however you like, but it's essential to stick with white wine vinegar both for neutral color and mild flavor. And you can add more zing by omitting the peppercorns and adding a few slices of ginger and a clove or two of garlic.

  2 smallish red onions, thinly sliced into rounds or half moons
      (about 2 cups)
  $1/_2$ cup freshly squeezed lime juice
  $1/_4$ cup freshly squeezed lemon juice
  $1/_4$ cup white wine vinegar
  $1/_2$ teaspoon kosher salt
  A few thin slices of lemon and lime (optional)
  A few peppercorns (optional)

1. Put the onion slices in a small heatproof bowl and pour in enough boiling water to cover, using a fork to gently press the onions down to immerse, just for a moment. Set a sieve or colander in the sink and drain the onions.

2. In the same small bowl, combine the citrus juices, vinegar, and salt; stir with the fork until the salt is dissolved. Add the onions and mix gently.

3. Cover and let sit at least 1 hour (ideally 3 or 4).

4. Transfer the onions and all of the juices to a small jar (best to keep the onions covered with the juices) with a tight-fitting lid and keep refrigerated for at least a few weeks.

POTATOES VINAIGRETTE

Makes 5 to 6 cups

Dressing the potatoes while they're steaming hot infuses them with a subtle, slightly piquant flavor. Leftovers keep well for several days and are delicious as a stand-alone cold or room-temperature potato salad (with or without some capers thrown in) and can also be incorporated into Warm Cannellini Quinoa Potato Salad (page 141), Salmon Niçoise (page 194), or your own tossed-together improv.

6 good-size Yukon gold potatoes (about 2 pounds)
Kosher or sea salt
I large shallot, minced
About $\frac{1}{2}$ cup Basic Vinaigrette

1. Scrub and trim the potatoes and cut them into 1-inch chunks. Pile the potatoes into a large saucepan and cover deeply with cold, heavily salted water; bring to a boil. Lower the heat and simmer the potatoes for about 15 minutes, or just until tender in the center.

2. Drain the potatoes in a colander, transfer to a large bowl, add the shallots, and dress the steaming-hot potatoes with the vinaigrette, stirring gently to coat without breaking up the chunks. Check seasoning

and adjust with additional salt and pepper as needed.

3. Let the potatoes sit at room temperature for about 10 minutes, gently turning them a few times.

4. Check and adjust seasoning again. Serve warm.

RIFF

SHIITAKE CAPER POTATOES: Instead of vinaigrette, toss the steaming-hot potatoes with a couple-few tablespoons of Shiitake Shallot Caper Butter (page 172).

GREEN POTATO SALAD: Cook and dress as directed; serve cold leftovers with a generous amount of Lettuce Pesto mixed in.

HERB-ROASTED POTATOES

Fresh out of the oven, these put up pretty good competition against French fries for chowdownability (see Riff). Leftovers on their own can be recrisped in the oven, but are never quite as good as freshly made— and aren't so great thrown into salads and such because they are a bit dry on the inside. However, I can't overstate how good leftover roasted potatoes are with any and all manner of eggs. We incorporate them into breakfast on an almost daily basis. And folded into a frittata? Hello, delicious one-dish dinner.

Note: Mix it up now and then by substituting yams for some or all of the potatoes.

6 good-size Yukon gold potatoes (about 2 pounds), cut into l-inch
 chunks

l tablespoon avocado oil, plus more as needed

Kosher or sea salt

Freshly ground black pepper

l to 2 teaspoons chopped fresh thyme or rosemary leaves

1. Preheat the oven to 400°F, with convection on if possible. Line a large rimmed baking sheet with unbleached parchment paper.

2. Spread the potatoes out on the prepared pan, drizzle with the oil, and

mix with your hands to coat. Season generously with salt and pepper, and sprinkle on the herbs.

3. Slide the baking sheet into the oven and roast the potatoes undisturbed for 15 or 20 minutes, until golden brown and a bit puffy. Roast 5 to 10 minutes longer, stirring or turning a couple of times to brown on all sides. Serve hot, with additional salt and pepper to taste.

RIFF

OVEN FRIES: Cut the potatoes into slabs instead of chunks.

LEMON-ROASTED BUTTERNUT SQUASH

Makes about 6 cups

Butternut squash has a divinely sweet flavor and silky texture, but it's a bit of a bear to prep. I'll out myself—I sometimes buy it in precut chunks. If you go for the whole squash, that's great—just be sure to peel that bad boy before you try to cut into it. If you want to incorporate the squash into other dishes (page 188), cut it into $1/2$- to 1-inch cubes so they'll be golden all over. Note that the smaller pieces will brown more quickly, so you'll need check the squash after 15 to 20 minutes and keep a close eye on it from that point forward, shaking the pan or using tongs to turn the cubes.

I butternut squash (about 3 pounds), peeled, seeded, and cut into
    2- to 3-inch chunks
2 to 4 tablespoons avocado oil
I to 2 lemons, zested and halved (optional)
Kosher or sea salt
Coarsely ground black pepper

1. Preheat oven to 400°F, with convection on if possible. Line 2 large baking sheets with parchment paper.
2. Divide the squash chunks between the two sheets, drizzle on 2 tablespoons of the oil, and turn the chunks to coat all over, adding more oil

as needed. Squeeze the lemon halves over the squash, sprinkle on the lemon zest, and generously season the chunks with salt and pepper.

3. Roast the squash about 25 minutes, until it begins to brown, then turn the pieces (spring-loaded tongs work well for jobs like these) and continue cooking about 20 minutes longer, turning once or twice more to brown on all sides, and checking often toward the end of the cooking time to prevent overbrowning. The squash is done when golden brown all over and the tip of small knife slides into the flesh with no resistance.

4. Check seasoning and adjust with additional salt, if needed, before serving the squash hot or incorporating it into another dish.

SAUTÉED ZUCCHINI WITH PESTO

Makes about 3½ cups

It's important to keep the zucchini moving while it cooks in the pan, otherwise some of the slices will be overcooked by the time the rest are done. If you're using frozen pesto, it will start to thaw a little while you cook the zucchini and melt the rest of the way once you add the cooked vegetables to the bowl. In summertime, make this with pattypans or other small seasonal squashes, which are naturally sweeter and more tender than zucchini.

I to 2 tablespoons Basil Pesto (or I to 2 frozen cubes)
I to 2 tablespoons butter or ghee
3 or 4 zucchini, thinly sliced into rounds or half-moons (about I½ pounds or 4 cups)
Kosher or sea salt
Freshly ground black pepper
2 tablespoons freshly grated Parmesan cheese

1. Put the pesto in a medium-size serving bowl.
2. Melt the butter in a large skillet over medium-low heat. Add the zucchini and season liberally with salt and pepper. Cook, stirring almost constantly and tasting frequently, and sprinkle in a little

more salt until any hint of bitterness gives way and the slices are tender, but not soft, and beginning to brown lightly at the edges, about 5 minutes.

3. Transfer the cooked squash to the serving bowl. If you are using frozen pesto, leave it to melt for a few minutes under the pile of hot zucchini, then mix gently to coat. Sprinkle generously with Parmesan before serving.

RIFF

PESTO TOMATO ZUCCHINI SALAD: Skip Step 1; in Step 3, transfer the cooked squash to a wide shallow bowl and let cool to room temperature, then gently toss with 1 cup Slow-Roasted Tomatoes followed by 2 to 4 tablespoons Pesto Vinaigrette. Serve at room temperature or chilled, with or without shaved Parm. Other delicious adds: leftover Potatoes Vinaigrette (page 183) and/or crumbled feta cheese.

DRY-ROASTED ZUCCHINI

Makes about 3½ cups

This simplest of quick and easy preps yields pleasingly light and tender slices that are perfect alongside any main and incorporate into other dishes beautifully.

3 or 4 zucchini, thinly sliced into rounds or half-moons (about 1½
    pounds or 4 cups)
Kosher or sea salt
Freshly ground black pepper

1. Preheat the oven to 400°F. Line 2 rimmed baking sheets with unbleached parchment paper.
2. Arrange the zucchini slices in a single layer on the baking sheets and season with salt and pepper. Bake 8 to 10 minutes, until slightly softened.
3. Transfer the zucchini to a serving dish, check seasoning and adjust with additional salt and pepper as needed.

Drizzle with extra-virgin olive oil, grate on some Parmesan cheese, and serve. It's also good lightly doused with any vinaigrette (page 164) or a Lemon Yogurt Sauce (page 173).

MORE GOOD EATS

KALE SALAD WITH LENTILS AND BUTTERNUT SQUASH

Serves 4

If you prepare the components ahead of time, this salad comes together in just a few minutes. It's also good with baby spinach or mixed baby dark greens; skip the marinating/massaging step.

One large bunch dinosaur kale
Kosher or sea salt
Freshly ground black pepper
I lemon, halved
$^{1}/_{4}$ to $^{1}/_{2}$ cup Basic Vinaigrette (page 164) or Citrus Vinaigrette
     (page 165), divided
I cup cooked French green lentils (page 142)
I cup Roasted Butternut Squash, cut into $^{1}/_{2}$- to I-inch pieces

1. Fold each kale leaf in half lengthwise and use a knife to slice along the full length of stem. Reserve the stems for another use. Slice the leaves lengthwise into long, $^{1}/_{4}$-inch wide strips. Gather the strips into a pile and cut crosswise into 3-inch long pieces.

2. Transfer the kale to a salad bowl, season with salt and pepper, and squeeze the lemon halves over the leaves (use a small sieve or your other hand to catch the seeds). Drizzle in 2 tablespoons of the vinaigrette and mix with your hands to coat. (At this point, the kale can be covered and left to marinate in the refrigerator for several hours or overnight. Doing so will reduce the amount of rubbing

time in the next step, or you might find it's not needed at all.)

3. Continue mixing the kale with your hands, rubbing the leaves between your fingers, for several minutes, until the leaves have softened considerably. (They will feel almost silky and be tender to the bite; if still fibrous, continue rubbing for a few more minutes.) Season the kale with more salt to taste (a little pinch at a time, until any hint of bitterness gives way).

4. Add the lentils and 2 more tablespoons of the dressing, toss to mix, then add the squash and toss lightly. Add more dressing as needed to coat everything evenly. Taste and adjust seasoning as needed with additional salt.

CREAMY CHICKEN SALAD

Serves 4 to 6

You could serve this on a bed of baby spinach or other dark baby greens, but it would be a lie of omission if I didn't tell you it's perfect with crisp, sweet hearts of romaine.

4 cooked and chilled boneless skinless chicken breasts, cut into smallish chunks

I cup toasted pecans or walnuts, coarsely chopped

1½ cups halved seedless grapes (or I cup chopped apple plus ½ cup dried cranberries)

½ cup coarsely chopped celery

I cup cooked and chilled farro

¾ cup Lemon Yogurt Sauce, plus more as needed

Kosher or sea salt

Freshly ground black pepper

4 cups coarsely chopped hearts of romaine lettuce

Juice of ½ lemon

1. Combine the chicken, pecans, grapes, celery, and farro in a medium bowl and toss to mix. Stir in the yogurt sauce. Season the salad to taste with salt and pepper.

2. In a separate bowl, toss the lettuce with the lemon juice and season lightly with salt and pepper.

3. Divide the lettuce among 4 shallow bowls and top each with a mound of the salad.

GRAIN SALAD WITH DRIED FRUIT

Serves 4 as a side dish

This pretty, fruit-studded salad is nutritionally complete on its own if you use protein-rich quinoa, but it's delicious and fortifying with whole wheat couscous, rice, or farro as well. Use a microplane for zesting the lemon; it makes it easier to avoid any bitter-tasting white pith.

2 cups cooked red quinoa (page 151)

2 stalks celery, diced small

1 scallion (white and tender green parts), sliced thin, or 1 small
    shallot, minced

1 cup mixed dried fruit, such as cherries or cranberries, currants,
    golden raisins, and finely chopped apricots

1/4 cup roasted unsalted pistachios, coarsely chopped

Freshly grated zest of 1/2 lemon

Juice of 1/2 lemon, plus more as needed

1/4 to 1/2 cup Citrus Vinaigrette (page 165), divided

Kosher or sea salt

Freshly ground black pepper

About 2 cups baby spinach or other tender greens

1. Combine the quinoa, celery, scallion, dried fruit, pistachios, lemon zest and juice, and 1/4 cup of the vinaigrette in a medium bowl. Mix well, and season to taste with salt and pepper.

2. If you have time, let the salad sit at room temperature or in fridge for at least 20 minutes.

3. Give the salad a good stir. Taste and adjust seasoning with a little more salt, if needed. If it seems a little dry, add a tablespoon or two

more of dressing and/or a squeeze more of lemon juice.

4. In a separate bowl, lightly dress the greens with a tablespoon or two of the remaining vinaigrette and lightly season with salt and pepper, tossing to mix.

5. Divide the greens among four salad plates or wide, shallow bowls, and top each with a mound of the grain salad.

RIFF

COCONUT GINGER GRAIN SALAD WITH DATES: For the dried fruit, use ½ cup finely chopped dates and ½ cup finely chopped candied ginger. Replace the pistachios with ¼ cup lightly toasted shredded coconut or crumbled coconut chips. Add a pinch of cinnamon, if you like.

FRUITY MINTY GRAIN SALAD: Use all dried apricots for the fruit, omit the nuts, and add 2 to 4 tablespoons finely chopped fresh mint leaves.

GARBANZO FARRO SALAD

Serves 4 as a substantial side dish

Follow this recipe to the letter and you have a delicious and fortifying salad in minutes. Also use it as a template: Try rainbow quinoa rather than farro; instead of bell pepper, go for roasted tomatoes or fresh sliced grape tomatoes (or jarred hearts of palm, drained and chopped); replace the basic vinaigrette with Pesto Vinaigrette (page 165), Pistachio Mint Pesto (page 168), or Lemon Yogurt Sauce (page 173).

2 cups cooked, drained garbanzo beans

I cup cooked farro

I sweet bell pepper (any color but green), diced

I cucumber, peeled, seeded, and diced

I to 2 stalks celery, diced (optional)

½ cup Basic Vinaigrette

Kosher or sea salt

Freshly ground black pepper

Combine all of the ingredients in a medium bowl, toss to mix, season to taste, and serve. Keeps well in an airtight container in the fridge for about 3 days.

BLACK BEAN AND CORN SALAD WITH AVOCADO

Serves 6 or more

This salad is a big hit at barbecues. It keeps well for a day or two as a make-ahead, but hold off on adding the avocado until shortly before serving.

2 cups cooked rice (pages 156–158)

1/4 cup Basic Vinaigrette (page 164) or Citrus Vinaigrette (page 165)

I lime, halved, plus more as needed

2 cups cooked black beans (page 138)

I cup fresh (or frozen and thawed) corn kernels, lightly cooked and well-drained

3 scallions, finely chopped (white and tender green parts)

I sweet bell pepper, any color but green, chopped

1/2 pint cherry or grape tomatoes, halved or quartered, or I cup chopped summer tomatoes

1/2 teaspoon cumin

Kosher or sea salt

Freshly ground black pepper

I avocado, diced

I to 2 tablespoons fresh cilantro leaves, chopped

1. Put the rice in a medium large bowl, add the vinaigrette, squeeze in the juice from the lime halves, and stir to evenly coat the grains with the dressing. Stir in the beans, corn, scallions, bell pepper, and tomatoes. Add the cumin, lightly season the salad with salt and pepper, and mix thoroughly. Add the avocado and cilantro and toss lightly. Taste and adjust seasoning as needed, with additional salt and pepper and/or additional lime juice.

2. If time allows, cover the salad and leave it sit at room temperature for 30 to 60 minutes (or longer, in the fridge), so the flavors get a chance to intermingle, before serving. Taste and adjust seasoning with additional salt and pepper and/or lime juice. Serve chilled or at room temperature.

WARM GRAIN SALAD WITH ROASTED ASPARAGUS AND CHARD

Serves 4 as a side dish

Precooked grain works great for this salad; just thaw (if frozen) and rewarm gently in the microwave or a steamer basket. The vegetables need to be quite small for the salad to come together nicely. To cut up the asparagus, I like to use kitchen shears because I can just snip the spears into bits without even turning them out of whatever container I've got them in. It's important to chop the chard into small pieces, no bigger than about ¼- to ½-inch square, so that it blends well with the other ingredients; any larger and it will be too leafy and interfere with the texture. The easiest way to chop it that finely is to first cut it into long thin strips, then turn the whole pile of strips 90 degrees and chop crosswise, forming nice little squares.

2 cups red quinoa (page 151), brown basmati rice (page 156) or other cooked grain, steaming hot

2 tablespoons Shiitake Shallot Caper Butter (page 172), plus more if needed

½ recipe Roasted Asparagus (page 176), cut into half-inch pieces

1 cup stemmed, finely chopped chard

Kosher or sea salt

Freshly ground black pepper

1. Put the hot grain in a medium bowl, immediately add the shiitake butter, and stir until the butter is melted and evenly distributed.

2. Add the asparagus and chard, and mix well to coat and warm every-

thing evenly.

3. Season lightly with salt and pepper, stir to incorporate, then taste and adjust seasoning with additional salt if needed. Serve warm or at room temperature.

SALMON SALAD NIÇOISE

Serves at least 4

You can go to town switching up the components here. I've made this with leftover cod. Instead of asparagus, I've swapped in roasted or sautéed zucchini or green beans (which is what you'd find in a classic Niçoise). Sometimes I throw in a cubed avocado or a cup of cooked farro—or both. In a pinch, I've replaced the salmon with cannellini or garbanzo beans. Any which way you do it, this is damned good eats. It makes an amazing thrown-together lunch if you've got a good selection of leftovers on hand. And if you spread the salad greens on a serving platter, then layer on the various other components, the situation becomes dinner-party gorgeous.

Tender baby greens

Kosher or sea salt

Freshly ground black pepper

Basic Vinaigrette (page 164)

6 to 8 ounces grape tomatoes, halved

$1/_2$ recipe Roasted (page 176) or Blanched Asparagus (page 175), cut into 1-inch pieces ($1^1/_2$ to 2 cups)

$1/_2$ sweet bell pepper, cut into $1/_2$-inch pieces

1 cup pitted good-quality olives

2 to 3 cups leftover Potatoes Vinaigrette or diced boiled potatoes, room temperature or chilled

2 to 3 hard-boiled eggs, sliced

6 to 8 ounces cold leftover cooked salmon, lifted away from the skin and crumbled into chunks

1 to 2 tablespoons capers (optional)

1. Put the greens in a wide, shallow serving bowl, season lightly with salt and pepper and dress very lightly with a little vinaigrette, tossing to coat.
2. Add the tomatoes, asparagus, bell pepper, and olives, drizzle on a little more vinaigrette, and toss to combine.
3. Add the potatoes, tossing gently to mix without breaking the potatoes apart. Do the same with the hard-boiled eggs and then the salmon.
4. Sprinkle on the capers. Taste and adjust the seasoning with salt, pepper, and/or a bit more dressing, if needed.

CHICKEN WITH PISTACHIO-MINT COUSCOUS

Serves 4

This right here is why make-ahead components rule. I make this freaking delicious salad happen in less than 10 minutes, almost entirely with easy components banked in my fridge or freezer—the couscous, chicken, and pesto—plus whatever nice salad greens I happen to have on hand. If the chicken and couscous are frozen, they do need to be thawed, which you can do by leaving them in the fridge for several hours or overnight, or by defrosting in the microwave. If you do defrost the chicken in the microwave, err on the side of overly slow and gentle so you don't dry it out—you don't even want to warm it up because the hot couscous will do that for you. The dish is great with plain chicken, but it's especially tasty if you've added a little citrus and/or some seasoning (such as cumin or smoked paprika) or herbs (such as oregano and/or mint) to the chicken so the meat is infused with a hint of flavor. Repurpose any leftovers for a slammin' lunch: filling for a pita sandwich or layered into a lunch parfait. Variations are pretty much endless.

$1/4$ Pistachio Mint Pesto (page 168)

$1/8$ teaspoon cinnamon, preferably good-quality Saigon

2 to 3 cooked chicken breasts (page 145), cut into 1-inch chunks (about 3 cups)

3 cups cooked whole wheat couscous (page 155), steaming hot

½ cup unsulfured dried apricots, thinly sliced

3 cups baby spinach, baby arugula, or other tender salad greens

Kosher or sea salt

Freshly ground black pepper

1. Put the vinaigrette in a small jar, add the pesto, put on the lid, and shake. Add the cinnamon and shake to thoroughly incorporate. (That's how I do it. You can also use a small bowl and a whisk.) Set aside.

2. Put the chicken in a large salad bowl.

3. Fluff the hot couscous, dump it into the salad bowl on top of the chicken, and give the mixture a few stirs just to combine. Give the vinaigrette a couple of shakes/whisks and pour all but about 2 tablespoons of it over the couscous mixture. Toss a few times to bathe the grains and the chicken in the dressing. Stir in the apricots.

4. Pile the greens on top of the mixture in the salad bowl, but don't toss everything together just yet. Season the greens with a pinch of salt and a grind of pepper, drizzle the reserved dressing over top, and give just that top layer of leaves a couple of light tosses with the dressing. Then toss the whole mixture to combine.

5. Divide among 4 wide, shallow bowls and serve immediately.

RIFFS

CAPRESE-ISH: Use classic vinaigrette instead of citrus; basil pesto instead of pistachio mint; omit the cinnamon; and swap in baby arugula instead of spinach; and sliced rounds of ripe tomato (in summer), halved cherry/grape tomatoes (other seasons), or Roasted Tomatoes (page 165) instead of apricots. Add slices of fresh mozzarella and a basil leaf snippets atop each serving, drizzle on some fruity extra-virgin olive oil, and season with a touch of kosher or sea salt and a grind of black pepper.

SALMON AVOCADO ROLL-INSPIRED: Use chunks of cooked, chilled (leftover) salmon instead of chicken, cold rice instead of couscous, soy ginger vinaigrette instead of citrus, and sliced avocado instead of apricots. You could go further and top each (grown-up's) portion with a dash or two of extra soy sauce, a dab of wasabi, and little pile of chopped pickled ginger. And you know those toasted seaweed snacks? Crumble one of those on as well. You're welcome.

HEARTY CHILI

Serves 6 to 8

Putting in a little veggie-chopping time—I'm talking 15 minutes, max— pays you back with multiple family-pleasing meals.

1 tablespoon avocado oil

$\frac{1}{2}$ red or yellow onion, chopped

2 cloves garlic, minced

2 medium carrots, chopped

2 stalks celery, chopped

$\frac{1}{2}$ large bell pepper, chopped

1 teaspoon kosher or sea salt, plus more as needed

$\frac{1}{2}$ teaspoon chili powder (use ancho or chipotle to add smoky depth)

$1\frac{1}{2}$ teaspoons ground cumin

$1\frac{1}{2}$ teaspoons smoked sweet Spanish paprika

$\frac{1}{2}$ teaspoon dried oregano

2 (18.3-ounce) jars diced or whole tomatoes, with juice

3 cups cooked black, kidney, or cannellini beans, or a combination, drained (liquid reserved)

1 cup cooked farro or other meaty grain

$\frac{1}{2}$ cup Roasted Tomatoes (optional, page 165)

1 to 2 teaspoons lime juice or red wine vinegar, plus more as needed

Toppings (your choice): cilantro leaves, diced avocado, grated Cheddar cheese, sour cream, and/or soft corn or tortilla chips

To serve (your choice): warm tortillas or steaming hot rice

1. Set a heavy-bottomed soup pot over low heat, add the oil and warm until shimmering. Add the onions and garlic and cook until soft,

about 4 minutes, stirring occasionally. Stir in the carrots and celery and cook 3 minutes. Stir in the bell pepper, salt, chili powder, cumin, paprika, and oregano and cook, stirring frequently, about 7 minutes, until the mixture is fragrant, and the carrots and celery are tender.

2. Stir in the tomatoes, using the spoon to smoosh them up against the side of the pot to break them up a bit. Stir in the beans, farro, roasted tomatoes, and lime juice or vinegar. If the consistency is thicker than you prefer, stir in some bean liquid or water. Bring the chili to a simmer and continue cooking, stirring occasionally and adjusting the heat as needed to keep it bubbling gently, for 30 minutes.

3. Taste and adjust seasoning with additional salt and lime juice, if needed. Season with salt to taste.

4. Serve hot, garnished with cilantro, avocado, grated Cheddar, sour cream; with corn chips or tortilla chips alongside; and/or atop a bowl of steaming hot rice or warm tortillas.

> Note: For the palate-pleasingest texture and flavor, scoop out $1\frac{1}{2}$ cups of the chili and transfer it to a blender. (Important note: If the pitcher of your blender is plastic rather than glass, let the chili cool to room temperature before pouring it into the pitcher. Remember that even if there's no way to get rid of all your kitchen plastic, one very effective way to reduce chemicals leaching into your food is to never combine plastic with any manner of heat, including hot food. It's the same deal if you opt to use a food processor or an immersion blender: If it's plastic, cool before blending.) Blend until smooth, then pour the mixture back into the pot. Alternative: Just bust out a metal potato masher and go at it till the chili reaches whatever consistency you like.

RIFF

CON CARNE: At the end of Step 1, add 1 pound ground turkey or beef, stirring to crumble, and cook until thoroughly browned, draining off excess fat, if needed. Follow Step 2, but omit $\frac{1}{2}$ of the beans and all of the farro. Ignore the tip about pureeing to thicken.

WHITE BEAN SOUP

Serves 4 to 6, with leftovers

This is plenty robust enough to serve as a meal unto itself. It's also reason No. 999 to always, always have a stash of basil pesto in the freezer.

2 cups cooked cannellini or other white beans

6 cups bean cooking broth, or low-sodium chicken or vegetable broth (or a broth and bean liquor combo)

2 carrots, chopped small

I cup Sautéed Zucchini with Pesto, chopped small

I cup Sautéed Chard, chopped small

I cup cooked farro

$1/2$ cup Basil Pesto (page 167), to serve

Parmesan cheese (optional)

1. Combine the beans and broth in a large soup pot and bring to a boil over high heat. Stir in the carrots, lower the heat to a simmer, and cook until the carrots are just tender, about 3 minutes.

2. Stir in the zucchini, chard, and farro, and heat to warm through.

3. Just before serving, dollop a bit of pesto into each bowl and top with a few gratings of Parm.

ROASTED TOMATO SOUP (DOGI)

Serves 4

Sweet and aromatic sautéed shallots are really well-suited to the rich taste of roasted tomatoes. Meantime, the milk cuts the acidity of the tomatoes. The combination results in a mellow but full-flavored soup—a delicious way to help clear out that veggie drawer. I often leave out the optional grains and, to make a meal that brings together the nutritional holy trinity, I serve the soup with a side of (leftover) triple-threat salad, like White Bean and Farro Salad with Spinach, Feta, and Olives (page 154) or Lentil and Couscous Salad (page 156) on a bed of baby greens.

4 teaspoons butter, divided

2 shallots, sliced or chopped

$^1/_2$ recipe Slow-Roasted Tomatoes (page 165)

$1^1/_2$ cups chicken broth or vegetable stock

$^1/_2$ cup milk

Kosher or sea salt

$1^1/_2$ cups chopped vegetables (mix of carrots, celery, potatoes,
cauliflower, even fennel bulb; or anything from your crisper
drawer; or you can substitute $^1/_2$ to $^3/_4$ cup cooked vegetables,
chopped small)

$^1/_2$ cup to 1 cup cooked grains (optional; brown rice, quinoa, or
small whole-grain pasta shapes work well; page 151)

1. Melt 2 teaspoons of the butter in a large saucepan over medium heat. Sauté the shallots until translucent and just golden, about 5 minutes. Add the tomatoes and stir them to soften, then add the broth and milk. Bring the mixture to a simmer and cook for 3 minutes to reduce slightly. Transfer the tomato mixture to a heatproof bowl and set aside to cool to room temperature.

2. Meanwhile, if you're using uncooked vegetables, lightly season them with salt, melt the remaining butter in the saucepan and sauté the chopped vegetables over medium-low heat until they are completely cooked and soft. (If using precooked vegetables, just stir them in with the cooked grains in Step 4.)

3. Use a food processor or immersion blender to puree the cooled tomato mixture until smooth. Pour the puree back into the saucepan.

4. Stir the cooked grains into the soup and cook over low heat to warm through, adding additional water or milk to thin as needed. Taste and season with additional salt, if needed, and serve hot.

CHICKEN SOUP WITH (CAULIFLOWER) RICE

Serves 6 as a main dish

This soup is dead easy and way more delicious than you might imagine. Savory, satisfying, and soothing for the soul. Try it. You'll see.

$1/2$ recipe (about I cup) Caramelized Onions (page 181)

4 cups low-sodium chicken broth, plus up to 2 cups more as needed

I teaspoon kosher or coarse sea salt, plus more to taste

3 Yukon gold potatoes, diced small

2 carrots, chopped

Freshly ground black pepper

$1/2$ recipe (about 3 cups) Cauliflower Rice (page 179)

3 cups cooked, shredded chicken (ideally Peppery, page 146)

5 ounces (about 5 cups) baby spinach

Lemon Yogurt Sauce, for serving

1. Combine the onions, 4 cups of the broth, and 1 teaspoon of the salt in a medium pot and bring to a simmer over medium-high heat. Add the potatoes and carrots, season generously with pepper, and simmer gently until the vegetables are tender, about 10 minutes.

2. Transfer the soup to a blender (cool to room temperature first if your pitcher is plastic rather than glass) and puree until smooth.

3. Return the puree to the pot, stir in the cauliflower and chicken, and cook over low heat just to warm through, thinning with additional broth and seasoning with more salt and pepper, as needed.

4. Put a big handful of spinach in the bottom of each of 6 wide, shallow soup bowls and ladle the soup over top. Swirl a nice big spoonful of yogurt sauce into each bowl just before serving.

EGGS POACHED IN TOMATO SAUCE

Serves 4

You can always skip the farro—or not—and serve with slices of really good toasted bread for shoveling the saucy deliciousness into your sweet little faces. Note also that instead of stirring in the greens, you pile a little mound of reheated greens into each bowl and scoop the sauce and eggs over the top (this works especially well with raw baby spinach). Ditto the grains. Or both, even. Also note: You can't count on everyone to take down both their eggs? Not a problem. See—and enjoy—the breakfast variation, below.

Avocado oil or ghee, as needed

I cup Sautéed Greens (pages 162–163), chopped small, or 2 cups fresh baby spinach

I cup cooked farro (page 153)

2 cups Roasted Tomato Sauce (page 166)

Kosher or sea salt

Freshly ground black pepper

8 large eggs

Freshly grated Parmesan cheese, or crumbled feta cheese, to serve

Chopped fresh Italian parsley leaves, to serve (optional, but makes it even tastier and totally gorgeous)

1. Set a large (minimum 10-inch), deep ovenproof skillet over medium heat and drizzle in enough oil that it coats the bottom of the pan when you tilt it side to side a couple times.
2. Add the greens and cook to warm through.
3. Stir in the farro and cook to warm through.
4. Stir in the tomato sauce and bring the mixture to a steady simmer. Season to taste with salt and pepper and turn the heat down to medium-low—just enough to keep the sauce at a gentle (not splattery) simmer.

5. Press the back of a spoon into the sauce to make as many divots as you have eggs to cook. One at a time, crack each egg into a small bowl, then slip it into its very own well in the sauce.

6. Cover the pan with a lid, leaving it a bit askew to allow steam to escape, and cook 8 to 10 minutes, or just until the whites are firm but the yolks are still nice and soft (keep a close eye on it or you'll end up with hard-cooked eggs, which isn't terrible, but IMHO is also nowhere near as yummy as soft and tender).

7. Scatter Parmesan and parsley all over the eggs and sauce; grind on some more black pepper. You can sprinkle a teeny bit more salt onto each egg—your call. Use a large serving spoon or ladle to scoop eggs and sauce into shallow bowls. Serve hot.

RIFFS

PUTTANESCA-ESQUE: In Step 4, stir in ½ cup pitted and sliced kalamata or Niçoise olives, 1 to 2 tablespoons capers, and, if you have some, a dab of anchovy paste (that stuff is pure magic—nobody will have any idea it's in there; all they'll know is it tastes bowl-lickingly awesome).

BREAKFAST OF CHAMPIONS: Just in case it isn't obvious without my saying so, this whole situation is a showstopper for brunch. But I also want to be sure to tell you that leftovers, gently rewarmed so the eggs stay somewhat tender, make a kick-ass breakfast. And if I also happened to have some bean dip (white or black, pages 169 and 171) or hummus (page 169) around, I'd add a dollop of that and dribble on some hot sauce. And I would not be sorry.

HUEVOS RANCHEROS NO. 2: Skip or keep the greens and swap in black beans and corn for the farro; instead of Parmesan and parsley, top with grated Cheddar, jack, or crumbled queso fresco and cilantro leaves. Serve with warm soft corn tortillas and put out salsa, hot sauce, and such for those who want it. Chopped scallions, slivered radishes, and diced avocados crank up the fiesta factor. You could even get a little wild and put out a dish of crumbled bacon or diced and pan-crisped chorizo as a bonus topping.

BUILD-A-CASSEROLE DINNER

Serves 4 to 6, generously

This kitchen-sink-type thing is why it makes sense to chuck smallish amounts of leftover bean-based dips and soups in the freezer (be sure to label, and keep such things in a particular corner so you find them when the time comes). You couldn't go wrong mixing in some shredded or chopped leftover cooked chicken or other meat. I've been known work in the remains of a pot of chili (page 197) or white bean soup (page 199). The point is, you can layer up whatever you've got around that doesn't totally clash (and if it does clash, maybe you can riff a different combo)—the only limit is the top edge of the pan. P.S. It's delicious with a fried egg on top.

Avocado oil or ghee

3 cups cooked quinoa (page 151) or other grain

1½ teaspoons ground cumin

Kosher or sea salt

Freshly ground black pepper

1 cup finely chopped or pureed Slow-Roasted Tomatoes (page 165), Roasted Tomato Sauce (page 166), or chopped fresh or jarred tomatoes

1 cup fresh or frozen corn kernels

1 to 2 cups leftover cooked vegetables, such as broccoli (page 177), zucchini (page 187), or finely chopped sautéed chard; or 2 to 4 cups fresh spinach (optional)

3 cups cooked black beans (page 139), or a combo of black beans and Chipotle Black Bean Dip (page 171), or chili (page 197, liquid drained)

4 ounces Cheddar or Monterey jack cheese, grated (about 1 cup)

To serve: diced avocado, thinly sliced scallions, fresh cilantro leaves, salsa, hot sauce, and lime wedges

1. Preheat the oven to 350°F. Lightly oil a 9" x 13" baking dish.
2. Spread the quinoa in an even layer across the bottom of the prepared

baking dish, sprinkle lightly with the cumin (mix lightly with a fork if needed), and season with salt and pepper.

3. Scatter the tomatoes, corn kernels, and leftover vegetables in an even layer on top of the quinoa. Layer in the beans, spreading to level. Top with an even layer of cheese.

4. Cover the dish tightly with foil and bake 30 minutes.

5. Uncover the dish and bake the casserole 15 to 20 minutes longer, or until juices are visibly bubbling and the cheese is melted.

6. Let cool 5 minutes before serving, with dishes of toppings alongside.

RIFF

LESS MEX, MORE MED: Replace the quinoa with farro, whole wheat couscous, or rice; instead of cumin, mix in basil pesto (page 167), dried oregano, or Italian seasoning; swap in fresh or cooked spinach for the corn; ditch the black beans and dip in favor of navy or cannellini beans and white bean dip, or garbanzo beans and hummus, or the remains of minestrone (drained); top with feta or mozzarella cheese instead of Cheddar. Top with pitted and sliced kalamata olives, chopped fresh Italian parsley, and maybe some finely chopped fresh mint or slivered basil leaves. Serve with pita or crusty bread.

BUILD-A-FRITTATA DINNER (DOGI)

Serves 4 to 6

This is somewhat soufflé-like hearty goodness is, hands down, my favorite one-pan dinner. Rarely a week goes by that some manner of frittata is not served for dinner at least once in my house. Leftovers, if there are any, make a phenomenal breakfast or lunch (reheated or not).

I to 2 tablespoons butter or avocado oil, or a combination of the two

8 eggs, lightly beaten

Kosher salt and freshly ground black pepper

Pinch freshly grated nutmeg (optional)

1½ to 2 cups cooked vegetables (ideally a combo and, for me, ideally one that includes caramelized onions, potatoes, and greens)

2 ounces cheese (crumbled feta or goat cheese; grated Cheddar,
   jack, or whatever)
Chopped fresh herbs, optional

1. Preheat the broiler with a rack positioned one or two rungs down
   from the top.
2. Heat the butter and/or oil in a 10" or 12" cast-iron skillet over medium-low heat just until the pan is too hot to comfortably hold your
   hand closely over the center of it for more than a moment.
3. Lightly season the eggs with a pinch of salt and a couple grindings of
   pepper. Pour the eggs into the hot pan and cook 3 to 4 minutes, or
   until set about halfway through. Scatter the vegetables evenly over
   the surface and cook 1 minute longer, then sprinkle on the cheese
   and the herbs.
4. Transfer the pan to the oven and broil the frittata for about 1 minute,
   just until the top is puffed and golden. Take the pan out of the oven
   and check the center of the frittata for doneness; if it's still a little on
   the wet side, put the pan back in the oven—with the broiler *off*—and
   close the oven door, leaving the frittata to finish cooking from the
   residual heat from both the iron pan and the oven.
5. Cut into large wedges and serve.

TIP

Refining your seasoning skills is an amazingly easy way to make everything you make tastier. Exotic salts are all the rage, and I, myself, am
enamored of pink Himalayan salt. Scattering on a little delicate flaky
salt like Maldon's can add a beautiful finishing touch to a dish, but on a
day-in, day-out basis there's no need to be fancy with your salt—just be
sure that instead of iodized, which has a metallic tinge, you use sweeter-
tasting kosher or sea salt. Season salads lightly with a little salt and pepper *before* dressing.

SIX

ROOM BY ROOM

HOME IMPROVEMENT TIME!

Don't panic—I'm using the phrase "home improvement" in a different way than it's usually meant. As lovely as it would be for all of us to be able to give our humble abodes an eco overhaul and rid our residences of hazmat-licious building materials, we do have to dwell in reality, where unicorns do not frolic about.

Here's the truth: Even if you built a new home from the ground up using nothing but sustainable materials and lots of other nontoxic, super expensive stuff, that still wouldn't get you a perfectly safe home environment.

Because there is also the matter of, just like real estate agents always say, location, location, location. If you were up for living in a yurt on an island way out in the middle of the subantarctic Indian Ocean, among the penguins and albatrosses, that would get you a safer home environment. But it still wouldn't be truly perfect because pollution has traveled to all corners of the globe.

So let's bring the bottom line back to the reality we actually live in,

PETE DROPS SCIENCE:

Chemicals can be remarkably persistent and mobile. How persistent? It depends upon the molecule. Some degrade rapidly. Some take decades. Some will be around in 1,000 years. How mobile? They outgas from products like plastics. They get abraded into dust. They get flushed down the toilet. There are many pathways that chemicals follow into the environment, and once out, some travel to the ends of the earth, carried by air or water currents.

One study published in 1999 showed that pesticides had made their ways into tree bark in some of the most remote places on the planet. Flame retardants are in crustaceans in the bottom of the Pacific Ocean's Mariana Trench (the deepest in the world). Glacial and Arctic ice contain many different industrial chemicals and pesticides, even though the uses are thousands of miles away.

shall we? Here are the very best and most effective moves you can make to minimize horrendous hormone-disrupting chemicals.

- Dial down the toxic exposures that are happening *inside* your home. (Yes, girl, they're happening.)
- Keep the toxic trespassers coming in from the outdoors to a minimum. (Uh-huh, it gives a whole new meaning to "home invasion.")

Yes, sweet mama, we are—once again—talking about a crazy cornucopia of endocrine disruptors that can potentially lower IQs, mess with gonads, trigger weight gain, short-circuit immune systems, and cause cancer.

And yes, you can dial them *waaay* down without driving yourself batshit crazy. I swear.

3 THINGS TO DO RIGHT NOW

There are so many ways to reduce the toxic footprint in your home that it can seem a little daunting, so I'm going to get you started with three relatively minor measures you can take today that will have major impact on your family's level of exposure. These three strategies work best together, creating a snowball effect that gains momentum once you get rolling. The first step, ditching disgusting chemicals and going greener with cleaning products, gives you a head start on the second step, which is improving air quality. Keep going, and as air quality improves, dust will decrease, and the third step—dealing with that dust—will become much easier too.

NO. I: OUT WITH THE STINKY STANK

Let's start with a quick sniff test. Take a deep breath and tell me what the air in your home smells like. Be honest.

Is it a scent you'd describe as "fresh"? Our lizard brains are hardwired to detect a poopy diaper at a hundred yards, so in a busy household there's no telling what your nose might register when you really stop and pay attention. Did somebody forget to take out the trash out last night, or is that a whiff of not-so-clean sock?

Not everything in life smells like a rose—and it *shouldn't*! Vast amounts of marketing and advertising dollars have been spent on conditioning us to be super self-conscious about what real life really smells like—so we think we need to buy products to cover up even the faintest funk. Many of those products are potentially harmful. *And* the fragrance formulas are "proprietary,"[139] which means companies don't have to disclose the ingredients, so it's virtually impossible to know what you're unleashing when you use conventional products.

PETE DROPS SCIENCE:

The "conventional" fragrance industry has several thousand ingredients they use to create artificial smells. Many of those are made from petrochemicals. None have been fully tested for safety, especially for interfering with hormones, i.e., endocrine disruption. And worse, the mixtures that are blended with those ingredients aren't tested for safety either. There is no requirement to do so. One of the most notorious chemical groups used in fragrances are the phthalates. If the label includes "fragrance," there is a strong possibility that phthalates have been added. These are linked to a wide array of health problems, including harm to male reproductive organs. The problem is particularly acute when exposure takes place in the womb. So if you're using perfume fragrances to attract a mate, be aware of unintended consequences.

DR. TANYA'S PRESCRIPTION:

If you are planning to become pregnant, avoid fragrances as much as possible. Both men and women with higher levels of phthalates, which are likely in fragrances, are less likely to conceive.

PETE DROPS SCIENCE:

Dr. Tanya's got that prescription right. And there's more: Studies indicate phthalates can also increase the risk of childhood obesity by altering how key genes are turned on.

"Fresh rain"? "Sea breezes"? "The delicate scent of clean linens drying in the sun"? They reek of lies to me. You know what those products really smell like? Endocrine-disrupting chemicals (EDCs)!

EDCs are B-A-D—and, lest you forget, when I say bad, I'm talking potentially "messing up your little boys' sperm" bad, "bring on early puberty" bad, "screw with your metabolism and/or your immune system" bad, and so on.[140] (Turn to pages 7–10 for the full refresher on EDCs.)

(And don't even get me started on shopping malls and hotels that pump toxic scents into the building. *Mmm*—I so love that feeling of being enveloped by clouds of endocrine disruption and cancer.)

Here's another example from the other end of the smell spectrum: One whiff of bleach used to be all it took to make me think "clean." Bleach does indeed do an amazing job of blasting away bacteria and whitening whites, but it's flat-out harmful, and that sharp chlorine-y smell is a hint of its capacity as a corrosive gas so potent, it has been used in chemical weapons.[141] Let me put it another way—evil people use chlorine (the main component in bleach) to actually kill people. If you can detect the smell of bleach, that is a sign it's already doing damage to your body. Ditto ammonia.

So we need to contend with the hazmat potential of both faux flowery fresh smells and other smells that say "clean" but actually mean "toxic."

DR. TANYA'S PRESCRIPTION:

Pregnant women should be cautious of fragrances because their presence has been associated with behavior problems and attention deficit disorder in children whose mothers have been exposed to the chemicals fragrances contain.

HOW TO DEAL

JETTISON THE FRAGRANCES. Okay. So here's what I want you to do to start minimizing the toxicity that comes with artificial fragrance. First off, get rid of the obvious offenders. Adios any and all scented candles. (I'm looking at you,

Yankee Candle.) Buh-bye, bottles of air freshener. Put those Plugins on a permanent vacation. And throw all those fragrance-filled gels and beads and scent-releasing sticks and decals in the trash. Kick it *all* to the curb—*now*. Why? Because products designed to release artificial scents into the air you breathe are likely to contain a class of chemicals called phthalates[142]—many of which are believed to interfere with hormones in the body and have been linked to declines in IQ and respiratory problems in children, poor sperm quality (among other reproductive problems), and many other health hazards.[143, 144, 145] (See page 5 for more about phthalates.)

> ### PETE DROPS SCIENCE:
>
> Styrene is a common additive to consumer products, and is included on a master list maintained by the International Fragrance Association of ingredients that perfume makers can use in fragrances. And in 2014, the National Academy of Sciences concluded that styrene can cause cancer.

There are many different chemicals that fall into the phthalate family, but even if you knew all the names this brood goes by, you aren't likely to see them listed on labels because manufacturers don't have to disclose when these—or other potentially harmful substances—are being used in their products.

So *wise up* and boot out all the "air-freshening" products you can find in your home. And congrats on making this extremely smart and ultra-effective move: You have just made a significant reduction in your whole family's toxic load. How's that for instant gratification?

If you need something that smells good, essential oils are lovely. You can use a room diffuser or make an easy-to-use room spray by combining 1 cup distilled water, $\frac{1}{4}$ cup witch hazel, and about 20 drops of your favorite essential oil combination in a spray bottle (shake vigorously before using).

GREEN UP YOUR CLEANUP. Depending upon which cleaning products you use, you can easily end up adding as much or more toxic shit than you're getting rid of because most commercial cleaning products out there

> ### DR. TANYA'S PRESCRIPTION:
>
> Fragrances often contain phthalates, which have a lower molecular weight; they leach easily and can be ingested, inhaled, or absorbed through the skin.

PETE DROPS SCIENCE:

The phthalate DEHP is probably the best studied of the phthalates, both in lab animals and in people. In animals, it causes what's become known as the phthalate syndrome, which includes reduced sperm quality and quantity, undescended testes, and a birth defect of the penis known as hypospadias, where the tube connecting the bladder to the outside world emerges on the shaft of the penis, instead of at the tip. Those are experimental data. You can't ethically conduct these experiments on people, but you can look for signs that these and related problems are statistically associated with phthalate exposure. And guess what—that's what scientists are finding. The most eye-opening of the studies shows that male babies exposed to DEHP in the womb have a shorter anogenital distance (AGD) than normal. AGD is the distance from the anus to the base of the penis. In animal experiments, shorter AGDs are associated with the effects noted above.

today are pretty poisonous—and not just in the obvious ways you'd expect caustic chemicals to be. Plus, once again, thanks to our government regulations (or lack thereof), manufacturers don't have to tell you all the stuff they've put into their cleaning solutions, unless you live in California.[146]

So here's what I want you to do to start getting a handle on the whole scenario: Flip the product around and take a look at the label on the back. If a whole side of the container is devoted to hazard warnings, just toss it—whatever cleaning effectiveness it might have is not worth the risk. Trade-offs, baby.

If you're willing to whip up some homemade cleansers, you'll find recipes sprinkled liberally throughout this chapter. But if you're not into making all (or any) of your own cleaning products (hey, we don't all have an inner hippie earth goddess!), there are loads of great products out there—see page 243 for a list of some of my faves.

CLEANING-LABEL GREENWASHING

Be on the lookout for seemingly positive words that may indicate that toxic chemicals are in the mix. Disingenuous language can be used to create the appearance of being environmentally responsible; this particular brand of bullshit is sometimes called "greenwashing."

NATURAL: There is absolutely no regulation of the use of the word "natural," so even products that are labeled "natural" may have artificial fragrances added to them. Manufacturers are at liberty to use the term however they like, so it is meaningless at best—and we know how unscrupulous a bunch those chemical companies can be, so *don't be fooled*.[147] "Natural" isn't used exclusively by brands that are trying to trick you. But it's a huge selling point that many companies exploit. You have to know which brands you can trust (see pages 243–245 for a list). And don't forget: Natural doesn't necessarily mean nontoxic—plenty of things in nature are quite toxic.

FREE AND CLEAR: This isn't a regulated term either, but it is a somewhat better indicator that a product is less likely to have added fragrances (and dyes). However, it's still possible that some scents may be in the mix to mask the smell of other ingredients; call the manufacturer if you want to be absolutely sure.

ORGANIC: In the world of household product labeling, there is no legal oversight on what organic means. Some manufacturers interpret the term as a chemist would to indicate that a product's ingredients are all carbon-based (and if that's the case, then petroleum-based ingredients could be included). However, if you see the "USDA Organic" logo, then all of the ingredients conform to the standards of the National Organic Program.

BIODEGRADABLE: This term basically just indicates that the product is designed to break down once it hits a water source, and the reality is that the resulting compounds may or may not be toxic.

PETE DROPS SCIENCE:

Chemical safety is tested one chemical at a time. But we live our lives being exposed virtually all the time to a busload of chemicals. No one has a clue as to how they interact. Any steps you can take to reduce the load on that bus is a step toward a healthier life. It's common sense.

DR. TANYA'S PRESCRIPTION:

When using essential oils around kids, be cautious. Dilute the oils if you can and use only one drop at first on skin (if you're using a diffuser, put it on the other side of the room). If your child seems in any way negatively affected, then stop it right away.

DR. TANYA'S PRESCRIPTION:

If there is a "free and clear" version of what you use, switch to that, as it's generally better and safer.

PETE DROPS SCIENCE:

One recent surprise is the discovery that cleaning agents called quats (quaternary ammonium compounds)—commonly used as cleaning agents in restaurants, food-processing plants, day care centers, schools, gyms, and hospitals—can harm the fertility of mice, including longer time to pregnancy, fewer pups, and more miscarriages. And it has just been found that just living in a cage in a room in which quats are being used as cleaners can cause miscarriages and birth defects, including some horrific impacts on brain development called neural tube defects. Both male and female parents are able to convey this effect to their offspring. Almost nothing is known about quats' impacts on people, but these are not good signs. Unfortunately, quats are rarely listed as ingredients. Sometimes you can find out on the product's Web site. You can always ask.

NO. 2: CLEAR THE AIR

If you've gotten a grip on the fragrance situation in step No. 1, you've already made a big improvement in indoor air quality. Now it's time to crank it up another notch because this is a hugely important part of making your home a lot less like a toxic dump site. And objective No. 1 is all about ventilation.

Unless you take steps to ensure your home is properly ventilated, the energy efficiencies that help lower your utility bills can also trap dangerous toxins in your home, where they recirculate and multiply in the air you breath. And there are plenty of them. According to the Environmental Protection Agency (EPA), the air pollution in your home can be two to five times more toxic than that of the outdoors (depending on where you live).[148]

I repeat:

> *The air inside your home could be two to five times more toxic.*

But where do these pollutants come from?

House dust is a big source of indoor pollution. Outdoor soil is one element in dust. Another is the indoor component of dust, which includes countless particles of organic matter—dead skin and hair, pollen, and pet dander, as well as all the ugly stuff that comes with dust mites. Those indoor particles get mixed in with dirt from the great dust bunnies hiding under your bed. But that's not all. There are toxic chemicals in that mix, too, itty-bitty by-products of various goods and furnishings you bring into your home. We'll delve into the horror show of household dust in No. 3.

In addition to dust, the air in your home can harbor mold, yeast, and bacteria—consider these the Four Horsemen of your air-quality apocalypse. All of these sources of indoor pollution can aggravate preexisting conditions like asthma, allergies, and chronic bronchitis, just for starters.[149] Additional sources of indoor pollution come from primary sources when something in your house creates direct contamination in the air (poorly vented fireplaces, stoves, and those fragrance-filled products we just talked about are all good examples of those). At the other end of the spectrum, there are secondary sources of pollution, created when something sheds fine particles into the air (fire retardants, which we'll talk about later in this chapter, are a good example of that type of pollution, as well as formaldehyde in furniture).[150]

HOW TO DEAL

OPEN SESAME. The first solution to the indoor air issue is supremely simple: Open a window. Yep. You read that right. It couldn't be easier and it really does make a difference.

One of the reasons opening the windows is so effective is that all

PETE DROPS SCIENCE:

Location, location, location. If you're living in Beijing and filtering your indoor air, it's safer inside. Or if you live downwind of a chemical plant. But very often, beyond these extreme circumstances, indoor air is more polluted. Levels of indoor air pollutants can build up because many of the products we bring into our homes are off-gassing, as are the building materials our homes are made from (think formaldehyde from plywood, VOCs from paint, etc.), and because air circulation may suck.

Here's something to think about: VOCs (volatile organic compounds) present in indoor air regularly can reach levels that cause cognitive impairment in people. Think about that as your kids are doing the night's homework.

DR. TANYA'S PRESCRIPTION:

As a pediatrician, I have seen an increase in kids with asthma and wheezing episodes. It's likely a mix of genetics and environment, but even small negative changes in air quality can make their lungs more susceptible to small airway irritation, inflammation, and wheezing.

DR. TANYA'S PRESCRIPTION:

For kids with allergic asthma, a HEPA filter is the best way to remove mold, pollen, and animal dander from the air and help your child breathe better.

that dust circulating in your indoor world never has an opportunity to break down the way it would if it were outside, where wind and sunlight and other forces of nature are at play. Essentially, without the wind to blow things along, your indoor dust accumulates in a temperature-controlled environment that protects it from degrading. Of course, that type of protection from the elements is good for your family, but not it if enables toxic dust to persist indefinitely. Open a window and the problem is temporarily solved. But forget everything I just said if you live very close to a freeway (hello pollution). If that is the case, keep reading.

HOWDY, HEPA. Obviously, it's not practical to keep all your windows open 24/7, so consider filtering the air you breathe to keep it fresh. If money is no object, you can go all out and install a high-end air-filtration system that will do a bang-up job cleaning the air inside your home. There are a lot of options to consider if you want to go that route. But I'm going to keep things here as basic and affordable as possible, so we're going to focus on portable HEPA air purifiers, which you can plug into a corner of any given room so they can start doing their thing: churning out clean air.

I'm a big fan of HEPA (High-Efficiency Particulate Air) filters. These bad boys of the air-filter world work by forcing air through a series of fine meshes that trap harmful particles of all sizes, including pollen, pet dander, dust mites, and tobacco smoke.

Once you decide which air-filtration units are right for your needs, you basically just plug them in and let them do their job. You can move them from room to room, if necessary, but they are designed to work best if you keep them on all the time. Make sure you replace the filters as often as recommended by the manufacturer so your air cleaner can keep on cleaning.

HOUSEPLANTS TO THE RESCUE

Toxic air pollutants in the home can include formaldehyde (a known carcinogen that can be emitted from off-gassing furniture), benzene (toxic to your blood and bone marrow, and released from glues, paints, furniture wax, and detergents with benzene added), and trichloroethylene (a neurotoxic solvent used in a variety of products). But get this: NASA has spent years studying the detoxifying effects of plants on indoor air quality to protect astronauts in space, so we have their rocket science (!) to help us improve the air in our homes. There are several common and easy-to-grow plants that do a good job filtering out toxicants. It would take a veritable forest to undo the damage of some environmental toxins, but every little bit counts and I'm all about the easy-to-grow greenery. Consider adding a few of the following to your windowsill.

PLANTS	TOXICANTS
Aloe vera	Formaldehyde
Areca palm	All indoor pollutants
Bamboo or reed palm	Benzene, formaldehyde, trichloroethylene
Boston fern	Formaldehyde
English ivy	Benzene, formaldehyde, trichloroethylene, xylene
Florist's chrysanthemum or peace lily	All indoor pollutants
Variegated snake plant	Benzene, formaldehyde, trichloroethylene, xylene
Spider plant	Formaldehyde, xylene

NO. 3: BUST THE DUST

Now we need to talk about the final leg of the top three changes that you should make a priority as soon as possible: must-do measures that will help you really keep dust to a minimum. Unfortunately, an air filter can't just suck everything out of the air for you, and whatever you don't get out of the air will eventually settle on your furnishings and floors. And when

PETE DROPS SCIENCE:

Benzene is a carcinogen linked to leukemia.

PETE DROPS SCIENCE:

Relatively short-term exposures of animals to trichloroethylene (TCE) cause a wide range of effects, including damage to the nervous system, liver, kidneys, blood, immune system, heart, and body weight. It is also associated with autoimmune problems in people.

DR. TANYA'S PRESCRIPTION:

For several reasons, children are more susceptible to environmental hazards that are inhaled. Compared with adults, they inhale more oxygen per pound of body weight, *and* their bodies are still growing and developing.

DR. TANYA'S PRESCRIPTION:

If you are exposed to industrial chemicals at work, make a habit of changing your clothes (leave them outside or in the garage, if possible), taking a shower, and washing your hair before you cuddle your kids at the end of the day.

you touch it, it can get into your body. Remember: The hard truth about dust (and all the other types of the environmental pollution in your house) is that it's more than dirty. It can be downright toxic. I hate cleaning, so this part isn't my favorite.

A joint study by the Natural Resources Defense Council, the Silent Spring Institute, and researchers from several universities recently identified 45 EDCs in everyday household dust, including flame retardants, phenols, phthalates, fragrances, and fluorinated chemicals[151] (see "Anatomy of a Dust Bunny" on page 219). It's difficult to estimate just how much exposure a person has to the chemicals in dust. Of course, reducing the amount of dust will reduce your exposure. There's really no way to avoid them completely, but the more of a dust-busting ninja you become, the more you'll protect your family's health.

In a cruel dose of irony, a clear pattern has emerged among people most frequently exposed to asbestos or industrial chemicals—our brave firefighters—and cancer. It seems that an even bigger on-the-job danger for them than fire is the toxic smoke produced when the flame-retardant–treated products we have in our homes burn.[152] Fortunately, due to public outcry, some of the more heinous fire retardants have been voluntarily phased out; but because these chemicals have an uncanny ability to linger, it's unclear how long their persistence may remain a problem in our lives. See page 234 for more about flame retardants in the household and what to do about them.

See page 234 for more about flame retardants in the household and what to do about them.

PETE DROPS SCIENCE:

If you want your child's brain to be the best it can be, begin staying away from flame retardants long before pregnancy. They interfere with how the thyroid hormone guides brain development and are linked to memory and learning problems and lower IQ. But the case against flame retardants merely starts there. They also are linked to delayed physical and mental development, earlier puberty, and reduced fertility.

ANATOMY OF A DUST BUNNY

While the composition of dust is unique to every household, the following 10 compounds were found in more than 90 percent of the samples from more than two dozen studies.

COSMETICS, LOTIONS, AND DEODORANTS

- MeP (phenol)
- DIBP (plasticizer)—also found in vinyl products

FURNITURE, BABY PRODUCTS, CARPET PADDING

- TPHP (flame retardant)—also found in electronics
- TDCPP (flame retardant)

NAIL POLISH AND PAINTS

- DBP (phthalate)

POLYSTYRENE BUILDING INSULATION

- HBCD (flame retardant)

SCENTED PRODUCTS

- HHCB (fragrance)

VINYL FLOORING

- BBP (flame retardant)
- DEHP (phthalate)—also found in food-contact materials
- DEHA (phthalate replacement)—also found in food-packaging materials

WHY I'M FIRED UP ABOUT FLAME RETARDANTS

One dangerous chemical that's probably hitching a ride on most of your indoor dust? Flame retardants. Thinking about them is enough to make my flaming red-haired head explode, and you should be pissed off about them, too.

These toxic chemicals (including polybrominated diphenyl ethers) routinely appear in thousands of everyday products, including computers, televisions, children's clothing, and furniture, where they can migrate into the air and eventually settle into your body.

Recent research indicates concentrations of these chemicals are more than 15 times higher than they were a decade ago, and their impact on your health is clearly negative. Exposure to flame retardants has been linked with thyroid disease,[153, 154] decreased fertility,[155, 156] lower IQ, and cancer.

HOW TO DEAL

Be all about the big picture. I've loaded the next section of this chapter with room-specific cleaning advice where applicable, but before you get into all that, you need a big-picture plan. After all, knowing exactly what to do (and how often) is the key to getting anything done.

Use the template below to make a chart that shows at a quick glance how often the main tasks need to be dealt with. I've coded the frequency with which you can tackle different spots around the house. One important thing to remember when making your own plan is to spread out the weekly and monthly tasks—ideally, just try to get a few things done every day.

	FLOOR	APPLIANCE	FURNITURE		
KITCHEN	Sweep Damp mop	Stovetop Microwave* Fridge Oven *deep clean	Counters Tables Chairs Cabinetry	Windows & blinds	Walls, baseboards & ceiling fans
BATHROOM	Damp mop	Sink Toilet Tub		Windows & blinds	Walls, baseboards & ceiling fans
LIVING ROOM	Vacuum	Electronics	Tables Upholstery Bookshelves & picture frames	Windows & blinds	Walls, baseboards & ceiling fans
BEDROOM	Vacuum & Damp mop	Electronics	Linens Pillows Mattress	Windows & blinds	Walls, baseboards & ceiling fans

KEY: **Daily** Weekly Every 2 weeks Once a month 4 times a year

Carpets should be professionally deep-cleaned every six to 12 months (ideally spring and fall; I recommend using Zerorez, a nationwide carpet-cleaning service that uses alkaline water instead of harsh chemicals.)

SHUCK THE SHOES

Shoes worn outside unavoidably collect dirt (an umbrella term for particles of pollution as well as pesticide residue, bacteria, and other unholy evils), and if they're left on when you come inside, those shoes distribute all that nastiness throughout your home.[157] And I really mean throughout. So maybe it's worth designating a spot near the door where all footwear is stowed. I realize this strategy isn't for everyone, but those who

DR. TANYA'S PRESCRIPTION:

Take off your shoes when entering your house; this is one of the best ways to avoid bringing toxic pollutants and chemicals (or anything else undesirable) into your home.

PETE DROPS SCIENCE:

A most excellent suggestion! Not only does it reduce the amount that's tracked in, but it also reduces the wear and tear that leads to more dust. And more dust means more opportunities to breath in or ingest contaminants.

use it swear that it keeps their floors considerably cleaner.

MAKE A CLEAN SWEEP

Time to zero in on specific concerns in the various rooms in your home. For each space, I've identified the biggest culprit of toxic contamination, and I am here to help you slay each of these beasts. Plus, for each room, I've furnished you with a trove of tips and tricks for greener cleaning that will make each and every one a healthier and happier place.

CLEANING UPS AND DOWNS

When you think strategically about the areas you'll need to focus on most frequently, think from the ground up. Your floor is where all the dust and dirt is bound to settle (eventually), and even as you're walking around your house in your bare feet, this dust easily gets redistributed in between cleaning. Plus, if you have small children in your house, you know that floor is basically ground zero for a bunch of hand-to-mouth activity.

Whenever you're deep-cleaning a room, start with the highest surfaces first—but make sure you're cleaning your floors more frequently than any other surface. This is the best way to get the most effective results from the time you put into cleaning.

GEAR UP

Being well-armed is half the battle when you're out to vanquish toxic household dust and dirt. Here's what I recommend you have on hand (if you don't already):

A HEPA VACUUM. Using the same air-filtering technology that we talked about in the previous section, any vacuum with a HEPA attached to it is going to do a better job of keeping the dust inside the canister versus blasting it back into the air.

MICROFIBER CLOTHS. Here's an advancement in the war on dust that's something of a mixed bag. These products (marvels of modern engineering!) are chock-full of superfine tendrils that can pick up particles that a regular cloth can't, so you can bypass all manner of toxic chemicals when you use one of these bad boys. However, they are made from plastic, so consider this a compromise of sorts.

DAMP MOPS AND STEAMERS. Forget those disposable pads you push around the house on a stick while squirting artificial fragrances all over your floor. Once you know about the dangers of EDCs, that type of cleaning solution becomes a true horror show. Instead, if you want a truly clean floor, you're going to need to get some washable mopheads. Another good alternative, if you have wood flooring, is to use a steam mop, which sanitizes without any harsh chemicals and helps surfaces dry quickly.

EXTENSION ROD AND SPRAY BOTTLES. These are real time-savers where damp-dusting is concerned. Clamp a microfiber cloth (or regular cloth) on the end of an extension rod and you'll have an easy way to reach all kinds of hard-to-get places; keep a few spray bottles on hand and you can give your cloth a healthy squirt (just simple water is usually enough to do the trick), which will maximize your ability to pick up dust with one clean stroke.

CELLULOSE SPONGES. Made from wood fiber, these are a great alternative to the common polyurethane sponges. And make sure to avoid anything that promises to be antibacterial or odor-free. That's usually a good indication that something has been doused in the poison known as triclosan (see page 228 for why you want to steer clear of that shit).

KITCHEN

This household hub has the potential to be the Grand Central Station of toxic exposure and its creepy cousin, cross-contamination. All kinds of hazmats can run amok, freely jumping from one spot to another, and ultimately onto the food you're about to put in your mouth. There's no question that this room is a top priority.

If you want to skip ahead to page 241, I'll give you my best advice on cleaning products to use to keep your kitchen as green and clean as possible. But there's one major hurdle sitting right in the middle of your kitchen that is so problematic, we need to talk about it first.

MONSTER HAZMAT: DRINKING WATER

H_2O? More like H_2 OM(EFFING)G!

For decades, we've been told everything was peachy keen with our water supply. And we've endured a healthy amount of scoffing from all sides at the very *idea* of spring water rather than tap water—and I'm not talking about the eco-perspective on the inarguable blight of disposable plastic bottles. I'm talking about official lectures about how irrational we were for not swallowing the idea that the public water supply was unquestionably safe. The nerve of us to suggest otherwise!

Then, along came Flint, Michigan: tragic and trust-annihilating. A community's entire water supply filled with lead because of corroded pipes. A slew of lawsuits, a few visits from the president of the United States, and the sad story has yet to find a happy ending—thousands of households remain years away from seeing their damaged water lines replaced. And unfortunately, analysis of the EPA's own data suggests that the problems in Flint, while extreme, likely represent just the tip of the iceberg. There are about 75 million homes across the country built before 1978, meaning they likely contain some lead plumbing and could become vulnerable to the same problem.[158]

And don't even get me started on the water-related risks associated with the fracking industry. Tap water that could double as lighter fluid? Are you freakin' kidding me?!

The reality is we are all at risk of having a contaminated water supply in some way or another. Consider the results of a recent study that analyzed more than 36,000 water samples collected by the EPA between 2013 and 2015. The researchers found 16.5 million people

have at least one of six different types
of perfluoroalkoxy alkanes (PFAs) in
their drinking water that meets or
exceeds the EPA's designated "safety"
threshold (linked to a variety of health
problems, PFAs are those persistent
chemicals used in food packaging that
we talked about in Chapter 3).[159] A recent report by the Natural
Resources Defense Council that looked at data from 2015 found more
than 80,000 reported violations of the Safe Drinking Water Act; close
to 77 million people were served by more than 18,000 of the systems
with violations.[160]

> **PETE DROPS SCIENCE:**
>
> Water filters are a good idea, but
> make sure you buy the kind that
> doesn't introduce another plastic
> into your drinking water.

If you rely on a public water system, you are depending on your local
civic employees to monitor the quality of the water they supply (in fact,
you should receive a consumer confidence report from them every July).
If you are one of the 10 percent of Americans relying on a private water
supply (as from a well), you're on your own as far as monitoring is concerned, so you need to have the source professionally tested annually.

The EPA's list of things that shouldn't be in your water is a long one:
more than 90 substances. The agency publishes this list, along with the
"safe" amount of each contaminant, on their website, and revises it about
every five years based on whatever new contaminants are cropping up.

That list is filled with all kinds of nasty things you'd never want to
touch, from microorganisms to the disinfectants designed to kill them, as
well as any number of chemicals, including pesticides, industrial pollutants, pharmaceutical drugs, and radioactive material. Yes. You read that
right. Radioactive material can pop up in
your water supply as a natural by-product
of erosion.

The EPA recommends having your
water tested if you suspect any problems
(signs include an uptick in gastrointestinal illnesses in your household).[161] You
can buy a kit to test your water or contact

> **DR. TANYA'S
> PRESCRIPTION:**
>
> Whatever water filter you choose,
> make sure you clean or replace it reg-
> ularly to avoid the accumulation of
> other unwanted things, like mold and
> bacteria.

WATER-FILTER WINNERS

Having sampled what's out there, here are the water filters and filtration systems I have found that remove the most contaminants:

Aquagear pitcher
Berkey
eSpring multistage UV water purifier
Megahome distiller
Pure Effect filters
Pur faucet-mount filter
Radiant Life multistage remineralizing reverse-osmosis system with nonplastic UV light
Radiant Life Series 6 whole-house filtration with Zeolite

your local health department, which might be able to conduct testing for free. But there's a really important reason to do this (even if you don't notice any overt problems) because your home's water supply may have unique issues. To figure out which type of water filter best fits your needs, first you need to know exactly what is flowing out of your faucets.

HOW TO DEAL

FIND A FILTER THAT FITS. Given how unlikely it is that you have pristine tap water flowing through your home's pipes. I'm going to suggest that everyone use a water filter of some kind or another for their drinking water. Depending on what your consumer-confidence report says, and whether you decide to pursue further testing, you may be able to rely on a simple filtering system (if there are only a few contaminants present, then you probably just need something simple to take out the chemicals your water-treatment facility adds in). However, if you are dealing with serious safety issues, a multistage filter may be a better solution.

Once you know the specific contaminants you're dealing with, go to nsf.org and use their terrific database to find a water filter that's best designed to suit your needs. You can plug in the individual contaminants and get a list of suitable filters that will make comparison shopping so much easier. Here's a general overview of the most common water-filtering technologies that are available:

Carbon: Generally, carbon filters come in two forms, carbon block and granulated activated carbon. You'll find this technology applied to everything from the basic pitcher-style water filter that you keep in your fridge to an elaborate whole-house filtering system. Not surprisingly, these filters vary greatly in their effectiveness, but the main reason they work is because activated carbon chemically bonds with contaminants as water filters through it. Some just remove chlorine and improve taste and odor, while others remove asbestos, lead, mercury, and volatile organic compounds (VOCs). Unfortunately, activated carbon is not so good at removing hazardous "inorganic" materials like arsenic, fluoride, hexavalent chromium, nitrate, and perchlorate.

REVERSE OSMOSIS: By pushing water through a semipermeable membrane that blocks anything larger than a water molecule, reverse osmosis can remove many contaminants not removed by activated carbon, including arsenic, fluoride, hexavalent chromium, nitrates, and perchlorate. However, because reverse osmosis does not remove toxic chemicals like chlorine and trihalomethanes, many reverse-osmosis systems include an activated carbon component to handle that part of the job. As with carbon filters, quality can vary tremendously.

WATER SOFTENERS: If you're living with "hard" water (indicated by the presence of minerals that can build up and damage your plumbing, appliances, and fixtures), a water softener will help to lower calcium and magnesium levels. It'll also remove barium and certain forms of radium from your water supply, but that's about it. They're not an effective choice for removing most other contaminants, and if dietary sodium is a concern for you, then a water softener may not be right for you. For the same reason, they're also not recommended for watering plants and gardens.

PETE DROPS SCIENCE:

Chlorine-based cleaning projects are made using a chemical called perchlorate. This is a powerful EDC that is also used as a rocket fuel that contaminates many drinking-water systems throughout the country. It is a thyroid disruptor. So right from the get-go, using chlorine bleaching products promotes endocrine disruption. Household bleaching products do not contain pure chlorine. They use sodium hypochlorite, which includes chlorine. Do *not mix* chlorine-bleaching products with other cleaning products, especially ammonium. That will release chlorine gas, which is fast and deadly. Exposure to sodium hypochlorite can cause headaches, dizziness, nausea, vomiting, coughing, and a sore throat. It is corrosive to the respiratory tract, eyes, and skin.

DR. TANYA'S PRESCRIPTION:

Avoid antibacterial stuff, in general. A good scrubbing with unscented soap and water is usually best.

PETE DROPS SCIENCE:

Triclosan is bad stuff. Avoid it. Read the labels on your toothpaste to make sure it's not an ingredient. Triclosan's use as an antibacterial in soap and body washes was banned by the FDA in September 2016. It would be a good idea to find out if any of the old stuff you have beneath the kitchen sink has triclosan in it. Dispose of it carefully.

GREENER KITCHEN CLEANING

We all know that kitchen cleanliness is the key to avoiding a literal shitshow—family food poisoning is no laughing matter. But what you use to clean items in your kitchen is just as important because eventually y'all are eating that, too. Here's how to keep it green.

KEEP DISHWASHING CLEAN. What is up with the lurid rainbow of candy-colored concoctions in the dishwashing-soap section of the cleaning aisle. You so do not need dye to wash your dishes. Or—for the love of God—artificial fragrances! They are almost all synthetic, endocrine-disrupting evildoers and some people can have skin reactions when using them. Instead, look for a dish soap that uses botanical extracts or essential oils because these are nontoxic and wash away safely.

In the dishwasher-detergent arena, beware of products made with chlorine bleach. They spew a bunch of chemical compounds in the air and can contribute to poor indoor air quality.[162] They aren't necessarily VOCs, but they do help perpetuate the vicious cycle of poor air quality. Plus, like regular dish soaps, those pouch-style products typically contain artificial dyes and fragrances that can leave a chemical residue on your dishware. Who wants to eat off of that?

AVOID ANTIMICROBIALS. This little marketing promise can be found on cutting boards, sponges, and even ice cream scoops, but in all likelihood it means that triclosan, a potent EDC designed to kill bacteria, has been engineered into the product. Many natural materials make inherently tough spots for bacteria to thrive, including stainless steel, bamboo, glass, and ceramic, so lean toward products made from these materials when you can.

USE SEPARATE CUTTING BOARDS. The reality is you can never have too many cutting boards. That said, make sure each board has a designated use. For example, avoid chopping vegetables on the board you use for preparing raw meat. Seafood and poultry each deserve their own surfaces, too. Disinfect your boards after each use with boiling water or white vinegar and let air-dry.

BATHROOM

The "powder room," "the John," "the family library," "the facilities"—whatever you call it, some seriously nasty business (and not the natural-but-necessary kind) can be happening in your bathroom. This room isn't just for potty purposes. It's also where y'all go to get clean, so you need to make it a top priority and put a stop to the toxically noxious nastiness being unleashed in the loo.

Aside from all the bodily function stuff (and the products with artificial fragrances you may be tempted to use to mask them), bathrooms provide the ideal climate (*wet*) for bacteria and molds to grow at an alarming rate, which can affect your health.

PETE DROPS SCIENCE:

If you live in the Indianapolis area and have a serious mold problem, you are in luck. This is the only place in the world where TAML catalysts have been commercialized to clean up household mold infections. This technique is the invention of one of the world's great green chemists, Terrence Collins, Teresa Heinz Professor of Green Chemistry at Carnegie Mellon University. It is safe, cheaper, and much faster and easier than any other technology. The company that has licensed the technology from Carnegie Mellon, Indiana Mold, as a demo video here: http://indianamold.com/attics.

DR. TANYA'S PRESCRIPTION:

If your kids have asthma or are allergic to mold, any mold in your home can aggravate their symptoms. If you see or smell mold, remove it as soon as you can.

MONSTER HAZMAT: MOLD

If you're living with a mold problem, letting it get out of hand can have serious health consequences. There are thousands of different kinds of mold, all efficiently multiplying and generating tiny spores throughout the great outdoors. It's just part of life, and hardly something to stress about...as long as that shit stays outdoors. When it starts to grow out of control inside your home, mold generates a telltale musty smell, and bathrooms (specifically showers) provide ideal growing conditions. *All* types of mold—not just the notoriously toxic black mold you may having been hearing about—can potentially make us sick by aggravating upper respiratory problems, like allergies and asthma.

Mold can be freakin' tough to get rid of once it starts growing indoors—and, let's just face up to the fact that this happens to all of us now and then (show of hands for those who hate shower grout?). Here's the thing you need to know: Most commercial cleaners marketed as preventions or remedies for moldy grout will *not* help you deal with the problem. In fact, they are likely to do more harm than good.

The primary reason they're harmful is due to one of the main ingredients: bleach. Mildew-busting products also commonly contain cancer-causing carbon tetrachloride and chloroform, plus a boatload of endocrine-disrupting fragrances. Talk about a toxic cocktail.

HOW TO DEAL

MINIMIZE MOISTURE. Mold thrives in wet areas, so consider ways to keep your bathroom as dry as possible. Proper ventilation is mold's mortal enemy, so install a dehumidifier if dampness is an issue in other parts of the house (any rooms in the basement are usually especially vulnerable). Ideally, you want to keep the humidity in your home under 50 percent.

HEPA HELPS. A HEPA air filter, like we talked about earlier in this chapter, is another great mold-fighting tool. Because mold spores love air travel, they can easily find their way to any wet spot, where they'll reproduce like there's no tomorrow. A high-quality HEPA filter will absorb these airborne spores and cut down on their ability to migrate and multiply.

PAY A PRO. If you do have a larger mold issue to deal with (anything area larger than 12 by 12 inches) or if you suspect that mold could be setting up shop in your heating and cooling system, it's better to get a professional involved than risk the chance of a mushrooming mold problem—which becomes a major health hazard and a huge expense to remediate.

MORE BATHROOM-GREENING STRATEGIES

While mold will always remain your major concern as far as your bathroom is concerned, there are other important ways to keep your bathroom green.

DISINFECTANTS: The truth is, disinfectants are important because gross things happen in our lives and we want to erase the memory of them. But you're right that botanical or mineral-based disinfectants are far safer than the standard alternatives. Look for active ingredients like hydrogen peroxide and thyme oil, which kill bacteria (and mold), and clean really well.

> **PETE DROPS SCIENCE:**
>
> How stupid can we be? Some of the chemicals used to accomplish this deed may cause developmental and reproductive effects, but the amount of testing that's been done to establish safety is almost nil.

> **PETE DROPS SCIENCE:**
>
> Ditto from above for possible environmental effects. We know almost nothing about the effects on fish, wildlife, aquatic invertebrates, or any aquatic plants.

PVC PRODUCTS: I'd also recommend you avoid polyvinyl chloride (PVC) shower curtains and liners. Sure, they come with all kinds of funky designs that make you feel hip and special. But at what cost? They can send hundreds of toxic gases into your air for months, which is definitely not what you want from your nice, steamy shower.[163]

TOILET PAPER: And remember all the problems with bisphenol A (BPA) that we talked about in Chapter 3? As it turns out the thermal receipts that are saturated with the stuff have contaminated our recycled-paper industry. Research indicates that recycled toilet paper contains trace amounts of BPA.[164] So look for brands made from more sustainable sugarcane or bamboo instead.

LAUNDRY

Remember that old television commercial with a teddy bear rolling around in a basket of clean clothes, cooing about how soft and snuggly they were? It just goes to show how manufacturers have been trying for years to play up the attractiveness of clean laundry in the hope of selling you more of whatever they're making.

PETE DROPS SCIENCE:

Take a whiff of the chemicals off-gassing from the PVC shower curtain. Or better, don't. What you'd be smelling is a phthalate that is suffused into PVC plastic to make it pliable. Otherwise it would be rigid. And a lot is put in to achieve the suppleness that's needed for a shower curtain. Phthalates undermine fertility, contribute to obesity, and are linked to lower IQ in kids when they were exposed in the womb.

PETE DROPS SCIENCE:

Recycled paper and cardboard contain bisphenol A. It gets in there because the receipt paper used at ATMs, gas stations, many stores, and airplane tickets are coated with very significant amounts of BPA. The BPA undergoes a chemical reaction with a dye that's imbedded in the paper when it prints, and the reaction turns the dye from clear to dark. That's the print you see. Then the receipts get thrown into recycled paper bins and it all gets mixed together. What a tragedy!

MONSTER HAZMAT: DIRTY DETERGENTS AND FABRIC SOFTENERS

Let's start off with a big myth-buster that may just blow your mind (don't say I didn't warn you). If you rely on commercial laundry detergents, you probably think that when you throw your clothes in the wash and pull them out a half hour later, they're considerably cleaner, right? [Insert obnoxiously loud buzzer noise here.] Unfortunately, you're wrong.

What happens instead reads like a crazy (and sinister) science experiment. Your laundry appears cleaner than it really is because those detergents have left behind chemicals known as optical brighteners that use your clothing to stage a high-tech light show (as well as a hefty dose of endocrine-disrupting fragrance to mask any residual body odors). The color of your favorite shirt now appears to be more vivid and bright, but it really isn't.[165] These chemicals, now handily inside the fibers of your garments, capture light and reflect it back, for an illusion of brighter color. Some of these ingredients can even make your clothes glow under a black light!

Plenty of health and environmental consequences come with this magic show. These chemicals can, as you might expect, migrate to your skin. Then, when you go into the sun, these chemicals can become irritating; for many people, this leads to a rash that looks like a sunburn.[166] And while we don't really have any studies (yet) to tell us what happens when these chemicals get into our skin, we do know that when they end up in our lakes and waterways, fish die.[167]

HOW TO DEAL

GO OLD-SCHOOL ON YOUR LAUN-DRY. Like most of the conventional cleaning products we've been talking about, one of the biggest problems with laundry detergent is that US labeling laws don't require manufacturers to list everything that goes into them.[168] To protect your health (and the environment), look for vegetable-based detergents instead. (See page 245 for a rundown on brands to avoid and brands on the better end of the spectrum—or make your own using the recipes on page 242).

> **PETE DROPS SCIENCE:**
>
> There are too many potential ingredients to comment upon. The one thing you can be certain of is that whatever testing has been done on safety is incomplete and inadequate.

> **PETE DROPS SCIENCE:**
>
> Would you choose to avoid bringing formaldehyde fumes into your home? Play it safe. Keep away from particleboard and plywood, unless it specifically is sold as formaldehyde-free. There have been big efforts to reduce the amount of formaldehyde emissions, but not all manufacturers have taken this path. It's especially problematic if, for whatever reason, you don't have good air circulation in your house.

The same goes for fabric softeners. Some derive water-repelling properties from animal fat; using them means you are covering your clothes with trace amounts of animal fat (reminds me of Lady Gaga's meat dress . . . num-num).

If you prefer your fabric softener in the form of dryer sheets, the pickings are *very* slim—almost all of the products out there contain at least one chemical of serious concern. That's why on the "Naming Names" list on page 243, you'll see that even products from some of the most widely trusted eco-brands are ranked flat-out *bad*.

Bottom line, this is a situation where the safest and most economical route is to make your own fabric softener (it is easy, I swear; see page 242 for instructions). And if that idea doesn't appeal to you, look into buying wool balls.

LIVING SPACES

From living room to dining room to family room (to the extent that we have separate spaces like these in our homes nowadays), living areas very likely have one thing in common: a collection of furnishings you've selected for comfort and function. It makes me sick just to think about it, but it's quite possible that many such items can, over time, make you and your loved ones sick.

MONSTER HAZMAT: OFF-GASSERS

That "new carpet" aroma that wafts up from a cushy new rug underfoot? Well, what you're smelling along with that newness is toxic fumes. New product odors like that indicate that some *serious* off-gassing is going down. From cleaning products to furniture and from floor coverings to house paint, there are many things in our homes that contain certain toxic chemicals that have a way of doing something that sounds about as nasty as it is: off-gassing. When your furnishings slowly release their own version of silent-but-deadly farts into the air, VOCs are at play; they have been linked to all kinds of health conditions, from skin irritation and respiratory conditions to liver and neurological problems, as well as cancer.

For example, do you have any laminate furniture made with particleboard? That cute end table may look great when it's brand-spanking new, but it's also been treated with a type of glue made with formaldehyde.[169] It will be spewing vapors for the next seven to eight years, with most of the off-gassing happening

> **PETE DROPS SCIENCE:**
>
> PFCs are toxic, and they don't break down. They are bad for your health in multiple ways, including association with obesity and undermining your immune system's ability to resist disease. PFCs are a risk for developing fetuses and infants. And they are horrific for wildlife, from fish to bald eagles to polar bears.

> **DR. TANYA'S PRESCRIPTION:**
>
> There are so many things in the environment that can negatively affect kids. Some we know and others will be discovered years from now. The best things parents can do is to limit exposure whenever possible.

in first year. Another common source of VOCs includes anything made with the fire retardants I mentioned earlier, which are loaded onto furniture and plastics to help minimize the risk of house fires—in theory, anyway.

Here's the problem in a noxious little nutshell: Manufacturers started loading fire retardants into foam back in the 1970s to comply with a California law that required upholstered furniture to withstand a small flame for 12 seconds. Approximately 5 percent to 10 percent of the weight of foam comes from these chemicals, which are implicated in a range of health concerns, from diabetes to memory loss and endocrine problems. Every time you plop down on your couch, you could be sending an invisible cloud of these chemicals into the air you breathe.[170]

And if your upholstery has a label claiming it's "stain-resistant," that means it's probably been covered in perfluorinated chemicals (PFCs), that same nasty chemical cocktail we talked about in the food-packaging chapter that can compromise your immune system and may cause cancer (among other things).[171] Sure, that grape juice spill won't soak into the fabric, but the health cost is far greater.

HOW TO DEAL

AIR IT OUT. So . . . if you suspect that something you've recently brought into the house might be shedding VOCs like a dog in August, make sure to follow that "open a window" advice I gave you earlier. Better yet, see if you can put whatever it is out in your garage for a few weeks. New products can off-gas for years, but will slow down with time, so this strategy definitely helps minimize the problem.

GREENER LIVING SPACES

SHAKE OUT THE DUST. You probably give your small area rugs a good beating outdoors now and then to shake loose the extra dust they collect. If feasible, show your throw blankets and pillows the same sort of tough love. You should still regularly wash them in hot water, but a good shake in between washings will help.

VACUUM REGULARLY. I know we've already talked at length about how your vacuum is your best ally when it comes to fighting your own personal dust wars. However, this advice is so important, it bears repeating here. Vacuum your upholstery regularly (including underneath the cushions) and open a window, if you can, while you're at it.

USE A LITTLE WATER. Unless you're using the aforementioned vacuuming equipment, it's best to add a little water to your cleaning routine so you can avoid kicking up more dust than necessary. A little spritz of water on your cleaning cloth or a barely damp mophead will pick up more dirt than a dry tool.

CONTROL THE CLUTTER. The fewer piles of paper, hoards of kiddie collectibles, and craft projects in progress, the less accumulated dust. Stow the stuff you really want to keep in storage bins. Get the rest of the family on board and reap the added bonus of cleanup time being *sooo* much easier when everyone's in the habit of throwing things in a bin rather than leaving them lying around on the floor . . . or table . . . or counter.

STEP UP TO BETTER FLOORING. Vinyl flooring (as in PVC vinyl flooring) is notorious for shedding toxic VOCs into the air, as can synthetic wall-to-wall carpet (which can also hold onto toxic dust and dirt in its deepest layers).[172] If possible, when replacing flooring, opt for wood, ceramic tile, cork, bamboo, linoleum, and washable throw rugs for less toxic options.

WORK UP A WISH LIST

This is one of those areas where the best you can do is approach it as a long process of gradual improvement because replacing everything at once is impractical, to say the least.

First ask yourself: When was this item made? Anything made before 1975 is less likely to have been saturated with toxic flame retardants.

Also, where was it made? Europe, Japan, and China restrict the use of formaldehyde in furniture for health concerns, and anything that indicates it is following EU standards is also probably a safer option.[173] Another good sign is anything bearing the Greenguard certification, which ensures that the materials used have low-emission levels.

In response to consumer demand, a slew of furniture retailers have pledged to sell items made without fire retardants (see page 239 for a list).

BEDROOM

Of all rooms in your house, this one—your private oasis, your sleeping haven, your last refuge from worldly concerns—deserves special care when it comes to minimizing potential toxic exposures. Assuming you're getting the proper amount of shut-eye, you're spending about a third of your life (more than 2,500 hours every year) simply catching Zzz's in bed—and kids sleep even more! In fact, if you consider how your waking hours are usually distributed in other rooms of the house, it's quite likely that you spend more time in your bedroom than any other.

MONSTER HAZMAT: MATTRESSES

Most conventional mattresses are made with a toxic nightmare of synthetic materials. I know: It's an outrage. But trust me—arm yourself with the right information (coming right up!) and you'll rest easy, knowing you've got a plan to do what you can to fix it. I promise.

Okay. Ready? Here's a quick rundown of the top four types of chemicals you may be (literally) up against in the mattress department:

FLAME RETARDANTS: These phosphated, brominated, chlorinated, or antimony-laden substances that we've been talking about in furniture are going to show up in your mattress, too (theoretically to make them safer, given that foam is quite flammable).

PHTHALATES: These endocrine-disrupting plasticizers are used in manufacturing a variety of mattress components. Though some phthalates have been banned, new and as-yet legal compounds are still on the market; their safety has yet to be determined.

VOCs: This is more of the off-gassing we already covered when we looked at living space. Living with a steady stream of these compounds can lead to breathing problems, among other health issues. VOCs are especially worth mentioning here because emissions tend to rise with heat—as in the kind of body heat generated while we sleep in our cozy beds.[174]

PFCs: Again with the fluorinated chemicals—I know! Mattress man-ufacturers rely on these chemicals for their excellent moisture- and stain-repellant properties (I'm looking at you, Scotchgard!). Of course, they've also been linked with attention deficit hyperactivity disorder (ADHD), hyperactivity, delayed gross motor development, endocrine and reproductive problems, as well as cancer, so that kind of puts a little pee in the bed in perspective, doesn't it?[175]

HOW TO DEAL

MANAGE MATTRESS ANXIETY. Obviously, there's a ton of undesir-ables that might be stuffed into your mattress and could be throwing off dangerous chemicals as you sleep. But it's also helpful to remem-ber that these emissions dissipate over time. The older your mattress, the less likely it is to be spitting chemicals, especially if it was made before 2007,[176] when fewer fire retardants were required. So if you do not need a new mattress, don't race out to replace the one you have right now.

KEEP IT COVERED. If you recently purchased a new mattress before reading this book and are understandably concerned about toxic off-gassing, consider getting an activated carbon pad to use as a mattress cover. They are designed to absorb chemicals in much the same way a carbon-based water filter works, but note that they're not designed to be placed directly on a bed, and they can't be washed so you'll need to encase them in a fabric liner first. If that seems a little over-the-top to you, a good allergen barrier mattress cover is another option.

LOOK FOR NATURAL LATEX. Memory-foam toppers can provide an interim solution to an aging mattress; however, while comfortable, they can throw off VOCs like there's no tomorrow. A much better option is to look for products made from natural latex, which ensures it's free of syn-thetic materials.

SHOP WISELY. When you do decide to buy a new mattress, look for Greenguard-certified products. This third-party label ensures that a prod-uct meets strict standards for minimal emissions. Likewise, mattresses made with certified organic ingredients are most likely to be free of fire retardants, formaldehyde, and petroleum derivatives.

FLAME-RETARDANT-FREE FURNITURE

Shopping for new furniture? Here's a handy list of companies selling flame retardant-free furniture.

AICO (Amini Innovation Corporation)
American Furniture Manufacturing
Ashley Furniture
Best Home Furnishings
Bradington Young
Broyhill
CR Laine
Century (Highland House Furniture)
Coco-Mat
Comfort Design
Craftmaster
Crate and Barrel (CB2, Land of Nod)
Dania
David Edward
Drexel Heritage
Dwell Studio
EcoSelect
Ekla Home
Endicott Home
EQ3
Fairfield Chair
Flexsteel Inds.
Furnature
Gus Design Group
Heritage Home Group Brands (Broyhill, Drexel Heritage, Henredon, Hickory Chair, Lane, Maitland Smith, Pearson, Thomasville)
Henredon
Hickory Chair
Hickory White
Highland House
Homeware
Hooker Furniture (Bradington Young, Homeware, Sam Moore)
IKEA
Interline (Scandinavian Designs, Plummers, Dania)
Kevin Charles Fine Upholstery (sold by City Furniture stores in Florida)
Kincaid Furniture
Klaussner (Comfort Designs)
Kristin Drohan Collection
Lane
La-Z-Boy (Kincaid)
Lee Industries
McCreary Modern (available at Crate & Barrel and Room & Board)
MotionCraft
Pacific West Furniture
Palliser Furniture
Pearson
Pine St. Interiors/EcoTerric
Plummers
Precedent Furniture
Roger + Chris
Sam Moore
Scandinavian Designs
Sherrill Furniture (Hickory White, Lillian August, Precedent, Motion Craft, Whittemore Sherrill, Mr. and Mrs. Howard)
Soma Ergonomics
Southern Enterprises (only some products are fire retardant–free)
Southern Furniture
Southern Motion
Stitch NYC (only some products are fire retardant–free)
Taylor King
Thomasville
United Furniture Industries
Vanguard Furniture (Michael Weiss, Thom Filicia, Compendium)
Viesso
Whittemore Sherrill Ltd.

Source: Center for Environmental Health

RECIPES FOR A GREENER HOME

HOMEMADE CLEANSERS 101

It's likely you already have a bunch of the ingredients you'll need already sitting in your pantry. We're talking about vinegar, salt, baking soda, and lemons...and maybe a little hydrogen peroxide and/or some essential oils now and then. I've put together a full list of what you'll need below. Stock up on whatever you don't have and you'll be ready to start using greener alternatives.

Baking soda
Borax
Castile soap
Coconut oil (fractionated)
Distilled water
Essential oils: citrus, lavender, and tea tree
Hydrogen peroxide
Kosher salt
Lemon
Olive oil
Rubbing alcohol
Vegetable glycerin
Vinegar (white and apple cider)
Washing soda

RECIPES FOR GREENER CLEANING

If you like the idea of sticking to some basic homemade cleaning products, try these recipes—they'll make your bathroom sparkle, promise.

TOILET CLEANER: Pour 1 cup white vinegar into the toilet and leave overnight, or come back a while later. When you return, sprinkle about 1 tablespoon baking soda around the bowl, then scrub.

GENERAL BATHROOM CLEANER: Mix $^2/_3$ cup baking soda with $^1/_2$ cup vegetable oil–based liquid soap, $^1/_2$ cup water, and 2 tablespoons vinegar. Store mixture in a jar or spray bottle and shake well before using.

UNCLOG A DRAIN: Pour $^1/_2$ cup white vinegar into a clogged drain. Let sit while you bring 2 cups water to a boil, then pour water down the drain.

SHOWER CLEANER: Soak a sponge in white vinegar, sprinkle with baking soda, and scrub.

WINDOW AND GLASS CLEANER: Mix $^1/_3$ cup white vinegar with $^1/_4$ cup rubbing alcohol and put in a 32 ounce spray bottle; fill the rest with water.

ALL-PURPOSE FLOOR CLEANER

- 4 cups white vinegar
- 1 gallon cold water
- 1 tablespoon vegetable oil (optional for wood floors)

Combine the vinegar, water, and vegetable oil (if using) in a large bucket. Damp-mop your floor and allow to air-dry.

WOOD POLISH You can always use coconut oil to clean wood and give it a shine, but if you want something a bit more powerful, try this recipe.

- $^1/_2$ cup apple cider vinegar
- $^1/_4$ cup olive oil
- 1 teaspoon coconut oil
- 1 tablespoon vegetable glycerin
- 1 tablespoon fresh lemon juice
- 30 drops essential oil (I prefer lavender)

Combine ingredients into a container. Rub a small amount into your wood furniture with a clean cloth, then buff. Store leftovers in a cool, dark place.

RECIPES FOR GREENER KITCHEN CLEANING

GENERAL DISINFECTANT: Mix 1 part vinegar and 1 part water in a spray bottle to clean everything from countertops to doorknobs, especially during flu season.

ALL-PURPOSE CLEANER: Mix 2 cups distilled water, $\frac{1}{4}$ cup castile soap, and 15 to 20 drops your favorite essential oil(s).

AIR FRESHENER: Mix $\frac{1}{2}$ teaspoon white vinegar, 3 drops of essential oil, and fill the rest of the 4 ounce spray bottle with water. Use a spritz or two whenever you want to freshen up the air around you.

WINDOW CLEANER: Mix $\frac{1}{3}$ cup white vinegar with $\frac{1}{4}$ cup rubbing alcohol and put in a 32 ounce spray bottle; fill the rest with water.

CLEANING WOOD CUTTING BOARDS: Cut a lemon in half, then sprinkle the cutting board with kosher salt and scrub. Rinse thoroughly. I like to condition my cutting boards with refractionated coconut oil once every 2 weeks.

CLEAN THE BLENDER: Throw half a lemon in the blender with some dishwasher soap and some water. Blend and then rinse thoroughly.

RECIPES FOR GREENER LAUNDRY

If you're interested in going the clean-and-simple route and want to try your hand at homemade laundry products, these recipes are the place to start. An added bonus: It's cheaper per load than the commercial stuff.

LAUNDRY DETERGENT: Combine 1 grated bar of castile soap, 1 cup washing soda, 1 cup borax, $\frac{1}{4}$ cup baking soda, 20 drops of a citrus essential oil, and 5 drops of lavender essential oil.

STAIN REMOVER: Combine 1 cup water, $\frac{1}{2}$ cup hydrogen peroxide, and $\frac{1}{2}$ cup baking soda. Apply to the stain and let soak for 30 minutes. (This works well on dark stains, including blood.)

FABRIC SOFTENER: Add one cup of white vinegar to the final rinse cycle.

DRYER SHEETS: Cut up some old cotton clothes into a bunch of scraps. Combine 1 cup white vinegar together with about 30 drops of your favorite essential oils in a big glass jar with a lid, and place the scraps inside (you want them damp, but not dripping). Use in place of dryer sheets, reusing the scraps and refreshing the vinegar and essential oils as necessary. Don't worry about the vinegar smell; it will evaporate in the dryer, but the essential oil smell will linger.

RECIPES FOR A SWEET-SMELLING MATTRESS

- ✤ If you're worried about mites, mildew, or bothersome odors taking over your mattress, apply some drops of lavender essential oil around the corners of the bed and in the middle.

- ✤ Forget about using a cleaning product filled with synthetic fragrances on your mattress, of all places. Instead, try combining 20 to 30 drops of your favorite essential oil with a box of baking soda. Sprinkle this mixture liberally on your bare mattress. Let it sit for an hour or so, then vacuum thoroughly. If you have some left over, this mix can also work double duty on upholstered furniture and carpets.

NAMING NAMES

CLEANING PRODUCTS

BAD

These are high-risk products, containing multiple high- and moderate-hazard ingredients, as well as unknown or proprietary mixtures that make it impossible to find out what's actually in there.

2000 Flushes
Ajax
Armstrong
Bissell
Caldrea
Cinch
Citrus Magic
Clorox
Comet
DampRid
Drano
Easy-Off
Fabuloso
Fantastik
Formula 409
Great Value
Green Works
Goof Off
J.R. Watkins
Kaboom
Legacy of Clean (by Amway)
Lemi Shine
Liquid Plumber
Lysol
Nifti (by Colgate)
Mop & Glo

Mr. Clean
Murphy
OdoBan
Old English
Parsons'
Pine-Sol Pledge
Safeway Bright Green
Scrub Free
Scrubbing Bubbles
Simple Green
Soft Scrub
SOS
Sno Bol
Spic and Span
Swiffer
Tilex
Ty-D-Bol
Weiman
Windex (by SC Johnson)

BETTER

These are moderate-risk products that have far fewer toxic chemicals than the *bad* category. Each contains no more than one high-hazard ingredient.

Air Therapy
Babyganics
Better Life
Bon Ami
Caldrea
CLR
Ecover

Ecover
Grab Green
LA's Totally Awesome
Method
Mrs. Meyer's
Ology
Seventh Generation
Sodasan
Sun & Earth
The Honest Company
Whole Foods Market
Young Living
Zep

BEST

The only products to make the cut here are free of all high-hazard ingredients and list no more than one moderate-hazard ingredient.

AspenClean
Attitude Cleaners
Aussan Natural
Biokleen
Borax
BuggyLove Organic
Charlie's Soap
Citra Clear
Dapple
Dr. Bronner's
Earth Friendly Products
Earth Mama
Eco-Me

Fit Organic
GreenShield
IGozen
Lion Bear Naked Soap Co.
MamaSuds
The Laundress
Truce

LAUNDRY DETERGENT

Look for biodegradable laundry detergents that contain no phosphates, perfumes, or dyes. These ingredients may irritate your skin and eyes; many are toxic and are suspected carcinogens.

BAD

This category consists of brands that use multiple toxic and/or questionable ingredients, including fragrances, artificial colors, preservatives like BHT, as well as sodium lauryl/laureth sulfate, polyethylene glycols, and quats.

Ace
All
Ariel
Arm & Hammer
Cheer
Dreft

Delicare
Downy Fabric Softener
Era
Gain
Green Works (Clorox)
Hero Clean
Ivory Snow
OxiClean
Persil
Purex
Snuggle Fabric Softener
Sun
Sunlight
Surf
Tide
Vaska
Vista
Wisk
Woolite
Xtra

BETTER

This category consists of brands or specific products that contain far fewer questionable ingredients on the moderate hazard scale, and no toxic synthetic fragrances.

All Stainlifters Free & Clear
Caldrea
Cheer Free
Dapple
Dropps

Ecos
Ecover
Method
Mrs. Meyers
Oxiclean Free & Clear
Planet
Presto
Simple Green
Seventh Generation
Sun & Earth (poor ingredient
    disclosure)
Sun Free & Clear
The Honest Co.
The Laundress (poor ingredient
    disclosure)
Tide Free & Gentle Powder

BEST

This category consists of brands
that use only low- or no-hazard
ingredients.

Attitude
Biokleen
Charlie's Soap
Eco Nuts
Eco-Me
Grab Green
Greenshield
J.R. Watkins
Molly's Suds
Nellie's
Odorklenz
Woolzies
Zum

DRYER SHEETS

Some of the chemicals in dryer
sheets that help make clothes feel
soft are also referred to as "asth-
magens" because they can cause
asthma to develop in otherwise
healthy people. Many of these
chemicals also have antibacterial
properties, but keep in mind that
freshly washed clothes are already
plenty clean.

BAD

All brands contain synthetic fragrance and/or dihydrogenated
palmoylethyl hydroxyethylmonium methosulfate. When something's a mouthful, it's not a good
sign. See Pete's comment on page
214 for the lowdown on this chemical and other quats.

365 Everyday Value (Whole
    Foods)
All Free & Clear
Arm & Hammer
Babies "R" Us
Babyganics
Better Life
Bounce (P&G)
Caldrea
Clutch
Cuddle Soft (Snuggle)
Downy (P&G)

Gain (P&G)
Great Value (Walmart)
Kirkland (Costco)
Member's Mark (Sam's Club/
  Walmart)
Method
Mrs. Meyer's
Purex
Seventh Generation
Snuggle
Soft Breeze
Stoneworks (Grab Green)
Suavitel
Sun & Earth
The Honest Co.
Up & Up (Target)

BETTER

This single brand is potentially *better* because, while I can't totally confirm ingredients, it's fragrance-free and doesn't contain sulfates, which would include dihydrogenated palmoylethyl hydroxyethylmonium methosulfate.

The Good Home Co.

BEST

No toxic synthetic fragrances or dihydrogenated palmoylethyl hydroxyethylmonium methosulfate.

Grab Green
PurEcosheet

PEST CONTROL

If you need some extra help controlling the bugs that are getting the best of your garden, there are many options available. Obviously, some are far better than others, so here's a list to take with you to the store.

BAD

These are products to avoid. They contain carcinogenic chemicals; can be hazardous to touch, especially for children; and may harm beneficial insect populations.

Ortho
Spectracide
Raid
Hot Shot
Bayer Advanced
Enoz
Sevin
Monterey
Bengal Combat

BETTER

These brands are EWG-approved products that contain safer concentrations of bug-repelling chemicals and essential oil choices. While usually safe for beneficial insects and for home use, always follow application instructions carefully.

Skin So Soft Bug Guard

Off!

Cutter

Repel

Terro

Monterey (check for neonicotinoids
  in some formulas)

Fairy Tales

Burt's Bees

Quantum Buzz Away

Bug Band

BEST

These products, which contain organic ingredients (mostly essential oils) also use trap and barrier strategies to help you better control garden pests.

Kosmatology

Oilogic

Baxter's Naturals

Garden Safe

Sokos

Organicide

Wondercide

EcoSmart

Repel (lemon eucalyptus oil–based)

NovaSource

Shake Away

Nature's Care

Babyganics

DoTerra Terrashield

Bonide

Now Foods

Borax

Parakito

Swamp Gator

Home Setinel

Garlic Scentry

Espree

Safer

Rocky Mountain Oils

Arbico Organics

California Baby

Baxter's Naturals

Chig-R-Blok

SEVEN

GREENER GROOMING

WELCOME TO THE CHAPTER that, for me, might most deserve to be subtitled "Are You Freakin' Kidding Me?"

I know—believe me, girl—this book sometimes feels like a nonstop WTF fest, but this chapter really takes the cake. And it was the hardest to write.

I've saved the whacked-out world of personal care products for last for two reasons.

First reason: because it is *majorly* confusing AF.

We are constantly inundated with advertisements that tell us that if we want to be clean, feel fresh, look pretty, and stay healthy, we need to apply an endless array of lotions and potions, cleansers and cosmetics, pads and wipes, and all sorts of other manufactured products. As if those products are *really* what makes the people in those commercials—with their shiny hair, clear skin, sparkling teeth, and slender waistlines—so happy and carefree.

Of course not. You know as well as I do that those commercials are complete and utter BS. Health and wellness, beauty and happiness don't pour forth from a bottle of body wash. Duh. But what you may not realize is that torrents of endocrine-disrupting chemicals and carcinogens

DR. TANYA'S PRESCRIPTION:

Fragranced products are often responsible for most skin irritation and allergies and are not recommended for pregnant women, small children, or children going through puberty because they often contain hormone disrupters and have the ability to affect their development.

PETE DROPS SCIENCE:

"Fragrances" is code for "we don't want to tell you what's in this because if we did, you might not buy it." Phthalates are often added to personal care products and hidden behind the "fragrance" word. Phthalates interfere with androgens, the male hormones like testosterone. A large scientific literature now links them to quite a diversity of health endpoints, especially problems with male reproductive health that begins with fetal exposure.

quite possibly *do*. That's right: Personal "care" products are potentially hazardous to your health. Double whammy: Make us feel bad about ourselves *and* maybe even kill us. What a low-down dirty industry we're dealing with here.

Ill effects from chemical-laced personal products can be as minor as a little skin rash, scalp flaking, or eye irritation that clears up once you stop using whatever product caused the reaction. But the risks go way beyond that when you're dealing with toxic chemicals. And make no mistake, my friend, that is exactly what we've got here: phthalate-laden fragrances and preservatives with known links to obesity, poor memory function, infertility, behavioral problems like attention deficit hyperactivity disorder (ADHD), thyroid issues, type 2 diabetes, and cancer. Sounds sexy, right?

And here's the part where it really gets confusing (and infuriating): Neither the Environmental Protection Agency nor the Federal Drug Administration have the authority to properly regulate the industries that produce the products we slather all over our skin[177] (the largest organ in your body, and a porous one at that) and even put directly inside our bodies (almost time to talk about "feminine care" items that might not belong anywhere near your hoo-ha, much less right up there). This is highly unfortunate and terribly unhealthy for American consumers. And get this: Many of our personal care products contain ingredients that have been banned in Japan, Canada, and the European Union.[178]

How can it be that we are so poorly protected? Well, here in the United States, companies manufacturing personal care products essentially regulate themselves. They handpick their own panels of experts and they determine for themselves what is "safe."[179] This approach to public safety is about as sensible as a preschool putting the toddlers in charge of snack time. Metaphors aside, safety testing and regulation of personal care products is a charade, and manufacturers get to package up their products however they want and sell them to us.

So it's on *us*—you and me, baby—to know a thing or two about selecting personal care products because that's how we can make safer choices that protect ourselves and our families from harmful chemicals.

The second reason I've left personal care products for last: because you should, too.

Girl, it's just like I told you at the beginning of this book. Food—and what it's packaged/cooked/stored in—comes first. That is the area in which you can make the most difference in your family's toxic load, and that's where it makes the most sense to focus your efforts. (Thus, that topic is the bulk of this book.) You can also take some basic measures to make your home environment safer and healthier, and that's exactly what we set you up for in the previous chapter. Now, let's

PETE DROPS SCIENCE:

When you absorb something through your skin (rather than digesting it), any contaminants automatically bypass your liver, which is your body's defense system. Instead, those toxins go straight into your bloodstream and can reach critical tissues at much higher concentrations than would happen via digestion.

PETE DROPS SCIENCE:

Not only are they banned in other regions of the world, but in multiple instances companies selling the same product in Europe as in the United States use different chemical ingredients, with ingredients banned in Europe used in the US formulation.

PETE DROPS SCIENCE:

Then when a university scientist discovers a harmful effect that the companies' experts missed, the company hires more scientists and lawyers to defend the product, often attacking the university scientist and manipulating data to confuse the public debate.

wrap things up by doing the same for personal care: mapping out a few simple steps to make significant improvements—without making yourself crazy.

Full disclosure: When I discovered the toxic vortex in my family's bathroom, I went full ostrich for a spell. Then, when I finally found the courage to pull my head out of the sand and take a good, hard look at our personal care products, I kinda sorta lost it.

Having been there and done that, and helped many others face the same quandary, I am here to help you skip that part. Stick with me and we'll make greening your grooming easy—well, as easy as letting go of some of your fave perfumes can be.

2 THINGS TO DO RIGHT NOW

NO. I: SAY "HELL, NO" TO SYNTHETIC FRAGRANCE

This here's the No. 1 monster hazmat to take down if you want to green up your family's grooming. Synthetic fragrances are made with a slew of endocrine-disrupting chemicals. These chemicals are typically not listed on ingredient labels because, although the Federal Fair Packaging and Labeling Act of 1967 requires cosmetics companies to list all ingredients on their labels, there's an exception to that rule (gargantuan loophole alert!) when an ingredient is listed as a "fragrance." With one little word, manufacturers legally bypass all the full

PETE DROPS SCIENCE:

Leah is alerting you to a loophole so big, you can send the space shuttle through it.

disclosure rules because fragrances are considered proprietary "trade secret" formulas.[180] Sussing out whether a personal care product contains chemical fragrance is a good way to evaluate its overall ingredient safety—where there's fragrance, you'll also often find other chemicals of concern.

HOW TO DEAL

KEEP YOUR SHOPPING CART
FRAGRANCE-FREE. Before you embark
on the enterprise of destinkifying the
products your family is already using, set
yourself up to shop smarter so you don't
inadvertently add to the problem by
bringing home even more artificially
scented products. When you shop, make
it a matter of course to check the ingredient label. And if you see the word

> ## DR. TANYA'S PRESCRIPTION:
>
> Fragranced products are responsible
> for most skin irritation and allergies
> and are not recommended for preg-
> nant women, small children, or chil-
> dren going through puberty because
> they often contain hormone disrupt-
> ers and have the ability to affect their
> development.

"fragrance"—or "perfume" or "parfum"—put it right back on the shelf.
Any one of those three words is a dead giveaway. That advice also goes
for multilevel marketing products. Learning to be just a little bit label
literate is a great way to prevent further fragrance hazmats from wea-
seling their way into your family's grooming routine. You can make it
extra easy on yourself by using the "Naming Names" lists (pages 273
through 291) to note particular brands you're looking for—and the ones
you need to avoid.

FERRET THE FRAGRANCE OUT OF YOUR FAMILY'S GROOMING
ROUTINE. When it comes to dealing with the products you already have, I
recommend taking the same approach as we did with processed food: Focus
on the front row—the products that are most constantly in use, such as
shampoos, soaps, lotions, toothpaste and various other oral care products,
hair gel and such, deodorants; plus your personal items, including everyday
makeup, facial moisturizers and cleansers, and feminine hygiene products.

Gather that daily stuff together, take a deep breath, and log some
label-reading time, keeping a sharp lookout for one of these three buzz-
kill words: fragrance, perfume, or parfum. Set aside any products that
flunk the fragrance test; they likely contain phthalates.[181] Then do a little soul-searching. It is quite possible that there are more ingredients
listed under the blanket term "fragrance," outnumbering those that you
see on the ingredient label.

PETE DROPS SCIENCE:

When the label says "fragrance," ask yourself whether you really need the product. And remember as you do that that the goal of advertising is to make wants seem like needs when they really aren't necessities. Do you need health for you and your family? Yes. Do you need fragrances that often are derived from petroleum? No. That simple question may save you a lot of grief if you apply it regularly.

PETE DROPS SCIENCE:

As outlandish as that might sound to someone just starting to read about this, it's a deep and legitimate concern.

If some of the flunkies feel like items you just cannot live without, or if you spent a ton of money on them and it makes you sick to think of chucking them, then put 'em back on deck until you find something better. (One *big* caveat here: If you discover that there is fragrance of any kind in any of your time-o'-the-month products, please, for the love of all things good and holy, kick it to the curb immediately. Then turn straight to page 272 for important info about the tender topic of how best to care for the goods down there, and get yourself some safer supplies next time you leave the house. Seriously. There's a whole lot more to fem care than just fragrance, but we will cover that soon.)

NO. 2: STREAMLINE AND SIMPLIFY

Try this concept on for size: If you're using more products on a daily basis than you have fingers to count, that's too much.

A consumer survey by the Environmental Working Group found that women use an average of 12 personal care products daily (containing up to 168 chemical ingredients). For men, the number of products was six (with 80-plus chemical ingredients). The group with the highest risk for off-the-charts exposure levels: adolescent girls, using on average 17 personal care products per day (with up to 180 unique chemical ingredients).[182] But get this: A related study in California followed a group of teenage girls and found the level of several dangerous chemicals in their bodies measured 25 percent to 45 percent lower after only three days of switching to fragrance-free products.[183]

So the point is this: If you can knock it down to 10 products (or less), you'll be making a huge difference in the toxic toll being taken by personal care products—*especially* if most of those products are fragrance-free.

HOW TO DEAL

TAKE INVENTORY. Take a mental spin through your daily grooming drill. Is there room to simplify? Do you really need to use a half dozen products on your hair every morning? Hey, far be it from me to judge.

CUT WHAT YOU CAN AND SWAP OUT WHATEVER SUCKS. Okay. So what's your count? Can you nominate a few candidates for elimination? For me, it turned out to be way easier than I thought to vote a few things off the island altogether, like the seven-step skin regime . . . who needs all that? But others I just couldn't do without, like my dry shampoo (that shit is the bomb diggity)—so some swaps had to be found. When I first looked at cutting back, one of my big concerns was budgetary; I just could not handle the prospect of trashing a bunch of high-end but hazmat-riddled beauty products. Once I narrowed down what I really needed, I purchased some better options and figured out how to make the others myself. This process took me almost a year, so don't worry if it takes you some time.

One thing I can tell you *not* to do: It's really not a good idea to try to replace everything at once because personal care products are, well, very personal; replacing them will be a trial-and-error process, and you

PETE DROPS SCIENCE:

The endocrine-disrupting chemicals found in personal care products are bad for both boys and girls. Sometimes the effects are bigger in one sex or the other. But frankly, the safety testing of products is so spotty that the safe assumption is that if we know there are adverse effects in one sex, the other will be impacted too. That's because both boys and girls (fetus, toddler, to teenager) have hormone systems that respond to both of the two classic sex hormones, estrogen and testosterone, as well as a host of other hormone signals. For example, estrogen during fetal development masculinizes the male brain.

PETE DROPS SCIENCE:

One of the scientific surprises that has come from research over the past two decades is that some endocrine-disrupting compounds can increase the risk of obesity.

DR. TANYA'S PRESCRIPTION:

Tween and teen girls use many personal care products simply because they believe this is what they should and need to use. They see them in ads and the media, and hear about them from friends. This can expose them to many unneeded products and chemicals. Truthfully, the list I give girls in my practice is fairly minimal: facial cleanser (depending on acne status), fragrance-free body cleanser (can double for shaving cream), sunscreen (chemical-free), fragrance-free body moisturizer (if needed), deodorant (as natural as possible), shampoo and conditioner (with as few chemicals and fragrances as possible). Hair products and makeup are minimal and as natural as possible. They just don't need it.

don't want to strand yourself with bad hair/greasy skin/stinky pits, for crying out loud. And different products work better for different people, so you gotta find what's right for you.

Instead, switch out one product at a time. When it comes to finding non-toxic products, check out Madesafe.org, which vets a wide range of product ingredients for carcinogens, endocrine disruptors, flame retardants, high-risk pesticides, toxic solvents, or harmful volatile organic compounds. Then they screen more deeply with a chemist for bioaccumulation, environmental degradation, aquatic toxicity, and animal harm.

HOW TO GO GREENER

Okay, so you get the gist here—many, if not most, of the products being sold to us for the very purpose of taking care of ourselves and our loved ones are laced with endocrine disruptors or other chemicals that are potentially hazardous to human health. The next step is to take a closer look at the items you want to keep in your routine, identify the ones that might need to go bye-bye, and find better replacements. Doing that just requires a bit of homework—and I've done a bunch of that work for you.

Whether you switch brands or go homemade, bear in mind that formulations may feel different because they are made with more natural ingredients than the commercial products you're leaving behind. And remember that you are trading *way* up healthwise.

HAZMAT HUNTING

Fragrance is just the tip of the personal care hazmat iceberg. Some of the monster toxics you should be most concerned about trying to avoid are actual ingredients, but others are by-products of chemical reactions (like 1,4-dioxane) or even naturally occurring elements (heavy metals). Many are bioaccumulative (they build up in the body and/or the environment over time rather than dissipate).

Like I told you at the beginning of the chapter, being selective and smart about grooming products is complicated AF. One of the things that makes it extra complicated is the need for synthetic ingredients because of mold (which is a hazard anytime water or aloe is an ingredient) and because of heavy metals (which can be present as a contaminant in various natural ingredients used for color). The upshot here is that the world of personal care products is very different than food: **Natural isn't necessarily better,** organic does not necessarily equal safe, and it is not necessarily a bad thing to see a few unpronounceably long ingredients on the label, because light use of safer synthetic preservatives (such as potassium sorbate and sodium benzoate) and dyes such as Red 7 Lake/CI 15850) is preferable to the risks posed by mold and /or heavy metals. These are compromises I think it makes sense to make. If you want to use lotions that are oil-based and contain no water,

DR. TANYA'S PRESCRIPTION:

Always flip products over and read the ingredients in everything, from what you put *in* your body to what you put *on* your body. Just because a product advertises that they support specific causes or "are natural" or "green," doesn't mean that they are.

#RETHINKTHEPINK

Pinkwashing is something that really makes me see red. When October rolls around every year, some of the brands that go pink for Breast Cancer Awareness Month also make and sell products laced with chemicals that are linked to—wait for it—breast cancer (plus endocrine disruption, etc). How is *that* for unconscionably cynical cause-related marketing? Don't let these sleazoids (I'm pointing at *you,* high-end hazmat peddlers: Clinique, Estée Lauder, Bobbi Brown, Donna Karan, and Darphin!) trick you into buying toxic shit in the guise of faux philanthropy. If you see pink branding on a personal care product (or any product, for that matter), scrutinize that ingredient label extra carefully.

you can easily find all-natural products that are safe (and plenty are listed on page 275). But if you like lotion that contains water, you either need to make it yourself—which is budget-friendly and surprisingly easy—or purchase a product that contains some manner of preservative. Or make sure you pay close attention to how old your personal care products are.

Here's a super-simplified, user-friendly rundown of some of the most important ingredient label clues to be on the lookout for. Relying on those lists means you don't have to worry about scrutinizing labels and identifying hazmats, but there are a bajillion products out there and it's important to be able to judge safety for yourself when the need arises.

HIGHEST HAZARD

1,4 DIOXANE, -ETHOXYLATED INGREDIENTS (ETHS), POLYETHYLENE GLYCOL (PEG), POLYSORBATES

WHY THEY'RE BAD: Known or suspected to cause cancer or birth defects[184]

WHERE THEY'RE FOUND: Shampoo, soap, and other products that get sudsy or foamy

WHAT TO LOOK FOR ON THE LABEL: Sodium laureth sulfate, PEG compounds, chemicals that end in "-eth" (like ceteareth and oleth) or "-xynol" (like nonoxynol or octoxynol), polysorbate

COAL TAR

WHY IT'S BAD: Toxic and carcinogenic[185]

WHERE IT'S FOUND: Dandruff shampoo, soaps, hair dye, lotion

WHAT TO LOOK FOR ON THE LABEL: Coal tar solution, coal, carbocort, coal tar solution, coal tar solution, crude coal tar, estar, impervotar, KC-261, picis carbonis, naphtha, high solvent naphtha, naphtha distillate, petroleum benzin

HEAVY METALS (SUCH AS ALUMINUM, LEAD, CADMIUM, NICKEL, AND MERCURY)

WHY THEY'RE BAD: Linked to reproductive, immune, and nervous system toxicity[186]

WHERE THEY'RE FOUND: Lightening creams, cosmetics containing natural minerals and dyes, deodorant

WHAT TO LOOK FOR ON THE LABEL: These are often contaminants that are not technically added so they're unlikely to be listed, but watch out for lead acetate, chromium, thimerosal, hydrogenated cottonseed oil, sodium hexametaphosphate, aluminum stearate, aluminum caprylate, aluminum chloride, aluminum acetate, aluminum hydroxide, aluminum oxide

PERFLUORINATED CHEMICALS

WHY THEY'RE BAD: Endocrine-disrupting, toxic to reproductive systems, carcinogenic[187]

WHERE THEY'RE FOUND: Anti-aging products

WHAT TO LOOK FOR ON THE LABEL: Polytetrafluoroethylene, polyperfluoromethylisopropyl ether, DEA-C8-18, perfluoroalkylethyl phosphate.

P-PHENYLENEDIAMINE

WHY IT'S BAD: Associated with allergic reactions that may affect skin, eyes, and lungs and can be severe enough to put some people in the hospital[188]

WHERE IT'S FOUND: Hair dye

WHAT TO LOOK FOR ON THE LABEL: p-Phenylenediamine, 1,4-benzenediamine; 1,4-phenylenediamine; 1,4 benzenediamine; ci 76060; oxidation base 10; p-aminoaniline; p-diaminobenzene; 1,4-benzenediamine (9ci); 1,4-diaminobenzene; 1,4-phenylenediamine; 4-aminoaniline

TALC

WHY IT'S BAD: Possibly linked to ovarian cancer when used in vaginal area; can be contaminated with asbestos if not tested (avoid inhaling!)[189]

WHERE IT'S FOUND: Cosmetics, body powders

WHAT TO LOOK FOR ON THE LABEL: Cosmetic talc, French chalk, talc (MG3H2 (SIO3) 4), agalite, asbestine, B 13, B 13 (mineral); B 13 (mineral), B 9, B 9 (talc), beaver white 200

HIGH HAZARD
ANTIBACTERIALS/ANTIMICROBIALS

WHY THEY'RE BAD: Known endocrine disruptors and environmental toxins; linked to cancer[190]

WHERE THEY'RE FOUND: Soap (liquid and bar), toothpaste

WHAT TO LOOK FOR ON THE LABEL: Triclosan, triclocarbon in the ingredients; if it says "antibacterial" or "antimicrobial" anywhere on the product, check to see if it says that alcohol is the active ingredient. That's okay.

FORMALDEHYDE

WHY IT'S BAD: Can cause skin irritation; linked to cancer[191]

WHERE IT'S FOUND: Soap/body wash, shampoo; liquid baby soap and shampoo

WHAT TO LOOK FOR ON THE LABEL: Formaldehyde, quaternium-15, DMDM hydantoin, imidazolidinyl urea, diazolidinyl urea, polyoxymethylene urea, sodium hydroxymethylglycinate, 2-bromo-2-nitropropane-1,3-diol (bronopol), glyoxal

ETHANOLAMINES

WHY THEY'RE BAD: Toxic and carcinogenic[192]

WHERE THEY'RE FOUND: Soaps, shampoos, conditioners, hair dyes, lotions, shaving creams, paraffin waxes, cosmetics, sunscreen, and fragrances

LABELED AS: MEA, DEA, TEA, triethanolamine, diethanolamine

HYDROQUINONE

WHY IT'S BAD: Linked to organ system toxicity, respiratory tract irritation, and cancer[193]

WHERE IT'S FOUND: Products for lightening/brightening skin, fading dark spots, etc.

WHAT TO LOOK FOR ON THE LABEL: Hydroquinone, tocopheryl acetate

PARABENS

WHY THEY'RE BAD: Endocrine disruption; linked to cancer and developmental and reproductive toxicity[194]

WHERE THEY'RE FOUND: Shampoos, conditioners, lotions, facial cleansers, deodorant, toothpaste, makeup

WHAT TO LOOK FOR ON THE LABEL: Ethylparaben, butylparaben, methylparaben, propylparaben, isobutylparaben, isopropylparaben, and any other ingredient ending in -paraben.

PHTHALATES

WHY THEY'RE BAD: Disrupt the endocrine system, harm the male reproductive system, can cause birth defects[195]

WHERE THEY'RE FOUND: Synthetic fragrance, hairspray, nail polish, makeup, shampoo, conditioner, facial cream and lotions

WHAT TO LOOK FOR ON THE LABEL: "Fragrance," "perfume," "parfum," BBzP, DBP, DEHP, DiDP

TITANIUM DIOXIDE (NANOPARTICLE)

WHY IT'S BAD: May cause cancer if inhaled (hazards of topical application/skin penetration unknown so caution is warranted because nanoparticles are unpredictable and can congregate around organs)[196]

WHERE IT'S FOUND: Sunscreen, cosmetics with sun protection

WHAT TO LOOK FOR ON THE LABEL: Powdered titanium dioxide, titanium dioxide

(Note: Avoid any sunscreen product that is not labeled "non-nano.")

TOLUENES

WHY THEY'RE BAD: Neurotoxic; potentially carcinogenic; exposure to vapors in pregnancy may harm developing fetus[197]

WHERE THEY'RE FOUND: Nail polish, hair dye

WHAT TO LOOK FOR ON THE LABEL: Benzene, methyl; benzene, methyl-; methyl- benzene; methylbenzene; toluol; antisal 1a; benzene, methyl-; methacide; methane, phenyl-

MODERATE HAZARD
AMMONIA

WHY IT'S BAD: May cause severe eye and respiratory irritation, skin
burns, kidney and liver damage, bronchitis and/or pneumonia[198]
WHERE IT'S FOUND: Hair dye
LABELED AS: Ammonia, ammonia hydroxide

PETROLEUM AND PETROLATUM

WHY THEY'RE BAD: May carry dangerous carcinogenic contaminants
(Note: White petroleum is not a dangerous ingredient, but any other
type is; plus the whole industry is dirty so I recommend avoiding any-
thing it produces.)[199]
WHERE THEY'RE FOUND: Lotion, cosmetics
LABELED AS: Petrolatum, petroleum jelly, paraffin oil, mineral oil

PROPYLENE GLYCOL

WHY IT'S BAD: Associated with allergic reactions that may affect skin,
eyes, and lungs[200]
WHERE IT'S FOUND: Vast range of personal care products
WHAT TO LOOK FOR ON THE LABEL: 1,2-dihydroxypropane; 1,2-pro-
panediol; 2-hydroxypropanol; methylethyl glycol; propane-1,2-diol;
1,2-dihydroxypropane; 1,2-propylene glycol; 1,2-propylenglykol (ger-
man) ; alpha-propyleneglycol; dowfrost; methylethylene glycol

WHY I'M ANTI-ANTIBACTERIAL

Triclosan (and its kissing cousin, triclocarban) are antimicrobial agents
found in many products (from clothing and kitchen gadgets to laundry
detergent, deodorant, and personal care cleansers). The triclosan promise is essentially that it keeps bacteria at bay. If you can forget for a
moment that it's a known endocrine disruptor and environmental toxin,
it may sound great that we have a chemical that can help protect us from
the invisible threat of microorganisms in our daily lives.

But, hello, reality: Most common illnesses (colds and flu) are caused by
viruses, not bacteria. Plus, triclosan is
rarely able to kill all the bacteria on your
skin, and those that survive learn how to
adapt, effectively turning into antibiotic-resistant bacteria.[201] That's bad. More
than 23,000 people die each year from
infections that defy our most potent antibiotic drugs.[202] Out of rising concern
about superbug bacteria, the FDA

> ## DR. TANYA'S PRESCRIPTION:
>
> White petroleum is perfectly safe to
> use because it has been specially
> refined to remove pollutants. Vase-
> line is a white petroleum brand you
> can feel safe using. I can't attest to
> generic petroleum jelly brands
> though. If your child has dry and irri-
> tated skin, plain Vaseline is fine.

recently banned the use of these antibacterial chemicals in hand soaps
and body washes starting in September 2017.[203] That's when they'll stop
being manufactured. But there's no telling how long this shit will stay on
shelves, so look alive and steer clear because—as per bloody usual—there's
a good chance the industry's replacement for triclosan will be a highly
regrettable substitution (translation: yet another hazmat du jour).

BODY

When you get right down to it, your body requires very little to be clean
and comfy. To avoid becoming stinky or sunburned, the main products
you'll need are soap, deodorant, lotion, and sunscreen. What you don't
need are products that can harm more than they help, like antiperspirants that plug your pores with aluminum (to stop you from sweating) or
sunscreens that put you at risk for breathing in nanoparticles (to protect
you from the sun).

DIY SKIN SAVERS

I buy most of my DIY supplies—in bulk—from Rose Mountain Herbs
(RoseMountainHerbs.com). I use certain ingredients, like castile soap

and essential oils, in homemade household cleaning potions, too, so it makes sense to keep a good quantity on hand.

BODY WASH: Combine $\frac{1}{2}$ cup castile soap, 2 tablespoons raw honey, 3 tablespoons glycerin, 1 teaspoon vitamin E oil, 1 teaspoon jojoba oil, and 10 drops of your favorite essential oil. Transfer to a pump bottle and refrigerate overnight before using.

BODY SCRUB: This body scrub is easy to make in small batches and leaves your skin super smooth after a shower. Combine equal parts of coconut oil and brown sugar in a small shallow bowl (just a few tablespoons of each is plenty for a couple of showers). Mash ingredients together with the back of a fork until a smooth paste is formed.

LOTION: Place $\frac{1}{2}$ cup shea butter in a small pan over low heat and stir in 2 tablespoons almond oil and 6 tablespoons coconut oil; heat until mixture is until melted. Transfer to a glass bowl and add 12 drops of essential oil (my favorites are ylang-ylang and orange). Refrigerate until cold, about 30 to 40 minutes. Whip mixture in food processor or blender until frothy. Transfer lotion to a small glass jar and store in a cool, dark place. It will last for about three months.

DIY DEODORANT

Combine $\frac{1}{3}$ cup coconut oil, $\frac{1}{3}$ cup arrow root powder, 2 tablespoons baking soda, and 13 drops of lavender essential oil. Whip in a blender for about a minute and transfer to a glass container. Refrigerate 30 minutes.

Note: If natural deodorant doesn't seem to work on you (translation: you totally reek—and mind you, I sure did!), I urge you to do the pit cleanse, which will unclog those poor armpit pores and make the natural deodorant work much better.

PIT CLEANSE

I am all about natural, but that doesn't mean I want to smell like a hippie from Haight-Ashbury. And guess what? After an armpit cleanse, the natural deodorant worked just as effectively as the conventional did.

You may need to repeat these steps five to 10 times a day at first, but I assure you that each day that number will decrease. My own cleanse ended after the fourth day (the average person takes between four to seven days to complete). Here's the four-step method that worked for me after I stopped using regular deodorant:

What you'll need:

I loofah
½ cup aluminum-free baking soda
    (or bentonite clay and cider
    vinegar, if you are sensitive to baking soda)
Soap and water
Any natural deodorant listed on page 277

PETE DROPS SCIENCE:

One unexpected problem—hand sanitizers increase the rate of absorption of some contaminants through your skin. Think of this: You are in a deli. As you enter, there's an inviting hand sanitizer waiting for you to press the plunger. You do. Then you get in line, place your order, and get a receipt with the number of your order. You hold it. If it's a receipt that uses thermal paper technology (which is really common), that hand sanitizer will increase your absorption of the bisphenol A that is lies on the receipt as dust, waiting to react to the ink embedded in the receipt that turns color when it interacts with BPA. BPA is one of the most notorious of endocrine-disrupting chemicals. It's bad news, especially for a developing fetus.

1. Use a loofah in the shower to remove dead skin and residue from your underarms.
2. Right after you step out of the shower, shake a little aluminum-free baking soda onto your wet armpits while they're still wet, then apply your natural deodorant.*
3. When you smell pit odor starting to rise, wash your pits with soap and water, and then apply another round of aluminum-free baking soda (or the clay mixture) followed by the natural deodorant again.

4. Repeat this process for up to two weeks or until your natural deodorant works for up to six hours.

If you are sensitive to baking soda, as some people are, mix 1 tablespoon bentonite clay with 1 teaspoon apple cider vinegar, then add 1 teaspoon filtered water to create a wet mixture (it will have the consistency of yogurt). Please note that bentonite clay has trace amounts of heavy metals. Use with caution. Store the mixture in glass and keep in cool place.

PREFERABLE TO PERFUME

In a laboratory analysis of a bunch of popular perfumes, the researchers with the Environmental Working Group and the Campaign for Safe Cosmetics found, on average, 14 undisclosed ingredients, many of which have not been studied for safety.[204]

Here are some cleaner scent options for you to consider:

LURK perfumes are made from 100 percent natural essential oils, resins, absolutes, and CO_2 extracts infused in certified organic jojoba and pure organic alcohol.

MOUNTAIN ROSE HERBS carries a huge selection of 100 percent pure, certified organic essential oils and softly scented hydrosols (flower waters).

RARE EARTH NATURALS provides 100 percent natural essential oil-based aromas, candles, diffusers, and more. Artisan-crafted in small batches, these products are made in the United States with products that are safe, synthetic-free, and responsibly sourced.

PETE DROPS SCIENCE:

Because the antibacterial additive triclosan has endocrine-disrupting properties, it has fallen out of favor with many consumers, In response, some personal care giants like Johnson & Johnson, Procter & Gamble, Colgate-Palmolive have started to use quats (short for quaternary ammonia compounds) in their place. Unfortunately, there's also research suggesting that while quats are not endocrine disruptors, some can impact your respiratory system and can have devastating impacts on fertility. Perhaps worse, the latest research with mice and rats suggests that ambient exposure to quats of either Mom during pregnancy or Dad prior to fertilization can lead to miscarriage and birth defects, including neural tube defects, in your baby. Simply being in a room where quats are used is sufficient to harm the rodents.

RICH HIPPIE uses old-fashioned methods to craft natural and organic perfumes.

PURE NATURAL DIVA carries synthetic free scents, as well as soaps, skincare, and more.

POUR LE MONDE has 100 percent natural perfumes in pretty bottles.

RED FLOWER sells an organic perfume concentrate and organic perfume oil roll-on.

GIVESCENT is made with a blend of oils and essential oils—free of alcohol, formaldehyde, parabens, phthalates, and sulfates. They are also cruelty-free and they donate a portion of every sale to Every Mother Counts and Women for Women International.

GODDESS GARDEN ORGANICS roll-on perfumes made from essential oils. Also carries sunscreen and facial care products.

SIMPLY AROMA, DOTERRA, and YOUNG LIVING are all great sources for essential oils.

TEETH

Clean teeth and fresh breath are more important than you might think. Proper oral hygiene plays a role in your health and may play a role in protecting you from heart disease, cancer, and diabetes. There's just no way around the need for using products as part of practicing good dental hygiene. But that doesn't mean you need to expose yourself to unnecessary and potentially toxic chemicals along the way. Here's a rundown of your best options.

DIY DENTAL CARE

TOOTHPASTE: Combine 3 tablespoons aluminum-free baking soda, 3 tablespoons coconut oil, 2 teaspoons Himalayan salt, 2 teaspoons xylitol, and 10 drops peppermint essential oil. Mash it all together till you get an even paste. Store in a cool area.

MOUTHWASH: Combine 1 cup filtered water, 2 teaspoons baking soda,

$^1/_2$ teaspoon xylitol, and 4 drops peppermint essential oil in glass container with a lid. Shake before using. Store in a cool area.

HAIR

According to some research, hairstylists are four times more likely to contract a chronic lung disease known as idiopathic pulmonary fibrosis.[205] And the risk is not limited to those who spend 40 hours a week working with these toxins. For example, over the last 10 years, the FDA has launched an investigation into a type of hair-straightening products known as "Brazilian" or "keratin treatments." Those products contain formaldehyde, a chemical the World Health Organization considers carcinogenic, and can result in serious hair damage and scalp burns. Even regular shampoos and conditioners can contain endocrine-disrupting phthalates and parabens. Here's what you need to know in order to make better choices among the near infinite number of options available.

DIY SHAMPOO AND CONDITIONER

Here are some great all-natural hair products you can make. If using a natural shampoo and conditioner combo seems to make your hair oily, try a different approach: Use the conditioner first and then the shampoo.

SHAMPOO: Combine $^3/_4$ cup liquid castile soap, $^1/_3$ cup coconut milk, $^1/_4$ cup honey, 2 teaspoons coconut oil, 1 tablespoon vitamin E oil, 25 drops *each* of lavender orange and ylang-ylang essential oils in a bowl, and mix until combined. Transfer to a bottle and shake. Refrigerate overnight.

Alternatively, if you want to try skipping the soap, you can try a baking soda rinse. Simply work about a quarter cup of baking soda through your locks (more or less depending on the length of your hair), and step into the shower. Rinse thoroughly. Don't do this too much or your hair will get oily. Twice a week is plenty.

CONDITIONER: Rinse your hair with ½ cup apple cider vinegar twice per week. Concentrate on your hair and not your scalp. Use this conditioner no more than twice a week or your hair may become oily.

HAIR TREATMENT: Rub a small amount of argan oil between the palms of your hands. Run your hands through your hair to distribute the oil, but concentrate on the tips.

FACE

Think about all the chemical shit we've already talked about. When you slather stuff like this on your face every morning, it is bound to have some kind of cumulative effect on your body, especially when you consider that the infinite combinations are never thoroughly tested to see how they interact. And as if that weren't enough, cosmetics frequently contain additional chemicals that help ingredients penetrate deeper into your skin. I do not consider "long-lasting" a selling point.

> ## DR. TANYA'S PRESCRIPTION:
>
> Personal care is a murky area. Although tons of products contain ingredients that are known endocrine disruptors, there are still so many brands that didn't seem to get the memo. This part of the industry isn't settled yet, meaning we don't know how much personal care products contribute or do not contribute to chronic disease and cancers. What I will say is I tend to focus my practice more on food and food packaging, where we know things can make an immediate impact in the health of your children. Personal care isn't an area I'm sure of yet, although whenever possible, it's still a good idea to avoid potentially dangerous ingredients from absorbing through your skin. So when it comes to the health of your family, this chapter is one where the most ambitious of mothers can follow, or leave it to later, when you can emotionally handle these changes.

That said, organic personal care products are not growing as fast as the food and clothing categories because it's a very difficult business. The world of personal care isn't as cut and dried as food is. It's überconfusing, to be honest. Formulating products that are effective and don't start molding is very difficult. Like, *very* difficult. And then finding natural dyes for blush and lipstick that don't have lead is even more difficult. (My friends in the beauty industry that actually test their shit

DR. TANYA'S PRESCRIPTION:

As I tell my patients, every healthy change, no matter how small, can benefit you and your family for the better. You may not be able to over-haul your entire household, but choose a few areas and go from there.

tell me this.) So I've tried to make it as simple as possible for you by showing you the best brands to consider. So if you have to go full ostrich like I did for a while, I get it. But whenever you do get started on this journey, just remember to take it slow and do one thing at a time. And perhaps focus on cleaning up your kids' personal care products before you tackle your own.

DIY CLEANSERS AND MOISTURIZERS

I love using my own simple handmade products for my daily facial routine. It's the only way to know for sure what I'm putting on my face. Most of these ingredients can be purchased easily from MountainRoseHerbs. com.

FACIAL CLEANSER: Combine $\frac{1}{2}$ cup grapeseed oil, $\frac{1}{4}$ cup castor oil, $\frac{1}{4}$ cup jojoba oil, and 15 drops of tea tree oil in an 8-ounce mason jar with a lid. Shake to combine. To use, simply massage a small amount of oil into your face and neck for about a minute, and then set a warm washcloth over your face. Let steam for a few seconds, then wipe clean. If you wear eye makeup, omit the tea tree oil so the cleanser will be safe to use around your eyes. Store in a cool, dark place.

FACIAL SCRUB: To exfoliate your skin safely, combine 1 tablespoon baking soda, $\frac{1}{2}$ tablespoon raw manuka honey, 1 drop of pure lavender essential oil, and 1 drop citrus essential oil in a small bowl. Gently massage the mixture onto wet skin and rinse thoroughly with lukewarm water. Pat dry and follow up with your favorite moisturizer.

FACIAL MOISTURIZER: I love a one-ingredient moisturizer, and coconut oil does the trick wonderfully. It has natural antibacterial and antifungal properties and works best as a nighttime moisturizer.

If you'd like a more complex moisturizer, combine 4 tablespoons grated beeswax, 1 teaspoon unrefined shea butter, and $1/2$ cup almond oil in a double boiler. Heat until mixture is melted. Transfer liquid into the blender and let it cool until mixture is room temperature. Meanwhile, in a separate bowl, combine 1 cup aloe vera gel, 12 drops ylang-ylang essential oil, and 1 teaspoon vitamin E. When the mixture reaches room temperature, start the blender and slowly add the aloe vera mixture. Transfer moisturizer to a glass container and use within six weeks.

DIY LIP BALM: Combine 3 tablespoons coconut oil, 2 tablespoons of cocoa butter, 2 tablespoons beeswax, and 3 drops of vitamin E oil in a glass measuring cup. Place the cup in the middle of a skillet filled with a few inches of water and warm gently over medium heat. The mixture will take about 15 minutes to melt completely. Remove from heat and stir in $3/4$ teaspoon (72 drops) of wintergreen essential oil. Use a medicine syringe to transfer liquid to 20 lip balm containers (you can buy these easily online).

HAIR COLOR AND NAILS

You know when you walk into a nail salon and all the technicians are wearing face masks and goggles? That's a sign you should reconsider whether a full set of nails is a wise idea. The reality is that people who work in hair and nail salons face serious health risks because of the products that are used in their industry.[206] The Occupational Safety and Health Administration publishes a list of a dozen different toxic chemicals that nail salon workers are regularly exposed to, including formaldehyde, toluene, and dibutyl phthalate.[207] For this exact reason, some people decide to go cold turkey with the salon visits in favor of the bare nail look. Or stop coloring their hair in favor of the natural silvery look. I'm going to let you decide where to draw the line. But hopefully these lists help you make a more informed choice about the products that are right for you.

FEMININE CARE PRODUCTS

To avoid putting potential toxins in your most private of places, ask yourself just a few simple questions: "Are they scented?" and "Are they bleached?" Answer yes to either of those questions and keep looking. Here's why.

Fragrances are loaded with phthalates, which can create a slew of problems we've talked a lot about already. And because your body's tissues down there are more permeable than other parts of your body, chemicals can enter your bloodstream through your vagina especially easily.[208] Bottom line: Steer clear of scented tampons, as well as scented pads, douches, and powders.

Bleaching creates a nasty by-product called dioxin, one of the most toxic substances on earth. While newer bleaching methods mean that the tampons of today have less dioxin in them than they once did, it's still there and the effect is cumulative.[209] Keep it out. Period (ha ha—but seriously).

FOR MORE INFORMATION ON PERSONAL CARE PRODUCTS

These three websites are well worth a visit:

MADESAFE.ORG. This third-party organization certifies products that you can use every day with confidence, knowing they are safely made from nontoxic ingredients. They also lab-test ingredients to ensure they are safe.

EWG.ORG/SKINDEEP. The Skin Deep database is an online safety guide for cosmetics and personal care products that combines ingredient lists with information from more than 50 standard toxicity and regulatory databases. The database provides easy-to-navigate safety ratings for tens of thousands of personal care products. And when you're out and about, make sure you've downloaded the EWG Healthy Living app on your phone to make informed shopping decisions. The app's barcode scanner can help you get detail about a product before you buy it.

SAFECOSMETICS.ORG. The Campaign for Safe Cosmetics is a project of the Breast Cancer Prevention Partners that provides a wealth of information about the chemicals to avoid in your personal care products.

NAMING NAMES:

SOAP AND BODY WASH

BAD

These brands are loaded with highly hazardous ingredients, such as unidentifiable fragrances, polyethylene glycols (PEGs), nanoscale titanium dioxide, parabens, p-Phenylenediamine, and propylene glycol.

Acca Kappa
Alaffia Authentic
Archipelago Botanicals
Aveeno
Bee and Flower
Burt's Bees
Caress
CeraVe
Cetaphil
Coast
Coastal Scents
CVS
Dial
Dove

Irish Spring
Ivory
Jergens
Johnson & Johnson
J.R. Watkins
Kiss My Face
Lever 2000
Neutrogena
Olay
Old Spice
Olivella
Palmers
Safeguard
SoftSoap
The Art of Shaving
The Body Shop
Thymes
Tone
Yardley
Yes To
Zest

BETTER

These brands use some moderate- or low-hazard ingredients, along with mostly natural/acceptable ingredients.

Attitude

Baby Dove Body Wash

Desert Essence

Dr. Woods Naturally

Earth Maiden Soap & Sundries

Kirk's Castile

Mrs. Meyer's

MoonDance

Nubian Heritage

One With Nature

Out of Africa

Shea Moisture

South of France

Sweet Grass Farm

Tom's of Maine

The Grandpa Soap Co.

The Soap Works

Weleda

BEST

These brands use only natural and low-hazard ingredients, with only essential oils for fragrance.

Auromere

Beautycounter

Biggs & Featherbelle

Dr. Bronner's

Dr. Desai Soap

EO

Farmaesthetics

Farmers' Market

Gemstone Organic

Kelly Teegarden

Level Naturals

Lusa Organics

Makes 3

Moon Valley Organics

Neal's Yard

Pacha

Pallas Athene

Plantlife

Remedies

Swanson

Zum Indigo Wild

LOTION

BAD

These brands use multiple high-hazard ingredients, including "fragrance."

Amlactin

Baby Magic

Baby Magic Bedtime Calming

Biosilk Therapy Original

Burt's Bees Milk & Honey

CeraVe

Curel Ultra Healing

Dial NutriSkin

Dove

Eos

Equate

Eucerin Original

Freeman C. Booth
Fruit of the Earth Cocoa Butter
Gold Bond Original
Gold Bond Ultimate Healing
Jergens Original
Jergens Ultra Healing
Johnson's Original Baby Lotion
Johnson's Bedtime Baby Lotion
Keri Nourishing
Keri Original
Lubriderm Advanced Therapy
Lubriderm Daily
Lubriderm Men's 3-in-1
Malibu Tan Hemp
Neutrogena Moisture Wrap
Neutrogena Sesame Lotion
Ocean Potion
Olay Ultra Moisture
Palmer's Cocoa Butter for Men
Perfect Purity
Queen Helene
Razac
St. Ives
Suave
Udderly Smooth
Vaseline Intensive Care
Vaseline Men

BETTER

These brands contain far fewer hazardous ingredients. Fragrance can be undisclosed but "phthalate-free."

Aveeno Active Naturals
Aveeno Active Naturals Baby
Aveeno Daily
Baby Dove
Cetaphil
Curel Ultra Healing
Giovanni
Giovanni 2chic
Mill Creek Baby Lotion
Puracy
Shikai

BEST

These brands contain no hazardous or very-low-hazardous ingredients.

Acure Body Lotion
Acure Yummy Baby Lotion
Avalon Organics
Babo Botanicals
Beautycounter
Bella Organics
Bubble & Bee
Carina Organics Baby Lotion
Deep Steep
Dr. Bronner's
Earth Mama Lotion
Earth Mama Body Butter
Episencial Babytime Soothing
    Cream
Now Solutions Sweet Almond
    Moisturizing Oil
Now Solutions Body Lotion

Nourish Organic
One Love Organics
Poofy Organics
Thinksport

DEODORANTS

Most commercial deodorants fight odor by killing bacteria and adding a layer of fragrance. Antiperspirants, on the other hand, inhibit sweat altogether because they contain aluminum, which temporarily plugs sweat ducts and keeps your armpits drier. However, one way the body releases toxins is through sweat, so that's why some theorize that using antiperspirants may raise breast cancer risk.[210]

BAD

These brands use high amounts of chemical fragrances, possible carcinogens, aluminum, petroleum, and allergenic ingredients that will affect sensitive skin.

Arrid
Axe
Degree
Dove
Gillette
Lady Speed Stick
Old Spice
Right Guard
Secret
Soft & Dri
Suave
Teen Spirit

BETTER

Products from these brands may contain some synthetic or unidentified fragrance ingredients, but instead of hazardous antiperspirant chemicals, they contain more natural solutions and essential oils.

Almay
Arm & Hammer
Ban
Jason Naturals
Kiss My Face
Mitchum
MoM Milk of Magnesia
Tom's of Maine
Weleda

DR. TANYA'S PRESCRIPTION:

Be careful when choosing deodorant for tweens and teens. There are a variety of natural/nonchemical versions that do work! Even for stinky teenage boys.

BEST

These brands use organic and natural antibacterial ingredients, like coconut oil, baking soda and/or and salts to control odor, essential oils, and more.

The Best Deodorant in the World
Bella Organics
Biotherm Deo Pure
Crystal
Earth Mama
Herban Cowboy
LavanilaA Miessence
Nature de France
Nature's Gate
Nourish Organic
Primal Pit Paste
Purelygreat Soapwalla
Schmidt's
Taylor's Pure & Natural

SUNSCREEN

Every day in America, 9,500 people are diagnosed with skin cancer.[211] So, no ifs ands or buts about it—sunscreen is essential. However, it is beyond absurd that so many of us block the sun's carcinogenic rays with products that are potentially carcinogenic (I mean, what the actual fuck?!). But don't forget that clothing counts in the sun-protection department, too. Wear hats and clothes labeled with a UPF (ultraviolet protection factor) to shield you from the sun's damage.

BAD

These brands use multiple high-hazard ingredients that can cause harm to various body systems via cancer, endocrine disruption, reproductive and central nervous system damage, and overall immune-system toxicity.

Australian Gold
Banana Boat
Block Up
Blue Lizard Original
Bull Frog
Coppertone
CVS
Equate
Hampton Sun
Hawaiian Tropic
Nature's Gate
Neutrogena
No-Ad
Pure Defense
Up & Up

BETTER

These brands contain far fewer hazardous ingredients.

All Good

All Terrain Aqua and TerraSport

Aveeno

Babyhampton Beach Bum

Be Natural Organics

Beauty Without Cruelty

Burnout

CeraVe

Coola Suncare

Nurture My Body

Ocean Potion

Star Naturals

Sunology

TruKid

Loving Naturals

True Natural

Raw Elements

Releve

Soleo Organics

Sunumbra

Thinksport and Thinkbaby

Zeb's Organics

BEST

Brands in this category are either free of questionable ingredients or contain only low-hazard ones.

Adorable Baby

Attitude Little Ones

Babo Botanicals

Badger

Bare Belly Organics

Beauty by Earth

Beauty Counter

Belly Button & Babies

California Baby

Dolphin Organics

Goddess Garden Organics

Jersey Kids

Kiss My Face Organics

TOOTHPASTE AND MOUTHWASH

BAD

These brands use fluoride (a neurotoxin) and other toxic or questionable ingredients, like triclosan, parabens, sodium lauryl sulfate, nitrites, and artificial sweeteners, flavors, and colors. Because these products go in your mouth, we are applying standards that are more in keeping with food-grade ingredients than those we use for other personal care products.

Aim toothpaste and mouthwash

Act mouthwash

Aquafresh toothpaste

Arm & Hammer toothpaste

Close-Up toothpaste

CloSys toothpaste

Colgate toothpaste and mouthwash

PETE DROPS SCIENCE:

And one of the most common ingredients in sunscreens, oxybenzone, kills coral at incredibly low concentrations. So those tourists snorkeling over Hawaiian and Caribbean reefs lathered up in sunscreen are contributing to the demise of a wonder of biodiversity.

Crest toothpaste and mouthwash
Euthymol toothpaste
Fluoridex toothpaste
Listerine mouthwash
Opalescence toothpaste
Orajel mouthwash
Parodontax toothpaste
Pepsodent toothpaste
PerioSciences toothpaste
Rembrandt toothpaste and mouthwash
Sensodyne toothpaste and mouthwash
Supersmile toothpaste
TheraBreath toothpaste and mouthwash
Ultrabrite toothpaste

BETTER

These brands are fluoride-free or offer fluoride-free products. They also avoid sodium lauryl sulfate and artificial flavors. Some products here contain bentonite clay; because this is a natural substance that is sometimes contaminated with trace amounts of heavy metals, I have indicated in parentheses any for which heavy-metals testing could not be confirmed.

Auromere toothpaste
Babyganics toothpaste
Briut Essentials toothpaste* (heavy-metal testing unknown)
Desert Essence toothpaste and mouthwash
Earthpaste toothpaste* (heavy-metal testing unknown)
Hello toothpaste
Kiss My Face toothpaste
Marvis toothpaste and mouthwash
Natural Dentist mouthwash
Now Food Xyliwhite toothpaste
Oxyfresh toothpaste and mouthwash
Sun Smile toothpaste
The Honest Co. toothpaste
The Dirt tooth powder* (heavy-metal testing unknown)
Tom's of Maine toothpaste and mouthwash
Uncle Harry's tooth powder* (heavy-metal testing unknown)

Usana toothpaste

Xlear Spry toothpaste and mouth spray

Xyloburst mouthwash

BEST

These brands use natural ingredients and are fluoride-free. Brands using bentonite clay have been tested for heavy metals.

Auromere mouthwash

Dr. Bronner's toothpaste

Earth's Best toothpaste

Green Beaver toothpaste

Hello Kids toothpaste

Jason toothpaste and mouthwash

Kingfisher Natural toothpaste

My Magic Mud toothpaste

Nature's Answer PerioBrite toothpaste and mouthwash

Nature's Gate toothpaste

Nature's Way mouthwash

Oral Essentials

PerioSciences mouthwash

The Dirt mouthwash

Weleda toothpaste

FEMININE PRODUCTS

This list includes tampons, single-use, and reusable pads and panty liners, and single use and reusable cups.

BAD

Products from the following brands contain either pesticides, EDCs, and/or toxins.

Always

Cardinal Health

Carefree

CVS Health

Kotex

Kroger

O.B.

Playtex

Signature Care

Stayfree

Tampax

U by Kotex

Walgreens

BETTER

These brands are not organic, so they may have pesticide residue, but they are free from chlorine, perfumes, and other toxic chemicals.

Charlie Banana

Glad Rags

Maxim

Seventh Generation Free & Clear

BEST

These brands are made from organic cotton, FDA-approved

medical-grade silicone, or other nontoxic materials.

Aiwo Cup
Anigan EvaCup
Anytime Cup
Athena Cup
Blossom Cup
Diamond Cup
Diva Cup
Emerita Organic
Femallay Cup
Femmy Cycle
Fleurcup
GladRags (organic cotton)
Goddess Cup
Gyn Cup
The Honest Co.
Intimina Lily Cup
Jolie Organic
IrisCup
L.
Lena
Lola
Lunette Cup
Maxim (organic)
MenstroCup
Moon Cup
Natracare
Natratouch
Orchidea
Organyc
Pink Daisy
Pixie Cup

Rose Cup
Seventh Generation
Organyc
SckoonCup
Veeda

FACIAL WASH AND MOISTURIZER

BAD

These brands use high-hazard ingredients, including synthetic fragrances that likely contain phthalates, ureas, parabens, PEGs, and tocopheryl acetate.

Acca Kappa
Ahava
Avalon Organics
Aveeno
Bare Minerals
Barefoot SOS
Basis
Beauty 360
Bioré
Bliss
Botanics
Burt's Bees
CeraVe
Cetaphil
Clean & Clear
Clearasil
CVS
Dermalogica

Dove

Dr. Murad

Earth Science

Equate

Eucerin

Formula 10.0.6

Fruit of the Earth

Garnier

Glytone

Jergens

Kate Somerville

Lab Series

Lindi

Lucky Tiger

Neutrogena

Nivea

Noxzema

Olay

Olivella

Organic Doctor

Origins

Oxy

Pacifica

Palmers

Paula's Choice

Philosophy

Pond's

Puritan's Pride

Purpose

Queen Helene

SebaMed

Simple

St. Ives

Vaseline

Vivant Skin Care

Wild Naturals

Yes To

BETTER

These brands are free of high-hazard ingredients; they use moderate- or low-hazard ingredients. Some use "fragrance" without 100 percent ingredient disclosure so we don't know what's inside.

Alba Botanica

Amara Organics

Bulldog

DHC

Everyday Coconut

Jason

Nubian Heritage

The Seaweed Bath Co.

BEST

These brands use only natural and/or low-hazard ingredients, with no fragrance other than essential oils, if any.

Acure

Attitude

Babo Botanicals

Badger

Beautycounter

California Baby

Desert Essence

Devita Natural Skin Care

Dr. Bronner's

Dr. Woods Naturally

Earth Maiden Soap & Sundries

Earth Mama

EO

Farmaesthetics

Garden Botanika

Gemstone Organic

Goddess Garden Organics

Honest Beauty

Juice Beauty

Kelly Teegarden

Kiss My Face

LuSa Organics

Mambino Organics

Mother Dirt

Myrrhaculous

Neal's Yard

North American Hemp

Nourish Organic

Novobellus

One Love Organics

Osmia Organics

Plantlife

Shea Moisture

TruKid

Weleda

SHAMPOO & CONDITIONER

BAD

These brands use an abundance
of highly hazardous ingredients

such as "fragrance" and moderate-
hazard ingredients (see list, page
262).

American Crew

Andre Walker Hair

Aussie Kids 3n1

Aussie

Aveeno Active Naturals

Aveeno Baby Shampoo & Wash

Axe

Bed Head

Biolage

Brazilian Keratin Therapy

Carol's Daughter

Clairol Hair Food

Clear Shampoo & Conditioners

Clean Freak Dry Shampoos

Dove

Dove Men+Care 2-in-1

Essence Ultime

Eucerin Baby

Equate

Fekkai

Galvin & Galvin London Kids

Garnier Fructis

Head & Shoulders

Herbal Essences

Herbal Essences Naked

Infusium 23

It's a 10

JHirmack Distinctions

John Frieda

Johnson's Original Baby Wash

Keratin Protein

L'Oréal Everpure

L'Oréal

Mane 'n Tail

Mixed Chicks

Mustela Bebe

Nexxus

Not Your Mother's Clean Freak
    (dry shampoo)

Old Spice 2-in-1

Pantene Pro-V

Pert 2in1

Prell

Psssst! Dry Shampoo

Redken

RenPure Solutions

RenPure Originals

Ricitos De Oro Baby Shampoo

Rusk

Selsun Blue

SoapBox Shampoos & Conditioners

SoCozy 3 in 1

Suave Kids

TresEmmé

Up & Up

Vo5

White Rain Kids 3 in 1

BETTER

These brands contain moderately
hazardous ingredients and perhaps undisclosed but "phthalate-
free" fragrance ingredients.

Alba Botanica

Baby Dove Shampoo

Babyganics

Babo Botanicals

Burt's Bees Baby Shampoo

Deep Steep

Now Solutions

BEST

Products in this group contain no
moderately or highly hazardous
ingredients.

Acure Organics

Alaffia Authentic

Attitude

Beautycounter

Bumble & Bee

California Baby

Carina Organics

Dessert Essence

Dolphin Organics

Dr. Bronner's baby shampoo & wash

Dr. Bronner's

Earth Mama

Earthley

Exactly! Organics

Fresh Monster Haircare for Kids

Johnson's Baby Naturals

Juice Organics

Laritelle

Miessence

Morrocco Method

Nine Naturals
Nubian Heritage
Puracy
Pure Haven Essentials
Rahua
Shea Moisture baby shampoo
    & wash
Shea Moisture
The Honest Co.
Thinkbaby
Thinksport

STYLING PRODUCTS

BAD

These brands use highly hazardous ingredients in a majority of their products.

Alberto VO5
Agadir
American Crew
Attitude Little Ones
Awapuhi Wild Ginger by Paul
    Mitchell
Biosilk
Boots Botanics
Bosley
Bumble and bumble
Cantu
Cantu Kids
Cheer Chics
Condition

Cristophe
CurlFriends
Curly Sexy Hair
Fairy Tales
Fekkai
Frizz Ease
Garnier Fructis
Global Keratin
Got 2b
Herbal Essences
ISO
It's a 10
Kenra
KeraFiber
Klorane
KMS
La Coupe
Marc Anthony
Michael O'Rourke
Mill Creek
My Secret Hair
Naturelle
Nexxus
Nothing But Curl
Pantene Pro-V
Paul Mitchell
Prive
Pureology
Redken
Sally Hershberger
Salon Grafix
Samy
Schwarzkopf

Samy Fat Hair

Sexy Hair Concepts

Smooth 'n Shine

Sta-Sof-Fro

Thicker Fuller Hair

Tigi Bed Head

TresEmmé

VaVoom by Matrix

Volumax

BETTER

These brands use fewer highly hazardous ingredients, along with numerous moderate- to low-hazard ones.

Andalou Naturals

Aquage

Aqua Net

As I Am Naturally

Aussie

Aveda

Axe

Bain De Terre

Beauty Without Cruelty

Biolage by Matrix

California Smooth

Carol's Daughter

CHI

Consort for Men

CVS

DermOrganic

Dove Style+care

Eden BodyWorks

Elasta

Enjoy Professional Hair Care

Eva NYC

Eufora

Fantasia IC

Final Net

Finesse

Focus 21

Free & Clear

Freeze It

GG Gatsby

Giovanni

Goldwell

Hair Rules

Herbal Essences Naked

J Beverly Hills

John Frieda

Joico

Kerastase

Kiss My Face

L'Anza

Living proof

L'Oréal

Marc Anthony True Professional

Mink Difference

Motions

Neuma

Nioxin

Not Your Mother's

Nubian Heritage

NuHair

OGX

OSiS+

Peter Lamas
Phyto
Professional by Nature's Therapy
Rave
Renpure Organics
Rusk
Sebastian
ShiKai Color Reflect
Simply Smooth
So Cozy
Suave
Suave for Kids
The Dry Look for Men
Toni & Guy Glamour
Trevor Sorbie
Unite
Vidal Sassoon Pro Series
Vitalis

BEST

Any questionable ingredients found here are on the low-hazard end of the spectrum.

Andalou Naturals
Aromatica
Beautycounter
Carina Botanical
Carina Pure & Natural
Healing-Scents
Herbal Choice Mari Organic
Little Green
Maia's Mineral Galaxy

Morrocco Method
Primal Life Organics
Qet Botanicals
Rare Elements

MAKEUP

BAD

These brands use multiple highly hazardous ingredients, such as fragrance and carcinogens. For brands that have only a particular product qualifying as *bad,* that product is specified in parentheses. Unless otherwise indicated, all brands on the "bad" list rank in the *better* category for eyeliners.

Benefit
Black Radiance (Eyeliners)
Boots No7 (Moisture Drench Lipstick)
Champneys
CoverGirl
Estée Lauder
Lancôme
L'Oréal
MAC
Maybelline
Physicians Formula
Revlon (Moon Drops Creme Lipstick)
Rimmel

Smashbox
Wet n Wild (Silk Finish Lipstick)

Stila
Too Faced

BETTER

These brands contain mostly low- to moderate-hazard ingredients; some may contain minimal amounts of high-hazard ingredients. For brands that have only a particular product that ranks as *better,* that product is specified in parentheses.

Afterglow
Almay
Anastasia Beverly Hills
Black Radiance
Bobbi Brown
Boots No7
Clinique
e.l.f.
Kat Von D
L.A. Colors
Maybelline (Color Sensation Lipcolor, SuperStay 24 2-Step Lipcolor)
Mineral Hygienics
NARS
Neutrogena
NYX
Physicians Formula
Wet n Wild
Revlon
Sephora

BEST

These brands contain the lowest amounts of toxins and carcinogens, if any. Many of these brands are certified organic as well. Note: Only the brands marked with an asterisk are sufficiently transparent about heavy metals—either they have information on their site about testing for heavy metals or have opted to used acceptable synthetic hues because they were unable to find enough natural hues without dangerous levels of heavy metals. This is not to say that brands without an asterisk do have heavy metals—just that they do not provide enough information for me to be sure. No company can claim to be heavy metal free because all processing contains contamination, however, the less the better. Therefore, I've ranked them on their other ingredients first and you can decide.

Au Naturale Cosmetics*
Batty's Bath *
Beautycounter *
BeeyoutifulSkin
Bella Mari

Cate McNabb

Coastal Classic Creations

Daisy Blue Naturals

Eco Lips

Everyday Minerals

Healing-Scents

Isoi

Living Nature

Logono

Maia's

Omiana*

Qet Botanicals

RawSkin Ceuticals

Real Purity

Rejuva

RMS*

Sally B's*

Sante

The Organic Face

Valana

W3LL People

Zao Certified Organic Makeup

HAIR COLOR

BAD

These brands are best avoided because they use carcinogens and other highly hazardous ingredients.

Clairol Nice 'n Easy with Color Blend Technology

Creme of Nature Exotic Shine Hair Color

Garnier Nutrisse

Garnier Olia

John Frieda Brilliant Brunette

Joico Vero K-Pak Color

L'Oréal Paris Preference Fade-Defying Color + Shine System

L'Oréal Paris Superior Preference Mousse Absolue Automatic Reusable Color

Redkin Color Extend

Revlon Colorsilk Beautiful Color

BETTER

These brands use far fewer hazardous ingredients, many of which are less concerning than other high- or moderate-hazard ingredients (i.e. the potential negative health effects are often less severe).

Arctic Fox

Clairol Nice 'n Easy Root Touch Up

Dark & Lovely

Fanci-Full

Garnier Color Styler Intense Wash-Out

Herbatint

Garnier Olia

John Frieda Color Refreshing Gloss

John Frieda Sheer Blonde Go Blonder

Just for Men

Lime Crime Unicorn Hair
L'Oréal Paris Professional INOA
    Ammonia Free
L'Oréal Paris Professional Majirel
L'Oréal Paris Root Cover
Madison Reed
Marc Anthony True Professional
Naturetint
Naturigin
Overtone
Pravana
Manic Panic
Redken Chromatics Beyond Cover
    Hair Color
Revlon Color Stay
Special Effects
Sun-In
Tints of Nature

BEST

These brands contain very low amounts of toxins and carcinogens, if any.

Desert Shadow
Light Mountain Natural Henna
Logona Herbal Hair Color
Morocco Method Simply Pure
    Henna
Palette by Nature
Rainbow Henna
Saach Organics
Sante Herbal Hair Color
Surya Brazil Henna Powder

NAIL POLISH

BAD

These brands use a variety of unacceptable toxic chemicals in their products, such as formaldehyde, formaldehyde resin, toluene, DBP, parabens, camphor, lead, ethyl tosylamide, xylene and/or triphenyl phosphate (TPHP).

CoverGirl
Essie
Maybelline
Milani
OPI
Orly
Revlon
Sally Hansen
Sephora
Ulta
Wet n Wild

BETTER

These brands have fewer toxic chemicals.

3-FREE (NO FORMALDEHYDE, TOLUENE OR DBP):

Beauty Without Cruelty
Keeki
Kleancolor
NARS
Poofy Organics (also camphor-free)
Pure ICE

Sheswai

Sinful Colors

5-FREE (NO FORMALDEHYDE, FORMALDEHYDE RESIN, TOLUENE, DBP, CAMPHOR):

Bliss Genius

Deborah Lippmann

Dr.'s Remedy

Ella+Mila

Ginger + Liz

Habit Cosmetics

Jamberry

Jenna Hipp

JINsoon

Julep

L'Oréal

Obsessive Compulsive Cosmetics

Piggy Paint

Priti NYC

RGB

Snails (also paraben-free)

Spa Rituals

Suncoat

Tenoverten

Void Beauty

Zoya

BEST

These brands have the fewest toxic chemicals.

7-FREE (NO FORMALDEHYDE, FORMALDEHYDE RESIN, TOLUENE, DBP, CAMPHOR, ETHYL TOSYLAMIDE, XYLENE):

Butter London

Londontown Lakur

LVX

Pacifica

Smith & Cult

Trust Fund Beauty

9-FREE (NO FORMALDEHYDE, FORMALDEHYDE RESIN, TOLUENE, DBP, PARABENS, CAMPHOR, LEAD, ETHYL TOSYLAMIDE, XYLENE):

100% Pure

Acquarella

Honeybee Gardens

Kid Licks

Scotch Naturals and Hopscotch Kids

Suncoat Girl

CONCLUSION

I KNOW I'VE THROWN a lot at you and you may want to run and hide right now, but here's the takeaway:

> *You have great power to affect change within your home and far beyond it, if you so choose.*

Years ago, my oldest son received a McDonald's certificate as a reward for improving in math in early grade school. I was furious that fast food was being promoted in his public school and decided I was going to do something about it. I showed up at the McDonald's' shareholder meeting, gave the CEO a piece of my mind, and then chastised McDonald's publicly for advertising their toxic junk food to my son in his public school.

Because I lead a thriving online community, my girls were listening and tweeting everything I said. My words were their words. I was standing up for them as well as myself, and because they amplified the message, I was quoted in national newspapers and media outlets all over the world.

I did it again the following year, but this time McDonald's was waiting for me. Get this: they had an armed guard following me around! This was obviously intended to intimidate me but it didn't work. What it told me most clearly was that *they were the fearful ones.*

Once more, my words were national news.

The following year, McDonald's was so afraid of losing control of their message that they changed the rules for shareholders meetings to prevent me, and others like me, from entering. For them, one mom and her voice are something to fear, because they recognize that the new age of transparency and female empowerment has arrived, and I represent millions of women who are speaking up.

I could tell you similar stories about Monsanto—so scared of me and my Mamavation blogger network that, as they were recruiting bloggers for a campaign, they called me out personally and made it clear I didn't align with them. Result: it just made me more more beloved and trusted by more information-hungry moms than ever! Thanks guys!

EDCs and the harm being unleashed by them throughout our environment and within our bodies are a very inconvenient truth for these types of companies—and, for us, EDCs have become a tragic fact of life. But the science that exposes these truths is not going to go away.

Big Industry and their friends will come down hard on this book, saying that my opinions mean nothing because I'm just a *mommy blogger*. They are guilty of framing the truth to suit their needs. Saying that about me is an attempt to discredit and trivialize me—and you. It is an act of fear. (Never mind that they employ communication professionals like me to get their messages out to the public.) Trivializing me and the small amounts of chemicals that can harm us is also how they trivialize you. You don't need to worry your pretty little head about all these things, they say. Take it from the big boys who know what they are doing. But I think you've had enough of the boys club. I certainly have. They don't get to win anymore. I have told you exactly what Big Industry doesn't want you to know. I've brought you straight facts from the scientific community—independent toxicologists and endocrinologists—that are *not* on the Big Industry payroll.

This book isn't about me. It's about you taking firm hold of power that is rightfully yours—as a woman, as a mother, and as a leader. You are a force to be reckoned with. Bottom line: their fear is warranted.

So what should you do?

1. Share this message with as many people that will listen to you.
2. Support the brands that are producing food and other consumer products in such a way that respects our families and the future of our children.
3. When you hear "dose equals the poison," say "small amounts matter."
4. Remember how powerful you are and don't be belittled!

Now go for it, sister, and make awesome happen!

ACKNOWLEDGMENTS

Without my husband Mark Segedie, I would not be able to do what I do. Thank you for all your patience, encouragement, trust and love.

Thank you to Pete Myers & Dr. Tanya Altmann who helped guide and support me along the way. You are the rock stars here! Thank you for sharing your knowledge and always being there for me.

This book is written in memory of my father, aunt and uncle: James Edwin Strand, Lynda Strand & Jan Borhaug—all close relatives that died of cancer. Cancer ripped my family apart years ago. I work hard everyday to keep that from happening to others.

Thank you to my mom who never broke my spirit and always encouraged me to find solutions to challenges. You're my best friend! And thank you for being the best nanny in the world!

Thank you to Carole & Ken Segedie, my in-laws, who are incredibly supportive and thoughtful...and who put up with my green antics. To my cousins Yvonne Thomas & Em Kucklick who are the closest things I have to sisters. To my other cousin Paul Borhaug who inspires me with his lifestyle in Norway avoiding single use items like paper towels and composting.

Thank you to the Mamavation team: Miriam Harris, Sally Ekus, Cheri Johnson, Ashley Saunders, Gina Badalaty, Tracy Warner-Skogstad, Michelle Evans, Tracy Loeppky, Laura Saville, Elizabeth Bruno, Alicia Benjamin, Angela Bishop, Cheri Johnson & Megan McClain. And thank you for the help reviewing Amy Ziff & Lindsay Dahl.

I've had so many amazing friends over the years that have helped me hone my passion: Robyn O'Brien, Zuri Star, Ashley Koff RD, Andrea Donsky, Lori Popewitz Alper, Lindsay Dahl, Jennifer McGruther, Henry

Rowlands, Pamm Larry, Joanne Liberty, Jeanae Osborne, Jeanie Swan, Kia Ruiz, Kristine Moran, Megan Carter, Lydia Steele Richmond, Angela England, Ashley Covelli, Carey Gillam, Maria Quijada, Monica Young, Rebecca Ga, Stacy Malkan, Susan Cann, Suzanna Marcus, Alicia Voorhies, Alyssa Curran, Doris Tan, Erin Davy, Anna Lappe, Hannah Crum, Kelly Olexa, Barbara Jones, Kristina Drociak, Gary Hirshberg, Mike Schade, Meredith Sloane, Mia Voss, Micaela Preston, Monica Olivas, Rachael Herrscher, Pauline Campos, Rachel Pitzel, Samuel Anthony Harwit, Stacey Ferguson, Tshaka Armstrong, Carlotta Mast, Alli Worthington, Aaronica Cole, Rachel Sarnoff, Paige Wolf, Marci Zaroff, Laura Batcha, Maggie McNeil. Mostly girl power. *winks*

But most of all, thank you to all of you. This book isn't about me, it's about you. Thank you for allowing me to be your girlfriend as you kick the shit out these hormone disrupting chemicals. You are awesome my dear. Just awesome!

ENDNOTES

Introduction Chapter

1. http://eur-lex.europa.eu/LexUriServ/LexUriServ.do?uri=CONSLEG:1976L0768:20100301:en:PDF
2. http://www.foodmatters.com/article/8-additives-from-the-us-that-are-banned-in-other-countries
3. https://ehp.niehs.nih.gov/121-a340/
4. https://www.ams.usda.gov/datasets/pdp
5. https://www.fda.gov/downloads/AnimalVeterinary/SafetyHealth/AntimicrobialResistance/NationalAntimicrobialResistanceMonitoringSystem/UCM442212.pdf
6. https://silentspring.org/research-update/toxic-chemicals-widespread-household-dust
7. https://madesafe.org/science/toxicant-database/phthalates/
8. https://www.smithsonianmag.com/science-nature/why-chemicals-us-are-still-innocent-until-proven-guilty-180959818/
9. https://www.cdc.gov/healthyschools/obesity/facts.htm
10. https://www.cdc.gov/ncbddd/developmentaldisabilities/about.html#ref
11. https://www.cdc.gov/nchs/fastats/asthma.htm
12. https://www.cdc.gov/ncbddd/adhd/data.html
13. http://home.allergicchild.com/prevalence-of-allergies-in-todays-world/
14. https://www.cdc.gov/nchs/data/databriefs/db291.pdf
15. https://www.niehs.nih.gov/health/topics/agents/endocrine/index.cfm
16. https://endocrinedisruption.org/interactive-tools/endocrine-basics
17. https://www.nytimes.com/2017/03/11/opinion/sunday/are-your-sperm-in-trouble.html
18. https://academic.oup.com/humupd/article-abstract/23/6/646/4035689?redirectedFrom=fulltext
19. http://journals.lww.com/greenjournal/Abstract/2017/05001/Increased_Incidence_of_Endometrial_Cancer.19.aspx
20. Our Stolen Future. Book by Theo Colburn & Pete Myers
21. https://ehp.niehs.nih.gov/wp-content/uploads/advpub/2014/10/ehp.1408163.acco.pdf
22. https://www.endocrine.org/-/media/endosociety/files/advocacy-and-outreach/important-documents/introduction-to-endocrine-disrupting-chemicals.pdf
23. https://www.ncbi.nlm.nih.gov/pubmed/27765541
24. https://academic.oup.com/edrv/article/33/3/378/2354852
25. Our Stolen Future, p. 169-170, 197, 205-7

26. Sent to pete (by-products of EDCs can be more dangerous than parent chemical)
27. Sent to pete (emerging field of epigenetics connected to asthma, autism, diabetes, obesity, infertility, reproductive diseases, cardiovascular dysfunction and schizophrenia)
28. Sent to pete (you can pass these issues down to your great great grandchildren)
29. Stolen Future (enter body when you are a fetus)
30. https://www.livescience.com/10957-pesticide-turns-male-frogs-females.html
31. https://www.nrdc.org/sites/default/files/safety-loophole-for-chemicals -in-food-report.pdf
32. https://www.nrdc.org/sites/default/files/safety-loophole-for-chemicals -in-food-report.pdf
33. https://www.cancer.org/cancer/malignant-mesothelioma/about/ key-statistics.html
34. https://www.scientificamerican.com/article/bpa-free-plastic-containers -may-be-just-as-hazardous/
35. https://dash.harvard.edu/bitstream/handle/1/8965615/Daum06 .html?sequence=2
36. http://www.ucsusa.org/our-work/center-science-and-democracy /promoting-scientific-integrity/bisphenol-a.html#.WigR_Tdrw2w
37. http://www.ucsusa.org/our-work/center-science-and-democracy /promoting-scientific-integrity/bisphenol-a.html#.WigR_Tdrw2w
38. https://www.cbsnews.com/news/toxic-secret-07-11-2002/
39. https://www.newyorker.com/magazine/2014/02/10/a-valuable-reputation
40. https://www.forbes.com/sites/bethhoffman/2013/07/02/gmo-crops -mean-more-herbicide-not-less/#700ba8733cd5
41. https://www.centerforfoodsafety.org/issues/311/ge-foods/about-ge-foods
42. https://www.huffingtonpost.com/carey-gillam/tests-show-monsanto -weed_b_12950444.html...
43. http://www.justlabelit.org/right-to-know-center/labeling-around-the-world/
44. Our Stolen Future pg 87-109
45. https://www.ncbi.nlm.nih.gov/pmc/articles/PMC2984095/
46. https://www.usda.gov/media/blog/2013/05/17/organic-101-can-gmos-be -used-organic-products
47. https://www.nytimes.com/interactive/2017/10/21/us/document-EPA -Chlorpyrifos-FOIA-Emails-to-NYT.html
48. https://www.huffingtonpost.com/entry/usda-drops-plan-to-test-for -monsanto-weed-killer-in_us_58d2db4ee4b062043ad4af84
49. https://www.self.com/story/trumps-budget-plan-endocrine-disruptors
50. http://www.cnn.com/2013/11/01/health/kraft-macaroni-cheese-dyes /index.html
51. https://blog.generalmills.com/2015/06/a-big-commitment-for-big-g-cereal/
52. http://www.dannonpledge.com/
53. https://www.npr.org/sections/thesalt/2016/10/07/497033243/perdue -goes-almost-antibiotic-free
54. http://www.chicagotribune.com/business/ct-mcdonalds-antibiotics -0824-biz-20170823-story.html
55. https://www.womensvoices.org/2017/06/12/sc-johnson-announces

-disclosure-368-allergens-cleaning-products/

56. http://saferchemicals.org/2017/03/07/target-raises-the-bar-for-retailers -in-driving-harmful-chemicals-out-of-products/

57. https://cvshealth.com/newsroom/press-releases/cvs-health-takes-major -step-to-address-chemicals-of-consumer-concern

Chapter One

58. Antibiotics, http://www.ucsusa.org/food_and_agriculture/our-failing-food-system/industrial-agriculture/prescription-for-trouble.html#.WiiJFDdrw2w,

59. hormones, https://www.fda.gov/AnimalVeterinary/SafetyHealth/ ProductSafetyInformation/ucm055436.htm and

60. GMO feed, http://www.beefissuesquarterly.com/beefissuesquarterly .aspx?id=5672

61. http://newsroom.heart.org/news/children-should-eat-less-than-25 -grams-of-added-sugars-daily

62. https://www.accessdata.fda.gov/scripts/cdrh/cfdocs/cfcfr/cfrsearch .cfm?fr=501.22

63. https://www.consumerreports.org/cro/magazine/2015/01/how-much -arsenic-is-in-your-rice/index.htm

64. http://news.berkeley.edu/2011/04/20/prenatal-pesticide-exposure-lower-iq/

65. https://ehp.niehs.nih.gov/1408197/

66. https://well.blogs.nytimes.com/2016/02/15/more-omega-3-in-organic -meat-and-milk-review-of-studies-says/

67. http://online.liebertpub.com/doi/abs/10.1089/fpd.2016.2161

68. https://www.reuters.com/article/us-health-chemicals-environment/ toxic-chemicals-tied-to-340-billion-in-u-s-health-costs-and-lost-wages -idUSKBN12H2KB

69. https://www.reuters.com/article/us-health-chemicals-environment /toxic-chemicals-tied-to-340-billion-in-u-s-health-costs-and-lost-wages -idUSKBN12H2KB

70. https://www.scientificamerican.com/article/does-artificial-food -coloring-contribute-to-adhd-in-children/

71. https://cspinet.org/new/201006291.html

72. https://www.nytimes.com/interactive/2016/10/09/magazine/blue-food -coloring-mars-company.html

73. http://ns.umich.edu/new/releases/1760-food-dye-can-cause-severe -allergic-reactions

74. http://adc.bmj.com/content/89/6/506.short

75. http://adc.bmj.com/content/89/6/506.short

76. http://www.nejm.org/doi/full/10.1056/NEJM100407283310414#t=article

77. http://abcnews.go.com/Health/california-woman-sues-pepsicos -tropicana-alleging-deceptive-advertising/story?id=15394357

78. http://time.com/3894216/trans-fat-hydrogenated-oil/

79. https://www.nytimes.com/2016/05/22/upshot/it-isnt-easy-to-figure-out -which-foods-contain-sugar.html, 66 lbs. Of added sugar each year, http://sugarscience.ucsf.edu/the-growing-concern-of-overconsumption /#.Wi2z4jdrw2w

80. https://academic.oup.com/biomedgerontology/article/65A/8/809/572081
81. https://archive.unews.utah.edu/news_releases/fructose-more-toxic-than
-table-sugar-in-mice/
82. https://www.health.harvard.edu/press_releases/too-much-fructose-a
-hazard-for-heart-health
83. http://www.heart.org/HEARTORG/HealthyLiving/HealthyEating
/Nutrition/Sugar-101_UCM_306024_Article.jsp#
84. http://www.cnn.com/2016/01/18/health/where-do-we-stand-artificial
-sweeteners/index.html
85. https://www.scientificamerican.com/article/does-artificial-food
-coloring-contribute-to-adhd-in-children/
86. https://www.ncbi.nlm.nih.gov/pmc/articles/PMC471857/
87. https://www.scientificamerican.com/article/bha-and-bht-a-case-for-fresh/
88. https://emergency.cdc.gov/agent/bromine/basics/facts.asp
89. https://www.ewg.org/release/most-us-apples-coated-chemical-banned
-europe-0#.WilpJTdrw2w
90. https://www.ewg.org/research/pcbs-farmed-salmon#.WilqEDdrw2w,
91. http://onlinelibrary.wiley.com/doi/10.1046/j.1365-2621.1998.3320139.x/full
92. https://www.reuters.com/article/us-usa-food-gmo-vote/u-s-gmo-food
-labeling-bill-passes-senate-idUSKCN0ZO08N
93. http://healthpsych.psy.vanderbilt.edu/HealthPsych/olestra_katie
.html#The%20Side%20Effects%20of%20Olestra
94. https://www.livescience.com/36206-truth-potassium-bromate-food
-additive.html
95. https://www.bcpp.org/resource/rbgh-rbst/
96. http://time.com/4291505/when-vegetable-oil-isnt-as-healthy-as-you
-think/, https://www.ncbi.nlm.nih.gov/pmc/articles/PMC4029104/

Chapter Two

97. https://www.ewg.org/research/many-fast-food-wrappers-still-coated
-pfcs-kin-carcinogenic-teflon-chemical#.Wil5Rjdrw2w
98. http://pubs.acs.org/doi/abs/10.1021/acs.estlett.6b00435
99. https://www.ewg.org/release/toxic-truth-about-new-generation-nonstick
-and-waterproof-chemicals#.Wil8Gzdrw2w
100. http://www.dispatch.com/news/20170213/dupont-to-pay-670-million-to
-settle-c8-lawsuits
101. http://www.sciencedirect.com/science/article/pii/S0013935116302407
102. https://ehp.niehs.nih.gov/1409143/,
103. https://theintercept.com/2017/06/17/new-teflon-toxin-found-in-north
-carolina-drinking-water/
104. http://www.ceh.org/new-report-kicking-can/
105. https://www.ncbi.nlm.nih.gov/pmc/articles/PMC2854718/?tool=pmcentrez
106. https://www.epa.gov/sites/production/files/2016-09/documents/vinyl
-chloride.pdf
107. http://saferchemicals.org/2014/05/26/styrene-and-styrofoam-101-2/
108. https://www.savesfbay.org/sites/default/files/Polystyrene%20fact%20
sheet_MASTER.pdf

109. https://www.ncbi.nlm.nih.gov/pmc/articles/PMC3222987/
110. https://www.epa.gov/sites/production/files/2016-09/documents/vinyl
     -chloride.pdf
111. http://saferchemicals.org/2014/05/26/styrene-and-styrofoam-101-2/
112. http://www.foodpackagingforum.org/news/chemicals-of-concern-in-the
     -circular-economy
113. http://www.nytimes.com/1993/02/10/health/wooden-cutting-boards
     -found-safer-than-plastic.html
114. https://www.ewg.org/research/many-fast-food-wrappers-still-coated
     -pfcs-kin-carcinogenic-teflon-chemical#.WimUhzdrw2x
115. http://www.foodpackagingforum.org/news/chemicals-in-coatings-of
     -coffee-to-go-cups
116. http://www.foodpackagingforum.org/news/chemicals-in-coatings-of
     -coffee-to-go-cups

Chapter Three

117. http://www.panna.org/human-health-harms/cancer
118. https://ehp.niehs.nih.gov/1408660/
119. http://www.cdpr.ca.gov/docs/enforce/residue/resi2015/rsfr2015.htm
120. https://www.ewg.org/foodnews/dirty_dozen_list.php
121. https://www.ewg.org/foodnews/dirty_dozen_list.php
122. https://www.ecowatch.com/pesticides-organic-farming-2292594453.html
123. G. Edwards-Jones, O. Howells, The origin and hazard of inputs to crop
     protection in organic farming systems: Are they sustainable? Arg. Syst. 67,
     31-47 (2001)
124. G. Zehnder, G.M. Gurr, S. Kühne, M.R. Wade, S. D. Wratten, E. Wyss, Arthropod
     pest management in organic crops. Annu. Rev. Entomol. 52, 57-80 (2007)

Chapter Four

125. https://www.cornucopia.org/dairy_brand_ratings/
126. https://www.ncbi.nlm.nih.gov/pmc/articles/PMC1367841/
127. https://ehp.niehs.nih.gov/1409518/
128. https://www.ncbi.nlm.nih.gov/pmc/articles/PMC3226524/
129. https://www.organic-center.org/wp-content/uploads/2016/07/TOC
     _Report_AntibioticResistance_FINAL.pdf
130. http://rspb.royalsocietypublishing.org/content/283/1831/20160150.full
131. https://www.cambridge.org/core/journals/british-journal-of-nutrition
     /article/higher-pufa-and-n3-pufa-conjugated-linoleic-acid-tocopherol
     -and-iron-but-lower-iodine-and-selenium-concentrations-in-organic
     -milk-a-systematic-literature-review-and-meta and redundancy
     -analyses/A7587A524F4235D8E98423E1F73B6C05
132. https://www.consumerreports.org/cro/food/how-safe-is-your-ground-beef
133. https://www.npr.org/sections/thesalt/2014/12/23/370377902/farm-fresh
     -natural-eggs-not-always-what-they-re-cracked-up-to-be
134. https://www.npr.org/sections/thesalt/2014/12/23/370377902/farm-fresh
     -natural-eggs-not-always-what-they-re-cracked-up-to-be
135. https://www.livescience.com/47032-time-for-us-to-ban-ractopamine.html

136. https://www.ewg.org/research/ewgs-good-seafood-guide/executive
-summary#.WinziTdrw2w

137. https://www.consumerreports.org/cro/2012/08/the-benefits-and-risks
-of-eating-fish/index.htm

138. http://www.who.int/features/qa/cancer-red-meat/en/

Chapter Six

139. https://academic.oup.com/edrv/article/30/4/293/2355049

140. Our Stolen Future

141. http://www.newsweek.com/syrias-use-chlorine-gas-and-weapons
-history-496568

142. https://www.fda.gov/Cosmetics/ProductsIngredients/Ingredients
/ucm388821.htm

143. https://www.ewg.org/enviroblog/2008/05/cheatsheet-phthalates#
.WioGHzdrw2w

144. https://www.niehs.nih.gov/research/supported/sep/2015/phthalate
/index.cfm

145. https://academic.oup.com/jcem/article/100/4/1267/2815068

146. http://sd33.senate.ca.gov/news/2017-10-15-governor-brown-signs
-cleaning-product-right-know-act-create-first-nation-label-law

147. https://www.livescience.com/1737-truth-green-cleaning-products.html

148. https://www.epa.gov/indoor-air-quality-iaq/inside-story-guide-indoor
-air-quality

149. http://www.aafa.org/page/air-pollution-smog-asthma.aspx

150. https://www.atsdr.cdc.gov/formaldehyde/home/index.html

151. https://www.nrdc.org/resources/not-just-dirt-toxic-chemicals-indoor-dust

152. https://www.sffcpf.org/single-post/2017/01/01/Exposure-to-Flame
-Retardant-Chemicals-Means-Firefighters-Face-Higher-Cancer-Risk
-Than-Previously-Thought

153. https://www.nrdc.org/resources/not-just-dirt-toxic-chemicals-indoor-dust

154. https://www.hsph.harvard.edu/news/press-releases/exposure-to-common
-flame-retardant-chemicals-may-increase-thyroid-problems-in-women/

155. https://www.reuters.com/article/us-health-fertility-flame-retardants/
flame-retardants-linked-to-infertility-in-women-idUSKCN1BA2OQ

156. http://www.sfgate.com/bayarea/article/Pregnant-women-s-exposure-to
-flame-retardants-11731559.php

157. http://time.com/4462892/couch-cancer-flame-retardants/

158. https://www.atsdr.cdc.gov/emes/public/docs/How%20to%20Reduce%20
Your%20Exposure%20to%20chemicals%20at%20home%20work%20
and%20play%20fs.pdf

159. https://www.epa.gov/lead/protect-your-family-exposures-lead

160. https://www.acs.org/content/acs/en/pressroom/cutting-edge-chemistry
/unsafe-drinking-waterredux.html

161. https://www.nrdc.org/resources/threats-tap-widespread-violations
-water-infrastructure

162. http://www.lung.org/our-initiatives/healthy-air/indoor/indoor-air
-pollutants/cleaning-supplies-household-chem.html

163. http://articles.latimes.com/2008/jun/13/local/me-showercurtain13
164. http://www.sciencedirect.com/science/article/pii/S0045653517307725
165. https://www.ptj.com.pk/Web-2010/07-10/PDF-july2010/Practical-Hints
     -AVM.pdf
166. http://www.nytimes.com/2010/12/30/business/media/30adco.html
     ?mtrref=www.google.com&gwh=F66323BF27670BFDB98E9A223E7
     696EF&gwt=pay
167. http://www.healthylivingmagazine.us/Articles/268/
168. http://sd33.senate.ca.gov/news/2017-10-15-governor-brown-signs-cleaning
     -product-right-know-act-create-first-nation-label-law
169. https://www.cpsc.gov/PageFiles/121919/AN_UPDATE_ON_
     FORMALDEHYDE-update03102015.pdf
170. http://time.com/4462892/couch-cancer-flame-retardants/
171. http://healthland.time.com/2012/01/25/exposure-to-common-chemicals
     -may-weaken-vaccine-response/
172. https://www.consumerreports.org/flooring/breathe-easier-about-your
     -flooring/
173. Not Just a Pretty Face: The Ugly Side of the Beauty Industry by Stacy Malkan
174. https://www.ncbi.nlm.nih.gov/pubmed/10637531
175. http://www.ourstolenfuture.org/Commentary/News/2003/2003-0622
     -SJMN-scotchgardreturns.htm
176. https://leginfo.legislature.ca.gov/faces/billTextClient.xhtml?bill
     _id=200720080AB706

Chapter Seven

177. https://www.washingtonpost.com/news/energy-environment/wp/2015
     /03/19/our-broken-congresss-latest-effort-to-fix-our-broken-toxic
     -chemicals-law/?utm_term=.cbe17b323aef
178. http://www.safecosmetics.org/get-the-facts/regulations/international
     -laws/
179. https://www.cir-safety.org/how-does-cir-work
180. http://www.safecosmetics.org/get-the-facts/chemicals-of-concern
     /fragrance/
181. https://www.fda.gov/Cosmetics/ProductsIngredients/Ingredients
     /ucm128250.htm
182. https://www.ewg.org/research/teen-girls-body-burden-hormone-altering
     -cosmetics-chemicals/detailed-findings#.Wi1EJzdrw2w
183. http://news.berkeley.edu/2016/03/07/cosmetics-chemicals/
184. https://www.ewg.org/skindeep/ingredient/726331/1%2C4-DIOXANE/#
     .Wi1JYzdrw2w
185. http://www.safecosmetics.org/get-the-facts/chemicals-of-concern/coal-tar/
186. http://www.safecosmetics.org/get-the-facts/chemicals-of-concern/lead
     -and-other-heavy-metals/
187. http://saferchemicals.org/get-the-facts/chemicals-of-concern
     /perfluorinated-compounds/
188. http://www.safecosmetics.org/get-the-facts/chemicals-of-concern
     /p-phenylenediamine/

189. http://www.safecosmetics.org/get-the-facts/chemicals-of-concern/talc/
190. https://ehp.niehs.nih.gov/ehp1788/
191. http://www.safecosmetics.org/get-the-facts/chemicals-of-concern
/formaldehyde/
192. https://www.ewg.org/skindeep/ingredient/702286/ETHANOLAMINE/#.
Wi1ZFDdrw2w
193. http://www.safecosmetics.org/get-the-facts/chemicals-of-concern
/hydroquinone/
194. http://www.safecosmetics.org/get-the-facts/chemicals-of-concern
/parabens/
195. http://www.safecosmetics.org/get-the-facts/chemicals-of-concern
/phthalates/
196. http://www.safecosmetics.org/get-the-facts/chemicals-of-concern
/titanium-dioxide-2/#_edn22
197. http://www.safecosmetics.org/get-the-facts/chemicals-of-concern/toluene
198. https://www.ewg.org/skindeep/ingredient/700353/AMMONIA
/#.Wi1j1jdrw2w
199. http://www.safecosmetics.org/get-the-facts/chemicals-of-concern
/petrolatum/
200. https://www.ewg.org/skindeep/ingredient/705315/PROPYLENE
_GLYCOL/#.Wi1kLzdrw2w
201. https://academic.oup.com/femsle/article/202/1/1/577908
202. https://www.cdc.gov/drugresistance/threat-report-2013/index.html
203. https://www.npr.org/sections/health-shots/2016/09/02/492394717/fda
-bans-19-chemicals-used-in-antibacterial-soaps
204. https://www.ewg.org/research/not-so-sexy#.Wi1lIDdrw2w
205. https://www.ncbi.nlm.nih.gov/pubmed/9869312
206. https://www.ncbi.nlm.nih.gov/pubmed/9869312
207. https://www.osha.gov/SLTC/formaldehyde/hazard_alert.html
208. https://www.atsdr.cdc.gov/emes/public/docs/health%20effects%20of%20
chemical%20exposure%20fs.pdf
209. http://www.who.int/mediacentre/factsheets/fs225/en/
210. https://www.scientificamerican.com/article/fact-or-fiction
-antiperspants-do-more-than-block-sweat/
211. https://www.aad.org/media/stats/conditions/skin-cancer

INDEX

Underscored page references indicate boxed text. **Boldface** references indicate illustrations.